SAN ANTONIO ON PARADE

NUMBER FIFTEEN:
Tarleton State University Southwestern Studies in the Humanities
William T. Pilkington, Series Editor

SAN ANTONIO ON PARADE
SIX HISTORIC FESTIVALS

JUDITH BERG SOBRÉ

Texas A&M University Press   College Station

Copyright © 2003 by Judith Berg Sobré
Manufactured in the United States of America
All rights reserved
First edition
The paper used in this book meets the minimum
requirements of the American National Standard for
Permanence of Paper for Printed Library Materials,
z39.48-1984.
Binding materials have been chosen for durability.

Library of Congress Cataloging-in-Publication Data

Berg-Sobré, Judith, 1941–
San Antonio on parade : six historic festivals /
Judith Berg Sobré.— 1st ed.
p. cm.
Includes bibliographical references and index.
ISBN 1-58544-222-4 (cloth : alk paper)
1. Festivals—Texas—San Antonio—History.
2. San Antonio (Tex.)—Social life and customs.   I. Title.
GT4811.S25 B47 2003
394.26'09764'351—dc21
2002012407

CONTENTS

List of Illustrations	vi
Preface	ix
Introduction	xi
Prologue: Two Parades in San Antonio, 1870 and 1898	3
Chapter 1. Marching, Watching, and Celebrating: How the City Grew	8
Chapter 2. Fourth of July: "Grand Display of Patriotism!"	35
Chapter 3. Juneteenth: "They Are What They Deserve to Be, Free"	51
Chapter 4. Diez y Seis: "How the Sons of Mexico and America Enjoy Liberty"	73
Chapter 5. Columbus Day: "San Antonio Joins in the Great American Festivities"	101
Chapter 6. Volksfests: "Germania and Columbia"	110
Chapter 7. Battle of Flowers Parade: "Fun with Fair Flora"	154
Chapter 8. Spring Carnival, 1900: "In Charge of the Businessmen's Club"	194
Epilogue: San Antonio on Parade	205
Notes	217
Bibliography	245
Index	255

ILLUSTRATIONS

Parade marshals and band in Military Plaza, July 4 (?), ca. 1870 *4*
Fourth of July parade entering Alamo Plaza, 1898 *6*
Bird's eye view of San Antonio, 1873 *13*
San Pedro Springs Park, 1880s *18*
Main Plaza, not yet paved *19*
Commerce Street, unpaved and unclean *20*
Improved Commerce Street, late 1880s *22*
Military Plaza as marketplace, before 1874 *26*
Travis Square, an Anglo-American plaza *28*
Map of San Antonio, 1883 *31*
Main Plaza's metamorphosis, 1890s *32*
Mexican War veterans, San Pedro Springs Park, 1884 *45*
Excelsior Guards, ca. 1902 *58*
J. M. Shelburn, Juneteenth marshal *65*
Clara McPherson, queen of the Juneteenth festival, 1898 *69*
Possible Juneteenth parade in Alamo Plaza, ca. 1971 *71*
Mexican American *jacal* *76*
Squatter's shack in Manhattan, ca. 1875 *77*
Speaker's stand, Diez y Seis celebration, ca. 1883 *88*
Lemp's beer wagon, in 1882 Volksfest parade *121*
Wolfram's Central Gardens, 1882 Volksfest *122*
Arbeiter Verein's float, 1882 Volksfest *123*
1890 German Day float: "Tuetons and Cimbri" *134*
1890 German Day float: "Alaric Conquers Rome" *135*
1890 German Day float: "The Kaiser Triumphant, 1870" *136*
1891 German American Volksfest *140*
1891 Volksfest float: "Germania and Columbia" *141*

New Braunfels Founder's Day parade, 1895 *142*
1891 Volksfest float: "Father Rhine" *143*
1891 Volksfest float: "Hagen Killing Griffons" *144*
1892 German American Volksfest *145*
1892 Volksfest float: "Landing of Columbus" *146*
1892 Volksfest float: "Presentation of Pocahontas at the English Court" *147*
1892 Volksfest float: "Washington Crossing the Delaware" *148*
1892 Volksfest float: "Alamo Heroes" *149*
1892 Volksfest float: "Santa Anna before Sam Houston" *150*
1892 Volksfest float: "The United States and All Nations" *151*
1893 Volksfest float: "Cinderella Tries on the Glass Slipper" *152*
Battle of Flowers parade, 1898 *160*
Decorated carriage in Battle of Flowers parade, 1897 *161*
C. M. McAmis on his decorated bicycle *162*
C. A. Goeth and friends with decorated mounts, 1893 *163*
Belknap Rifles drill team *167*
Flower-decorated steamer truck *168*
Decorated Alamo facade *171*
San Antonio Zouaves *182*
Mrs. Hermann Kampmann's decorated carriage, 1897 *183*
Decorated carriages in Battle of Flowers parade, 1898 *184*
Chapa and Dreiss's "Battleship Texas" float, 1899 *188*
Commerce Street with illuminated arches *200*
King Alegria, his queen, and their court, 1900 *201*
Fallen arch at Commerce and Navarro Streets, 1900 *203*
Fortunato Villareal *208*

PREFACE

In April, 1975, during my first year teaching art history at the fledgling University of Texas at San Antonio, I was asked to be a float judge for the Battle of Flowers parade. I found the experience intriguing. In 1972, I had heard a presentation by the late Arnold Rubin at the College Art Association's annual meeting analyzing the Tournament of Roses. This was at that time a wonderful new approach to the study of popular ephemera as art history, in a field that had been dominated by orthodox studies of the "major arts" by great masters. That had piqued my interest too. An initial study of the first ten years of the Battle of Flowers with a fellow scholar in history, Mark Farber, carried out in 1979–80, remained unpublished. By the time I got back to the article in the late 1990s, Farber had left academia, and my own interests had widened from art history to cultural history and from the Battle of Flowers to a study of how nineteenth-century San Antonians celebrated civic holidays. This book is the result.

In retooling myself into a cultural (though still visually oriented) historian, I was given great and generous help along the way. Several people read chapters and gave valuable advice. These include David Johnson of the University of Texas, San Antonio (UTSA); Oscar Gooden, historian of Saint Paul's United Methodist church; San Antonio historical columnist Paula Allen; Texas historian Frank Jennings; and genealogical historian Theresa Gold.

Other people who shared their expertise with me were Robert Klier of the Beethoven Männerchor, who let me examine the bust of Beethoven that had been paraded in the 1890 Volksfest; Hector Cardenas of the San Antonio Fire Department (now retired); Frank Christadoro of the Christopher Columbus Society; and Reg Little of Alamo Fireworks.

Invaluable aid in library and archival research was provided by Dora Guerra, now at the Alamo but formerly librarian of UTSA special collections; her successor at UTSA, Dennis Medina; Tom Shelton and Chris Floerke at the Institute of Texan Cultures; Eva Milstead and Beth Standifird at the library of the San Antonio Conservation Society; Rebecca Huffstetler at the Witte Museum; Warren Striker and Martha Utterbank at the Daughters of the Republic of Texas

Library at the Alamo; and various staff members of the Texana department at the San Antonio public library.

I owe a special thanks to Vera Williams Young of the Carter-Taylor-Williams Mortuary, who was so generous in sharing visual material on early Juneteenth Festivals (and who is presently working on her own study of Juneteenth in South Texas). Four of the five very rare photographs relating to Juneteenth are from her.

I received encouragement from several dear friends and colleagues who were able to provide insights into local history: Steven Vollmer, Maggie Valentine, Charles R. Hoffman, Bruce Winders, Maria Watson Pfeiffer, and Michaele and David Haynes.

Lastly, I must thank my daughter, Miriam Shoshana Sobré, for her ruthless editing of my first draft. Without her keeping me in line, this text would be a lot longer, more obscure, and less interesting!

INTRODUCTION

Between 1866 and 1900, the city of San Antonio grew from an isolated, rather exotic town of diverse ethnic and social groups to a complex, cosmopolitan city. The city's civic festivals, six of which will be explored here, evolved and changed along with the city itself. The rise and development of these festivals echo similar events in other cities in the United States during the nineteenth century and the contemporaneous infancy of the American pageant movement, with its emphasis on patriotism and culture as expressed in spectacle.

In South Texas, this development could only have taken place after the Civil War. San Antonio had a chaotic history during the first half of the nineteenth century, and it was far too unstable for citizens to stage annual festivals (though they occasionally thought about it). Religious celebrations were different: they could be celebrated in times of disorder and stress; in fact, they often throve under such conditions, when people prayed for better times and celebrated narrow escapes or miraculous rescues. Civic festivals, on the other hand, needed the routine of stability in order to be planned on a yearly basis. The usual impetus for such celebrations in the United States was patriotic, even though they may have only begun years after the event that inspired them and often commemorated a pivotal moment that became elevated over time to the status of myth. Various patriotic declarations fitted the bill nicely. In other cases, if such an event was not available, one was appropriated for the purpose.

In the nineteenth century, many of these celebrations commemorated events among particular ethnic groups, emphasizing both the country or culture of origin and their present Americanization. San Antonio's festivals reflected a general trend of ethnic toleration in the United States after the Civil War—the celebration of the melting pot ideal that brought the best of the "old country" to the culture of the new.[1] And so, on the day of the festival, the principal downtown streets and plazas belonged to the group staging it, no matter what their economic and social situation in the everyday "real" world. They proudly displayed themselves and their contributions to their fellow citizens in a street parade. Afterward, in a public celebration held in a city park or similar venue, they offered traditional food, orations in both their native tongue and in English, anthems, salutes, fireworks, sports contests, and balls. The parades were free to all; something might be charged for food or dances, but the cost was nominal. Inclusion rather than exclusion was the rule of the day.

In the following chapters, we will follow the progress of six different festivals put on by various ethnic or societal groups during the period from 1866 to 1900: the Fourth of July, which might be supposed to be the most inclusive; the African American Juneteenth; Diez y Seis (celebrating Mexican independence); Columbus Day (celebrated by the city's small Italian American community); the German American Volksfest; and the Battle of Flowers, organized by the city's upper-middle-class women.

This particular group of festivals was chosen because each consisted of a parade that in most cases was joined by a park festival that could last up to three days. The Volksfest, Diez y Seis, the Fourth of July, and the Battle of Flowers celebrated the three dominant ethnic groups of the period in San Antonio (German American, Mexican American, and Anglo-American). The Italian American and African American groups were much smaller but, for reasons we shall examine, decided to emulate the festivals of their more populous brothers and sisters. On the other hand, some of the city's other smaller ethnic groups were excluded from this exploration, because their festivals (when they had them) were different. The city's Irish, for example, celebrated Saint Patrick's day as a religious holiday, with a procession culminating in a solemn Mass, rather than with the raucous parades seen in the Northern and Eastern United States. The small Franco-American community, on the other hand, opted to celebrate Bastille Day—a likely patriotic candidate—with a banquet.

Festivals are a feast for the senses. Visual messages are conveyed both by the marchers and the decorated street and park. The smells and tastes of foods reach participants, as do the odors of fireworks, horses and donkeys and their manure, and warm bodies. Marching bands play music, which is heard along with the shouts and exclamations of spectators (and maybe marchers too) and the boom of fireworks and military salutes. Do all these things change as the urban environment changes? What was the experience of marching or watching like in 1866? How was it different in 1898? How do these festivals reflect the cultural and urban growth and makeup of the city and its inhabitants? Do they change and evolve as the city evolves? Do they create their own myths and enduring iconographies?

In order to try and visualize these festivals and parades and what drove them, it is important to look "from the inside out," through contemporary writings, photographs, engravings, documents, and especially newspaper accounts. These celebrations often made the front page. To understand why, we must first examine how San Antonio developed and grew during the period between 1866 and 1900. Through this we will see how various communities within the population, whether Anglo-American, African American, Mexican American, Italian American, or German American, shifted within their own identities and within their relations to each other and to the changing city as a whole. In looking at the festivals in this way, we must often assume the views and prejudices of both celebrators and viewers. For this is the way the culture was both understood and reflected at the time, even if we are inclined to disagree with the participants more than a century later. In short, we must hearken back to an age when manifest destiny was the philosophy and "progress" the favorite catchword.

SAN ANTONIO ON PARADE

PROLOGUE
TWO PARADES IN SAN ANTONIO, 1870 & 1898

Alamo Fire Company No.1—the members of the company will assemble at their engine house, at 7 o'clock on the morning of the 4th, where they will form and march to the Alamo Plaza, and take their place in the procession.

After the procession, spectacle &c., shall have been concluded, the company will march back to the engine house and will there be dismissed.
—*San Antonio Express*, July 1, 1870

The Fourth of July was celebrated in San Antonio yesterday as it has never been celebrated before in Texas. Something like 5000 people manifested their patriotism by marching together in a procession that seemed to extend over endless distances. This procession in itself formed a spectacle, such as has not before been presented in this city, and it was but the inauguration of a patriotic demonstration which was continued all through the day and until late at night.
—*San Antonio Express*, July 5, 1898

1870

Alamo Plaza at 7:30 in the morning on July 4, 1870, was dusty and already showing signs of the coming heat of the day when parade participants came together and lined up, ready to march. Leading the procession were the marshals, rancher R. D. Bonnett, policeman Alejo Perez, and lumberman and volunteer fireman Hans Degener. They rode on horseback in formal dress with top hats. A band, pioneers, and a color bearer marched next. Then came a contingent of military from the local army post. County, city, and state officials who happened to be on hand followed. Members of the three white volunteer fire companies in dress uniforms marched, pulling along with them their firefighting equipment, decorated with red, white, and blue bunting.[1] Their star was Fire Company 2's shiny steam pumper, the *William Menger*, named after its hotelier purchaser, who was also the fire chief. It was barely two years old and the first such in the city. There

Parade marshals and band in Military Plaza, July 4 (?), ca. 1870.
Courtesy Witte Museum, San Antonio, Texas

was also a hook and ladder company made up of members of the Turnverein, a gymnastic and athletic club of German origin. The Beneficiary and Laborers' Associations, with their badges, and Tejano members of the Club Mexicano-Texano came next. Schoolchildren marched in a body. At the end of the procession were two African American organizations, the Colored Laborer's Association and the Loyal Union League. As a postscript, any citizen who cared to participate was welcome to join in.[2]

The route of the parade took them over the unpaved streets and plazas through the heart of the city, where citizens who had already been up and about for several hours lined the narrow and irregular sidewalks. They first marched around Alamo Plaza, then proceeded up Commerce Street, crossing its wooden bridge over the lush San Antonio River. Arriving at Military Plaza, they circled it as well and then returned to Alamo Plaza via Market Street. In Alamo Plaza they disbanded in front of the Menger Hotel, where Stanley Welch read the "Declaration of Independence" and S. G. Newton delivered an oration.

After the parade, members of Fire Company 1 and their guests proceeded on foot, on horseback, or in carriages about a mile and a half north of the plazas, up Acequia Street to San Pedro Springs Park, where the company hosted a barbecue. This was preceded by another reading of the "Declaration of Independence," by Capt. W. H. Houston, who stood on the park's speaker's platform surrounded by the firemen and thirty-eight young ladies representing the states of the union. The hot afternoon was occupied by concerts by various German singing societies of the city, and another address was delivered at 5 P.M. by Gen. William H. Young. The park activities reached their height with a ball at 6, winding up with a free lunch thrown by Gustav Duerler, proprietor of the park, at 9 P.M.[3] Meanwhile, downtown, there were two additional balls, one at the Menger Hotel, the other at the Casino Club. The celebrations terminated with a fireworks display.

Though the city's African American population was welcome in the parade, integration did not extend to the activities that followed. Members of the Loyal Union League and their families, and families of the children who attended the Colored School, had their own picnic at Guenther's Mill, south of the city.

1898

Nearly a world away in size was the Fourth of July parade held in San Antonio in 1898.[4] At that moment, the city was in the patriotic frenzy of the Spanish-American War, and word had just been received of the destruction of the Spanish fleet at Santiago. Enthusiastic spectators lined the streets and filled second- and third-story windows en route by 8 A.M, an hour before the procession was to start. Once again, the early-morning weather was hot, but the streets were considerably less dusty thanks to paving. Spectators and marchers alike were apparently willing to have the parade begin at the more fashionable, if warmer, hour of 9. The parade was a mile and a half long and so big that it was split into three divisions. The first consisted of the military, including Confederate and Union veterans marching side by side; twelve troops of U.S. mounted cavalry; three bands; city and county officials; members of the Cuban Club; and large contingents of the fraternal orders of the Elks, the Knights of Pythias, and the Odd Fellows; plus the United Commercial Travelers in full regalia, toting symbols and insignias. In the second division were various German American *vereine,* or clubs, of veterans, athletes, marksmen, and gardeners; several singing societies; and lodges of the German fraternal orders of the Sons of Hermann and the Knights and Ladies of Honor. The second division also included trade unions, with a band and a commercial float sponsored by Joske Brothers' Department Store. The third division had everyone else's societies: Catholic groups

Small portion of Fourth of July parade entering Alamo Plaza, 1898.
Courtesy U.T. Institute of Texan Cultures

of both sexes, including orphans, and Irish, Italian, French, and the numerous Mexican mutual aid societies. The now-professional fire department marched here along with their horse-drawn equipment, augmented by a contingent of ex–volunteer firemen. The rear was brought up by a couple of cowboys and finally, as in 1870, any other citizens who cared to march. Missing were organizations representing the city's African American population.

The parade started just to the north of Alamo Plaza, on Avenue D, at 9:15 A.M. Marchers proceeded west on Houston Street, now paved with hexagonal mesquite blocks, as were the other streets on the route, crossing San Pedro Creek and passing by the old cemetery. They then turned south on San Saba and east on Commerce, circling the narrow plaza then called Paschal Square on the way. At Military Plaza, they marched around City Hall. Proceeding on to Main Plaza via Treviño Street, they circled it as well, passing the handsome new neo-Romanesque courthouse and the recently planted garden, trees, and fountain in its center. They then continued on up Commerce Street, crossing the now-sluggish San Antonio River on the ornate iron Commerce Street bridge, to finish at Alamo Plaza.

The city's extensive electric streetcar system took festival-goers to two venues for further celebration. Five thousand people chose San Pedro Park, where at 3 P.M., William Dobrowolski read the official notices of the American victory at Santiago. Judge Edward Dwyer then read the "Declaration of Independence." There were also additional patriotic orations in Spanish and English, mostly relating to the Spanish-American War. Athletic contests followed.

Twenty-five hundred people, mostly German Americans, repaired south of downtown to Riverside Park to hear a concert by Carl Beck's Band, view a shooting exhibition by Adolph Toepperwein, and applaud Casino Club president Conrad Goeth's reading of the "Declaration." Orations followed in English and German, and the fete concluded with dancing and a fireworks display.

In some ways, these two festivals, separated by twenty-eight years, were quite similar in their route of march and their musical, military, fire-department, and civic-society components. In general, the parades and the concomitant orations, food, contests, dances, and fireworks echoed a pattern that had been firmly established in the United States for civic celebrations since the first half of the nineteenth century.[5]

The specific composition of the two processions differed somewhat, but that was because of the change in demographics in the city over thirty years. In 1870, the population was a little over twelve thousand people, with German Americans, Anglo-Americans, and Mexican/Spanish Americans making up its bulk, and a minuscule black community. By 1900, the city topped fifty-three thousand inhabitants, with Anglo-Americans in a firm majority, the Germans well on their way to joining with them socially and culturally, a dwindling Hispanic component, and a proliferation of other ethnic groups, though none great in number. The black community was flourishing but still set apart. The greater size and elaboration of the 1898 parade mirrored these changes, following the growth of the city. For by the end of the nineteenth century, San Antonio had become a substantially different place physically, culturally, and in its relationship with the rest of Texas and the United States. To understand these dramatic changes, and how they affected local celebrations, we must first examine how the city grew during the last third of the century.

CHAPTER 1
MARCHING, WATCHING, AND CELEBRATING
HOW THE CITY GREW

Twenty-five years ago we visited this city [1861]. Then it was little more than a collection of hovels. The howl of the cayote [*sic*] and the whoop of the Comanche could be heard almost from the plaza. The brawny Mexican and festive cow-boy held high carnival in all the public places. Murder, robbery, rape and villiany [*sic*] were of nightly and almost hourly occurrence. The adobe house, the Mexican cart, and the walking arsenal met the gaze on every side. The beautiful river wound its course through the ugly, filthy, uncouth streets, and was spanned by only a few old rickety wooden bridges, and a peaceable man, not to mention a decent lady, dreaded to walk the rough cobblestone, muddy streets in daytime, let alone at night. But twenty-five years have passed . . . and "presto!" change has been pronounced. Where stood the old adobe huts, magnificent stone and brick buildings are to be seen. Instead of the yell of the Comanche, you hear the scream of the locomotive all around the city. Where the unsightly Mexican cart met the gaze, you now see the beautiful and convenient street cars, with their sleek, fat mules and their jingling bells. In place of the mesquite thicket . . . you see fine, broad avenues, lined on either side with beautiful and stately residences, surrounded by magnificent groves or shade trees and lovely gardens of flowers. . . . The little old rickety wooden bridges have disappeared, and in their stead a hundred magnificent bridges now span the beautiful stream. . . . Where you then met the walking arsenal in the shape of a drunken cow-boy, or the murderous desperado, you now meet the sober, courteous, polite policeman, with his club and badge of office, who is ever ready to give any information you want. As for his protection, you don't seem to need that.
—S. R. Whately, *History and Guide of San Antonio, Texas*

Admittedly, this assessment of San Antonio's progress as a city, written for the National Press Association's thirteenth annual convention, goes beyond the hyperbolic to near hysteria, and many of its facts are exaggerated (the city, for example, never had cobblestone streets, not to mention one hundred bridges). But it does give some idea of the dramatic changes that occurred in San Antonio in just a quarter of a century.

True stability and growth only happened after the Civil War. San Antonio's earlier history was chaotic. Though established in the eighteenth century as both a garrison town and the eventual site of five missions, the site was at the northernmost reaches of Spain's colonization and would remain on its frontier. Its lush river made it an oasis in an otherwise inhospitable area. During the late eighteenth and early nineteenth centuries, its population of immigrant Canary Islanders, Franciscan missionaries, Mexican soldiers and their families, and the occasional settler from the United States remained basically the same. It had its ups and downs but had changed little with Mexico's independence from Spain in 1823.[1]

More Americans began to trickle in after this date, and the declaration of an independent Republic of Texas led to turbulence. Indeed, this was to supply the city's urban mythology with its "finest hour," the fall of the mission/fort of the Alamo in 1836. Even after Texas was incorporated into the United States in 1845, there was little improvement. San Antonio still remained remote. Its main trade routes led east to the Gulf Coast and south to Mexico, both being served by ox-drawn transport carts. Its mainstay was still agriculture, nourished by the river and the irrigation system of ditches (*acequias*) introduced by its earliest settlers. Comanche raids and a cholera epidemic in 1849, a consequence of the pollution of the *acequias,* kept the level of instability high.

True change began only when a sizeable number of German settlers arrived, part of a larger immigrant group to Texas. By the mid-1850s, the city's population was equally divided among Germans, Anglo-Americans, and the descendants of several waves of Spanish and Mexican colonizers, augmented by a small number of African American slaves (mostly domestic servants).

Eastern chroniclers of visits to San Antonio at this period noted its exotic air. The urban plan was still based on its original Hispanic/Roman model. Most of its public and economic life revolved around its three dirt plazas, Main and Military to the west of the river, Alamo Plaza with its dilapidated ex-mission to the east. All three were surrounded by low buildings, mostly adobe in the western plazas, with flimsier *jacales* near the Alamo. The latter—not that different from tropical dwellings elsewhere—were made of wooden poles, thatch, and mud. A livery stable and lumberyard constituted the plaza's main businesses. On Main Plaza was the eighteenth-century church of San Fernando, which by this time was in disrepair, its cracked bell making only a "clunk."[2]

Richard Everett, visiting in 1859, found several surviving Hispanic customs very intriguing, notably the cockfights and the way women and children bathed naked in the river. He also commented on the local ladies dressed in loose, cool garments, free of the tight corsets of their more "civilized" counterparts. Most of all he relished the dances called *fandangos,* where the poorer members of the Mexican American population mixed, danced, and courted, all under the vigilant eye of the older matrons, who also sold refreshments. What seemed lascivious to him was really quite decorous, though far in appearance from an East Coast grand ball.[3] Everett and other, subsequent visitors also remarked on the leisurely pace of the Mexican American lifestyle, which had very different priorities from the fast-paced Protestant ethic. They condemned this way of life as "indolent." Frederick Law Olmsted, who had passed through San Antonio two years earlier, noted that slaveholders looked upon the Mexican Americans with suspicion for their willingness to work for low wages and their habit of fraternizing with African Americans.[4] However, the former would be classified in the color-conscious hierarchy of the day as "white."[5]

More familiar to the visitor's gaze would have been the modest German limestone cottages, with their shutters and neat gardens. Indeed, it was the Germans who brought European culture and "civilization" to South Texas. Many of those who came were educated intellectuals, refugees from the revolution of 1848, and often politically liberal. They rapidly formed a mercantile, professional, and small-business middle class. They also brought with them many cultural institutions from home. They formed choirs and *vereine,* interest groups of which much will be said later. They established a German-English school in 1858 and in the same year constructed a social club, the Casino Association, whose building included a theater. Not surprisingly, they also built San Antonio's first breweries.

The city continued to maintain a garrison. The U.S. military headquarters, located downtown in a building built by the Vance brothers on Houston Street, provided the launch and supply point for a string of forts across wild West Texas. The officers socialized with the more genteel elements of the increasing Anglo-American population, who joined the Germans in mercantile activities.[6]

By this time, the town was beginning to grow into something bigger. A solid wood and iron bridge replaced the earlier wooden one on Commerce Street, the main business artery. Houston Street was created in 1851 by bridging the river and joining two earlier routes, Paseo to the east and Rivas Street on the west bank. A new market house was built on what was appropriately named Market Street. A volunteer fire company was formed in 1854. Plans had been made to illuminate the streets with gas. Two newspapers, the *San Antonio Zeitung* (later the *San Antonio Staats-Zeitung*) and the *San Antonio Herald,* were regularly published by the end of the decade. The city even had the second-oldest public park in the

United States (after Boston Common) at San Pedro Springs, about a mile north of downtown, though it was still largely undeveloped.

The coming of the Civil War stopped everything in its tracks. The military garrison surrendered as Texas joined the Confederacy, and Southern troops took over the Vance building. This alignment was not without controversy. Some of the Germans opposed secession and slavery; a number went for the duration of the war to Mexico, where such human servitude had long been abolished. Anglo-American Union sympathizers went north.[7] But people from all the dominant ethnic groups fought on both sides: August Santleben, August Siemering, and Wilhelm Thielepape, Germans all, fought for the Union. So did Anglo-American John Bolton and Mexican Americans Antonio P. Rivas and Juan E. Barrera. Among those who enlisted with the Confederacy (aside from many of the Anglo-Americans, who had come from other Southern states) were Mexican Americans Juan T. Cardenas and Francisco N. Sanchez and German American businessman Hermann D. Kampmann.

Those who remained at home were spared the direct devastation of war, except for a number of prominent citizens who were imprisoned for Unionist sympathies. But the lack of enthusiasm for the war grew as each year passed without a resolution. The battles raged far from San Antonio, but the lucrative trade with Mexico suffered from Union blockades, though it was still clandestinely successful.

After the war, the city was reoccupied by the victorious Union. San Antonio, like other formerly Confederate towns, suffered from the shortages and martial law of Reconstruction, and the years immediately after the war left it in bad economic straits. The planned gas illumination only lit a few streets in 1866; this was one of the only innovations, as there was no money available for anything else. And to add to local misery, there was a second cholera epidemic in the same year.

POSTWAR SAN ANTONIO, 1866–77

In the late 1860s and early 1870s, San Antonio still remained pretty much as it had been before the war. The city was unconnected to others by railroads. Stagecoaches remained the only means of public transportation—and the trip to or from Austin took seventeen hours, including meal stops.[8]

Visitors in the early 1870s were still intrigued by the exotic character of the city. "San Antonio," wrote Edward King in 1874, "is the only town in the United States which has a thoroughly European aspect, and it is more, in its older quarters, like some remote and obscure town in Spain than like any bustling villages of France or Germany."⁹

The city's plan was still dominated by its Spanish/Roman origins, with its three unpaved plazas. But its character was gradually changing. On Main Plaza, San Fernando Church was finally under expansion and restoration, beginning in 1867. It would achieve the status of a cathedral in 1874. The plaza's second-most impressive structure was still the two-story French Building, erected in 1856, but it was joined by another, Frost and Bro., in 1872. The older adobe buildings built by the most important Mexican American families were gradually replaced by one- or two-story structures of a commercial nature in the Anglo-American style. Most of them now contained either dry goods establishments or saloons. The Plaza Hotel, the stopping place for stagecoaches, was the most prominent building on the plaza's north side. The atmosphere in the plaza itself was often raucous. Medicine shows flourished at night, as did less savory activities.¹⁰ Many transients were attracted to the plazas, a result of the cattle drives that reached their peak in the 1870s. Others arrived as a result of the burgeoning wool trade, beginning in 1873, which was to help fuel the city's economic revival.

Military Plaza was nearly as gamey. It still retained something of its early character as the Plaza de Armas, the military post of colonial times. Though public executions had long vanished, the notoriously noxious jail, called the "Bat Cave," still remained. The not-so-sinful *fandangos* also disappeared, to be replaced by far more disreputable saloons. Though ox trains and prairie schooners of military supplies for the western forts still departed from and sometimes camped in this plaza, it was also beginning to develop its character as an open-air market.

Alamo Plaza, on the other side of the river, was somewhat more marginal. The derelict Alamo, rather fancifully rebuilt by two German engineers in 1849, now served the U.S. Army as a military munitions depot. The Menger, originally a brewery, had been expanded into a hotel in 1859. The Vance brothers, who had built the Vance House, had their own emporium here, as did the dry goods firm of Bresel and Briam. In the plaza's center was the decidedly unfragrant meat market and a storage house for volunteer fire equipment.

Streets, according to the original Spanish/Roman plan, ran at right angles to the plazas, east-west or north-south. The principal east-west artery was Commerce Street, which bridged the river. The street itself was narrow and, like the plazas and all other city streets, unpaved. Sidewalks on Commerce Street were extremely narrow, making pedestrian life hazardous.¹¹ The streets were no better on the wider Houston Street, or on Market Street or any other street for that matter.

Bird's eye view of San Antonio, 1873, by August Koch.
Courtesy Witte Museum, San Antonio, Texas

At this time, the principal north-south thoroughfares, such as Soledad and Acequia Streets, were west of the San Antonio River, which snaked around Commerce, Market, and other thoroughfares. Though there were several bridges over the river, its course often abruptly terminated smaller streets. All plazas and streets were either dusty or muddy, depending on the weather, and were often riddled with potholes.

Though unpaved, the one exception to the dirt expanses of the plazas was Travis Plaza, to the north of Houston Street. It dated far later than the other three, having been laid out on land gifted to the city by Samuel Maverick in the 1850s. It was originally surrounded by genteel private houses of wood or limestone, many with front gardens. What set it apart was its grassy center. From the start it was more a park or square on the Anglo-American model than a Hispanic plaza; soon it would be renamed Travis Square.

The river itself remained lush. An abundance of trees grew along it. Many houses that backed onto the river had lawns that sloped down to its banks. Naked Mexican women and children were replaced by decorous bathhouses for the more modest Anglo-Americans and Germans to enjoy.[12] But beautiful though it was, the river could, on occasion, be dangerous. It flooded the city in 1819 and 1845 and once more in 1865, when it washed out the Houston Street bridge. In fact, all of the local water sources could be lethal: ordinances were constantly made to keep people from dumping waste—including animal carcasses—into the river, the creeks, and the *acequias*. Polluted water led to disease, as the cholera epidemics proved. At this period, bacterial theories were just beginning to be explored, and for the most part, people could only tremble and wait when disease threatened. Newspapers of the period are full of horrific chronicles of the spreading of epidemics, and the death of children from diphtheria, measles, and whooping cough was common.[13] Though the city was spared the periodic attacks of yellow fever that scourged Galveston, the typhoid that afflicted Jim Bowie at the Alamo continued to flare up over the years. Even though inoculation against smallpox existed and was in widespread use, the poorer segments of the population remained unvaccinated, and cases were frequent. Cures tended to be patent medicines, dubious creams, or tonics often laced with alcohol or laudanum, which boasted that they would eliminate such ailments as "scrofulous ulcers," "colds, coughs, sore throat, influenza, and bronchitis." There was also Dr. E. C. West's Nerve and Brain Treatment, "a guaranteed specific for Hysteria, Dizziness, Convulsions, Fits, Nervous Neuralgia, Headache and Nervous Prostration caused by the use of Alcohol and Tobacco."[14]

Such epidemics were, at the time, expected and feared everywhere in the United States and Europe. Actually, considering this, San Antonio enjoyed a reputation as a healthful place to live. Though hot in the summer, its winters were generally mild, and for this reason it had become a refuge for people suffering from tuberculosis and boasted several sanatoria.[15]

The city was still small enough at this period that people lived mostly within walking distance of downtown, if not downtown itself.[16] They tended to cluster in neighborhoods according to their ethnicity, though these sometimes shifted. In the early 1870s Anglo-Americans and others of European extraction tended to settle to the north, except for the Germans, who occupied the near south side and the east. The Mexican American population was generally to be found west of San Pedro Creek, in neighborhoods with such labels as "Chihuahua" and

"Laredito." The still relatively small number of African Americans were scattered in various pockets around the city, usually in those areas that the others felt were undesirable. The style of dwellings differed according to the population. Along wealthy King William Street, the more prosperous Germans built solid wooden or stone houses, as did their Anglo-American counterparts to the north. Many of the poorer Mexican Americans still lived in *jacales*. The growth in the number of wooden structures made for increased fire danger. By the mid-1870s, there were five volunteer fire companies, two of these being "colored."

As the 1870s progressed, businesses began slowly to expand, mostly toward service-oriented industries. There were now many more dry goods stores, which outfitted cowboys for cattle drives, many of which began in San Antonio. Two of the biggest occurred in 1870 and 1871, and memoirs of the period describe cowboys actually driving longhorns through the city's streets.[17] These same dry goods stores also supplied people from the outlying ranches, not to mention local inhabitants, as well as members of the military, who remained an important presence. Several of the dry goods merchants, notably Thomas C. Frost, the Groos Brothers, and Daniel and Jesse Oppenheimer, began to do some informal banking on the side, making small loans and keeping money for clients. Gradually, all of them would establish true banks.

Somewhat more fashionable shops were to be found on Commerce Street, along with other businesses, including saddleries, a bookstore, hardware stores, an ice cream parlor, jewelry stores, and the offices of the *Freie Presse Fuer San Antonio* and the *San Antonio Express*.[18] At this period, San Antonio was still a very multilingual place. Shopkeepers had to be capable of doing business in several languages, sometimes simultaneously. Downtown was where everyone amicably mingled.

While few were really wealthy, many inhabitants began to prosper, and the much-vaunted "progress" was pursued along ethnic lines. The Germans remained shopkeepers, but many were skilled artisans; they would make up most of the nascent labor unions. Some diversified and became rich "capitalists," like Hermann Kampmann. Others, such as Ferdinand Herff and Berthold Hadra, were respected physicians. Max Lindner and Friedrich Kalteyer prospered as pharmacists. The Anglo-Americans were also merchants and provided the city with its lawyers, many of whom entered politics. Some became successful as stockmen; still others took advantage of the growing wool trade to become commission merchants. The Mexican Americans were a heterogeneous mix. They included established landowning families, descendants of the early Canary Islanders, the Spanish garrison, and Mexican settlers. Somewhat lower on the social scale were small artisans. At the bottom of the heap were the day laborers. African Americans generally segued from domestic servitude to domestic service. People of every nationality and origin ran the city's numerous saloons.[19]

In this pre-electric and pre-air-conditioning period, daily life, particularly in summer, proceeded in a far different manner than it would a century later. From June through September, with the relentless heat, it was the custom to rise very early—at 4 A.M—to work while it was cool. Marketing was done generally before sunrise: the meat market in Alamo Plaza opened at 3 A.M. and closed by 7 A.M. because of the flies. Everything shut down in the sweltering afternoon, to resume again in the nominally cooler evenings. Houses were sited to catch the prevailing southeastern summer winds. In the cooler months and shorter days of winter, people rose later, and the workday came closer to that of more northerly cities. The heat explains the early-morning start for the parades of high summer, such as Juneteenth and the Fourth of July.

Social life depended on ethnicity and class. Most Anglo-American women found the plazas, with the exception of Travis Square, to be disreputable. Much of their social life was conducted in their homes, where visiting on given afternoons was an accepted social custom. In summer, they took carriage rides in the cool of the morning or late afternoon. Socializing also took place within the churches that were rapidly increasing in number.[20] Harriet Spoffard remarks on the lilt in everyone's English, which came from their Spanish-speaking environment, as well the slow leisurely pace of life that allowed the town "still to retain its fantastic charm instead of joining the march of improvement."[21] Many of the men joined fraternal organizations such as the Masons (first established in San Antonio in 1848) and the Odd Fellows, which were just coming into their heyday.

German Americans had many organized activities. Like their Hill Country cousins, they founded choirs such as the Beethoven Männerchor. The various choirs participated in *sängerfests* (singing festivals) with other similar groups both in and out of town. They had also brought with them the custom of *vereine*, special interest clubs where like-minded men could meet. They too had their fraternal organizations, such as the Sons of Hermann. German Americans also dominated the white volunteer fire companies. The Casino Association flourished and, among other events, provided space for respectable dances. Protestants, Jews, and Catholics of German origin had their own religiously affiliated societies, but they also mingled in many of the previously mentioned activities. All of them also frequented the numerous beer gardens that dotted the city to the south, north, and east. These often featured band concerts and other wholesome entertainments and were considered family fare.

African American social life revolved around churches, which were to become even more important as the African American population increased. Like the others, Mexican Americans also tended to socialize among themselves and according to class. Religious festivals were popular, as were various sorts of dances. From early in the century, however, a number of upper-class Mexican Americans were intermarrying with Catholics of other origins; thus their identities became somewhat diluted as they crossed ethnic lines.[22]

Though they might frequent them by day for grocery and other shopping, respectable ladies of every ethnicity avoided Main and Military Plazas by night. The bars on these plazas were very rowdy, with celebrating stockmen and cowboys, many of the latter being transients with little stake in the city. Entertainment within the bars was firmly for men only. The sorts of diversions that went on nightly in the plazas were also suspect: patent-medicine vendors, itinerant magicians and tumblers, at least one open-air dentist, not to mention soliciting streetwalkers and plenty of gambling.[23] Throughout the early to mid-1880s this would all continue.

The great oasis for one and all was San Pedro Springs Park. Valued for its tranquil air and natural beauty since the eighteenth century, it had been set aside as a public park in 1851, gaining a few concessions by 1858. But this beautiful haven (with its two springs forming the origin of San Pedro Creek) had been ruined during the war, when the Confederates used it for a prisoner of war camp.[24] Its real development came when J. J. Duerler leased and began to develop it in 1866. He built five artificial lakes with footpaths surrounding the natural springs and planted trees to augment the pecan grove already there, as well as tropical plants and flowers. In this sylvan setting he constructed a two-story bandstand, a mineral museum, and a small zoo. After his death from a fall in 1874, his son, Gustav Duerler, took over the park's management. He added a racetrack and two dancing pavilions, an open-air one up on a small rise and an enclosed one on flatter ground.[25] Though various beer and food concessions operated in different periods, admission to the park was always free.

San Pedro Springs Park soon became a favorite Sunday venue not only for the German American community but for everyone else too. It became the preferred

San Pedro Springs Park, with visitors viewing a baseball game, 1880s.
Courtesy Witte Museum, San Antonio, Texas

place to hold group activities, athletic competitions, and, eventually, patriotic celebrations. It played, as we shall see, a prominent role in many of the city's festivals.

Such was the city up until 1877. It was still relatively isolated from the rest of the United States, still closer to its Hispano-Mexican origins, but it had already assumed a multiethnic character that gave it its peculiar charm and drew interested tourists hardy enough to make the journey. Though different groups lived in their own clusters, there was a remarkable interaction and ease of communication among them, quite different from the ethnic strife in other contemporary American cities. San Antonio had also achieved a stability that would make the regular celebration of annual urban festivals possible, though these were still relatively few in number, restricted to Fourth of July celebrations, Diez y Seis, and probably the earliest Juneteenths. Such festivals would have provided community-wide family-oriented diversions at a period when few municipal entertainments existed.

What would it have been like to watch one of these parades in this period? At times viewing would have been hazardous, to say the least. The narrow, rutted sidewalks along the downtown streets offered little space to congregate; the second stories of Commerce Street buildings offered a safer view. Down on the

Main Plaza, not yet paved, after a rainstorm. *Courtesy Witte Museum, San Antonio, Texas*

streets and plazas there would have been an additional hazard: the spattering of mud or flying dust. Indeed, in this period of unpaved streets, several Fourth of July parades had to be canceled because of excessive mud (this would continue into the 1880s). On the other hand, the 1877 parade had to be cut short because of the heat, even at the early hour, and dense blowing dust.[26] But of course, all of what we now consider hazardous and difficult was an accepted and unremarkable aspect of daily life. San Antonio was still a small town, so that most of the viewers would have known most of the marchers as friends (or occasionally enemies) and neighbors.

For marchers, there were additional pitfalls: potholes in the roads and plazas could make for broken axles and turned ankles, while avoiding manure was a constant challenge. It is also not clear if streets and plazas on the parade route were always actually cleared of the everyday vehicles that normally cluttered them.[27]

The routes of march were often governed by the twists and turns in the river and its limited number of bridges. This explains, for example, why the 1870 Fourth of July parade, returning to Alamo Plaza via Market Street, had to turn north on Casino Street to Commerce Street to cross the river.

Commerce Street, unpaved and unclean. *Courtesy Witte Museum, San Antonio, Texas*

"PROGRESS" TRANSFORMS THE CITY:
SAN ANTONIO, 1877–90

The year 1877 marked a watershed for San Antonio. On February 11, the Sunset (later the Southern Pacific) Railroad finally reached the city, and the arrival was celebrated with a torchlight parade and two days of celebrating. Five years later, it would be joined by the International and Great Northern Railroad and, in 1887, the San Antonio and Aransas Pass Railway. San Antonio was now accessible to the rest of the United States, and the consequences would be far-reaching. Many Eastern Anglo-Americans, both from the North and the South, would arrive, reinforcing their cultures and philosophies. By 1880, the population ratio had begun to shift with its dramatic increase to 21,207. Germans and Anglo-

Americans still retained the lead, at 7,610 and 7,800 respectively, but the Mexican American population remained essentially what it was in the 1850s, at 3,470. African Americans had increased in number to 2,178. Other nationalities were still fractional: the 1879–80 city directory of San Antonio lists 25 Spaniards; 25 Italians; 310 French; 60 Swiss; 17 Hungarians; 32 Dutch, Belgians, and Swedes; 178 "Polanders"; and 2 Chinese.[28]

Perhaps even more important for the city's infrastructure than the railroad connections was the inauguration of the mule-drawn San Antonio Street Railway on June 22, 1878. Its first line connected Alamo Plaza to San Pedro Springs; now revelers of modest means could ride to their favorite playground without plodding the mile or so from downtown in the heat.[29] The stage was set for physical expansion of the city beyond its downtown nucleus. By 1890 four major streetcar lines plus several short lines would span the entire metropolis and would continue to extend to the ever-growing suburbs. By then, all of these lines were electrified

Modern improvements came immediately. The first telegraph line had already been laid by the army in 1876. A water-pumping station was established in 1878 near the headwaters of the San Antonio River; it would be joined by a second, downtown pumping station in 1884.[30] This was an unfamiliar novelty to homeowners; they had to be educated in how to use faucets, and at first, patronage for the service was poor.[31] Gaslight was finally extended over most of the city in the late 1870s, and by 1881 the first electric company was formed. Still, electric lighting would not become widespread until alternating current was introduced by the Berg Power and Electric Company in 1887. A bigger iron bridge with fine towers replaced the earlier one on Commerce Street, and by 1890, the river would be traversed by fifteen spans, all but four iron.[32] But these bridges now crossed a smaller river. The new waterworks pumped water out of the river, and artesian-well drilling led to the demise of most of the *acequias*. By 1900, the San Antonio River, once so verdant and free-flowing, would be reduced to a "sluggish trickle through lime and silt."[33]

Perhaps most important for everyday negotiation, a campaign to pave the downtown streets had begun. Many were "macadamized"—graded and paved with crushed stone.[34] Outlying streets, for the moment, were simply graded, the more traveled ones receiving gravel. Most distinctive, however, were five miles of city streets that received a paving of hexagonal mesquite blocks. This was first introduced in 1882.[35] It became more widespread by the end of the decade, encompassing Commerce, Market, and Houston Streets; Main and Military Plazas;

Improved Commerce Street, with mesquite block paving and utility wires, late 1880s. *Courtesy Witte Museum, San Antonio, Texas*

and most of Alamo Plaza (except its northern end, which remained unpaved). Mesquite is a hard and durable wood, but there were problems created when blocks were pounded unevenly by heavy transport traffic.[36]

Along with the progress of improvements came a building boom. Taller business blocks were constructed, beginning with the three-story Dullnig block at Commerce and Alamo Streets and the Crockett block on Alamo Plaza. Hermann D. Kampmann's three-story bank on the corner of Commerce and Soledad was under construction by 1883. The five-story Maverick Bank, located at the corner of Alamo Plaza and Houston Street, replete with steam elevator and luxurious bar, was begun the following year.[37] Trade with Mexico received its official seal when Dr. Plutarco Ornelas, the first Mexican consul for the city, opened his office in 1879.

Although promoters such as Stephen Gould in 1882 and Andrew Morrison in 1890 predicted a bright future in manufacturing and industry for the city, this never happened.[38] Establishing a pattern that continued through the next century, San Antonio's economy was already based on three factors: banking and merchandising, the tourist industry with its connected services, and the military.

In the 1880s, banking and merchandising were booming. Surrounding ranches were now fenced in with the invention of barbed wire; as controlled breeding waxed, the era of the great cattle drives waned. Brokering of livestock, and their products of wool and hides, thrived, and by 1881 San Antonio was the state's leading wool center. Fortunes were made as commission merchants by local brokers such as the firm of Chabot and Cresson, Louis S. and Henry Berg, and Sam Bennett. The coming of the railroads allowed for more efficient shipping of goods, and once the city was connected to the Gulf Coast and Mexico by rail, the picturesque cart trade vanished. As fortunes increased, the businessmen who made them increased their empires by diversifying. Louis S. Berg, besides being a commission merchant, served as an alderman in 1881–82; was a founder of Temple Beth-El in 1874; built a woolen mill; ran a cotton gin; served as vice president of the Lone Star Brewing Company; founded the Berg Power and Electric Company; and, after moving to New Orleans in 1904, became president of the Mobile, Jackson and Kansas City Railway. Hermann D. Kampmann, who took over the Menger Hotel upon the death of his father, also served on the board of the San Antonio Water Works, was vice president of the San Antonio Street Railway Company, and was president of the Lone Star Brewing Company and the San Antonio Gas Company.

Politically, the city became increasingly complex. Administration increased from four political wards to eight. Bryan Callaghan Jr., who began his career as a lawyer and police recorder, became mayor in 1885. He would hold this post off and on into the twentieth century. He also ran an extensive and tight political machine, which, whatever its nefarious side, allowed many of the city's improvements to be made, particularly in the later 1880s.[39]

All of these changes certainly affected the city's everyday life, for worse and for better. Main and Military Plazas continued along their colorful and disreputable way, particularly at night. If the number of celebrating cowboys declined with the demise of the cattle drives, there was still a rowdy proportion of "transients." Some were respectable, such as tourists and consumptives in town for treatment, but many had a more dubious reputation. The city directory of 1878–81 lists 3,000 as a "floating population" among its total population of 20,000.[40]

Except for tuberculosis sufferers (who were housed in sanatoria), recovering invalids, and the more genteel tourists (who stayed, when possible, at the Menger), most of these transients seemed to concentrate in the plazas. Several hotels had been built on Main Plaza that specifically catered to those in the livestock trade, including Hord's (later the Southern), the Central, and the Saint Leonard.[41]

Main Plaza also housed a number of newer, bigger saloons and gambling houses, the most notorious being Jack Harris's Vaudeville Theater. It was located upstairs from Sim Hart's Cigar Store, on the plaza's corner with Soledad, and boasted gambling, a well-stocked bar, a vaudeville show, and accommodating ladies. It had a reputation for attracting the rough and the lawless even more than other, surrounding barrooms. Here, three famous shootings and four resultant deaths took place. The first was the killing of Harris himself by Ben Thompson, city marshal of Austin, in 1882 (the two had been feuding for some time). Two years later, Thompson himself was killed at the Vaudeville, along with his friend John "King" Fisher, in a shootout with Jack Harris's successors at the saloon, Billy Simms and Joe Foster, and a policeman, Jacobo Coy, who worked part-time at the bar as a special policeman and bouncer. Foster, wounded in the fray, later died also. These events led to one of San Antonio's enduring urban legends, giving their location the nickname of the "fatal corner."[42] But other killings occurred on the plazas at the same time. Typical of these was that of Benedict Schwartz, who was murdered in his pawnshop on Military Plaza in 1882 by an unknown thief. There is nothing inherently unusual in this except for the fact that Schwartz had himself killed a fellow Jewish immigrant, Sigmund Feinberg, several decades earlier in a quarrel and had gone unpunished for the deed.[43]

The entertainment available on the plazas continued to be for masculine consumption. Jack Harris's Vaudeville Theater was not the only place that featured bawdy acts; so did the Fashion Theater on Military Plaza. More opulent saloons and gaming houses blossomed, including the White Elephant, located next door to Vaudeville Theater, and others close to Main Plaza on Soledad Street. Theaters also sprang up to the west of the plazas, in an area that also housed the city's thriving red-light district.

Main and Military Plazas continued to be places of bustling activity. Military Plaza became an open-air market, which sold everything from hay to produce to trinkets, reminding tourists of plaza markets in Mexico. This was further enhanced by the heyday of the open-air Mexican food stands, intriguing visitors with their spicy food, so different from the blander American fare. In the 1870s, such dishes had been confined to informal eating places in the western *barrios* of

Laredito and Chihuahua; now they could be enjoyed al fresco.[44] This was, in reality, working men's modest fare, intended to serve the market merchants, but to intrepid visitors, it became a culinary adventure. The entire plaza market, along with the Alamo and the four ruined missions to the city's south, were then an obligatory destination for tourists, oases of Hispanic culture within an increasingly Americanized city.

Something of the colorful nature of Military Plaza at this period is evoked by Stephen Gould's description of it in 1882.

> The Plaza is a large open square surrounded by business houses and crossed by the street railway. On the east side of the Plaza, after leaving room for the passage of vehicles between the curbstone and the central space are long lines of tables . . . here one can purchase fresh vegetables during the entire year. The butter, poultry and eggs department is located on the north of the vegetable stands, while south of them are the Mexican lunch tables, where one can get a genuine Mexican breakfast with as good hot coffee as can be found in the city. Those who delight in the Mexican luxuries of tamales, chilli [sic] con carne, and enchiladas, can find them here cooked in the open air in the rear of the tables and served by lineal descendants of the ancient Aztecs. All the tables are without roofs, so that a pleasant morning must be selected for this visit in order to make it enjoyable, but rain or shine the tables are there and served by their regular attendants, who reap a considerable profit from their business.
>
> The West side of the central portion of the Plaza . . . is reserved for the wood, cotton, wool, hay, grain and produce wagons. . . . [These] are placed in perfect order and lines, so as to preserve the adjacent street lines, and along these are found Mexicans squatted on the ground before small squares of cloth and canvas on which are small piles of the Mexican necessaries, peppers, and wild fruits, and nuts in their season. The bird peddlers are also here in full force. . . . Mexican women monopolize the bird selling and are adepts at it. Indeed the Mexican women are as a rule better traders than the men.[45]

At the same time, however, more provisions were being made for a public evening life for the more delicate and respectable. Alamo Plaza, with its streetcar turnaround, was already becoming the most decorous of the three original plazas. The malodorous meat market was demolished in 1881, while the opulent Opera House, with its exclusive San Antonio Club upstairs, opened in 1886. There followed a veritable flood of drama, comedy, melodrama, and opera. Its

Military Plaza as marketplace, before 1874. *Courtesy Witte Museum, San Antonio, Texas*

grand inauguration featured the American soprano Emma Abbot in Donizetti's *Lucrezia Borgia,* followed by a whole repertoire of grand opera.[46] During the mid- to late 1880s, such well-known actors and actresses as Thomas Keene, Edwin Booth, Joseph Jefferson, James O'Neill, Kate Claxton, and Minnie Maddern (later Mrs. Fiske) appeared there.[47] A varied fare of light operas, musical extravaganzas, melodramas, minstrel shows, lectures, mind readers, and an occasional chamber music group was also featured.

Beer gardens also became even more popular, the most opulent of all being Scholz's Palm Garden, also on Alamo Plaza, three stories high, replete with a respectable billiards parlor and adorned with many potted palms. It opened with a grand concert in 1885. Outdoor performances were also given at Muth's Concert Pavilion and Beer Garden on Grayson Street, not far from the military post. Varying family-oriented activities took place at Wolfram's Central Gardens, which had been established in the early 1870s and was still going strong. Its location was unique, just south of Market Street, where the river looped back on itself to form a peninsula known as "Bowen's Island." Because it had only one entrance off of Garden (later Saint Mary's) Street, it remained a pastoral spot in the middle of the expanding city.

Other cultural and religious institutions also reflected the urban growth of San Antonio. Though the *San Antonio Herald* had ceased publication, the irreverent Republican paper the *San Antonio Light* appeared on the scene in 1881 to counter the more establishment-oriented *San Antonio Express.* The *Freie Press Fuer San Antonio* continued to flourish, and various Spanish-language weeklies were also published, as well as at least one modest, intermittent, African American one. The number of public schools increased, including a high school, to augment already existing private academies.[48] There was a proliferation of places of worship of all denominations. Three of them found homes on Travis Square, including the city's first synagogue, Temple Beth-El; the First Baptist Church; and the elegant Saint Mark's Episcopal Church. The former two were constructed in the 1870s, the latter somewhat later. Travis Square itself completed its construction. An iron fence surrounded its lawn, trees were planted, paths traversed its green expanse, and its center was graced by a commemorative monument.

Shopping also became more convenient. Several small enterprises in retail blossomed into veritable palaces of commerce. The earliest was the hideous emporium of Honoré Grenet, abutting the Alamo and masking what remained of its long barracks with fake crenelation. After 1884, it continued to exist, only slightly less gaudy in appearance, as Hugo and Schmeltzer. Wolfson's, which began as a

Travis Square, an Anglo-American plaza with grass, trees, and a commemorative monument. *Courtesy Witte Museum, San Antonio, Texas*

modest dry goods store on Main Plaza, had expanded considerably. It eventually evolved into a full-fledged department store on west Commerce Street. Beginning its existence as a small store on Austin Street, Julius Joske and Sons became Joske Brothers when it moved to the corner of Alamo Plaza and Blum Street, where in 1886 the cornerstone was laid for what later would be known as "the big store."

The military had finally moved from downtown—northeast to Government Hill, where a quartermaster's depot was constructed on land donated by the city beginning in 1876. The site would continue to expand throughout the rest of the century, being renamed Fort Sam Houston in 1890. San Antonio continued to be a strategic military center during this period, still oriented toward the forts of West Texas.

The residential areas followed the basic pattern of the previous decade, except that they were more spread out, with African Americans still confined to the least desirable areas both on the east and west sides and in the quarry area to the northeast of downtown.

The changing face of the city made viewing and marching in parades a very different experience than it had been in the previous decade. The buildings were taller, but there were also tall utility poles with their many crossbars supporting electrical and telegraph wires, which would have impeded some upper-story views. Electric streetcars also required overhead wires. The sidewalks had been rebuilt, but with the exception of Houston Street, downtown streets were still narrow, and the growing population would only have increased viewing crowds. The *San Antonio Light*'s account of the 1885 Volksfest parade gives an idea of what spectators had to endure, citing would-be viewers stacked along the sidewalks and every available window and balcony jammed. One enterprising fellow shinnied up to a parapet over the door of Lockwood and Kampmann's Bank, where he perched precariously, but with a good view.[49]

Given the packing in of people, it is not clear if anyone would have been able to notice it at parade time, but stores along the processional route began to decorate their buildings in honor of the day.[50] Typical of the period, as the idea of visual pageantry spread not only in San Antonio but elsewhere in the United States, bunting and evergreens were the festoons of choice.[51]

In the 1880s, with the introduction of floats in the parades, there was an additional hazard. The electrical, streetcar, and telegraph wires that crisscrossed the streets limited the height of floats, and it was not unusual for an overambitious one never to survive the first intersection. Though paving did away with axle-breaking potholes, the much-vaunted mesquite block paving, when worn or uneven, could break axles equally well, as could streetcar tracks.

It is probably not a coincidence that the flowering of urban parades around the downtown plazas in the mid-1880s coincided with the roughest period around the plazas themselves. One can only wonder how, during the torchlight processions that marked Diez y Seis, respectable viewers in Main and Military Plazas put up with the drunkenness and prostitution and noise emanating from the surrounding saloons. Part of the job of retaining order fell to the parade marshals, but the conditions probably also accounted for the large contingents of mounted police and military troops that marched in processions of the time.

Larger crowds were also a certainty at the associated celebrations, most usually held at San Pedro Springs Park. This was due not only to the increase in population but to the fact that the railroads were often induced to offer special rates to interested outlanders on festival days; the streetcar company would put on extra cars to bring people back and forth to the park.

SAN ANTONIO: AMERICAN CITY, 1890–1900

The changes in the appearance and the functioning of the city became even more profound in the last decade of the century. By 1890, San Antonio was the largest metropolis in Texas, with a population of 37,673 people; this would increase to over 53,000 by the century's end. Anglo-Americans were now soundly in the majority. While citizens of European extraction continued to prosper, there was considerable downward mobility in the dwindling Mexican American population at this time. African Americans were given few opportunities to improve their lot: their segregated schools were poorly equipped, and they were still confined to the city's marginal dwelling places.[52]

The main economic driver was still San Antonio's status as a market for range stock, cotton, and wool, though the wool market would virtually vanish after government tariffs were imposed in 1894. Proximity and trade with Mexico were still important, but hoped-for manufacturing opportunities never materialized. Encouragement of the city as a commercial center led to the holding of international trade fairs from 1888 through the early 1890s at spacious fairgrounds on the river, south of downtown. Adjacent to the fairgrounds was a new park, Riverside, which would become a second festival site. Though not as extensive as San Pedro Springs Park, it boasted a dance pavilion. Tourism continued to boom, increased by several thousand seasonal residents from the cold North who spent the five winter months in the city.[53] The military post at Fort Sam Houston continued to expand and to play a vital role in the region's economy. San Antonio had also become an attractive venue for trade and organizational conventions.

Perhaps the most obvious outward sign of the city's Americanization was the gentrification of Main and Military Plazas. In many ways, Military Plaza ceased to be a military plaza after 1892, when the city hall (designed by M. O. Kramer "in the style of the Renaissance") was completed right in its central space.[54] Mesquite block paving had replaced the dirt, and trees and grass surrounded the new structure. The outdoor market moved west of San Pedro Creek, as did the Mexican food vendors. William Corner described their sad deportation in 1890: "These al fresco restauranteurs have been hunted by electric lights and city improvements

Map of San Antonio, 1883. *Courtesy San Antonio Conservation Society*

from Plaza to Plaza, until now a poor remnant of them may be found still further west on Milam Square near the grave of the hero, whilst a few others cling tenaciously to a coign of vantage on Alamo Plaza to the east."⁵⁵

Main Plaza was equally transformed. A glamorous, neo-Romanesque courthouse designed by Alfred Giles replaced the old cattlemen's hotels on its southern

Main Plaza's metamorphosis, including mesquite block paving, utility poles, and formal garden, 1890s. *Courtesy U.T. Institute of Texan Cultures*

boundary, while surrounding buildings to the east assumed a greater air of respectability.[56] The infamous site of the Vaudeville Theater, which had burned down in 1886, was now occupied by taller commercial establishments. Most dramatically, the open expanse just to the west of the streetcar tracks, where both the cathedral and the courthouse fronted, was now occupied by a park, much like that on Travis Square. It was replete with footpaths, trees, and flowers, thus completing the metamorphosis of the Mexican plaza into a European-style urban square.

A similar park was established at the southern end of Alamo Plaza, across from the expanded Menger Hotel and the "Alamo Chapel."[57] A grandiose federal building and post office, described as being "Richardsonian Romanesque [in style] with a touch reminding one of Lombardy and the south of France," was built on its north side.[58] Except for the ugly Hugo and Schmeltzer building, the other commercial establishments in Alamo Plaza were solid, modern, two- to three-story buildings that housed a diverse assortment of businesses.

Plenty of older dwellings were still to be found around downtown, though adobes were fast disappearing. There were still *jacales* scattered around the city, particularly in the Mexican American barrios.[59] New neighborhoods continued to spring up as the streetcar lines expanded. There were modest houses to be found everywhere and an increasing number of larger ones in the city's northern suburbs. These new neighborhoods were generally located on the treed hills and restricted to Euro-Americans; they carried such picturesque names as Beacon and Prospect Hills, Grand and Belle Views, Park and Oakland Terraces, and South Heights.[60] Alamo Heights was being laid out at this time, with the inauguration of the Alamo Heights streetcar line.[61] African Americans, particularly those who were Baptist, began to concentrate on the east side. With the expansion of the city into suburban areas, the complexion of its daily life was changing. Whereas in the early 1870s everyone lived in or within walking distance of downtown, the downtown area increasingly became the place where people went to work, shop, or be entertained—respectably at the Opera House or the newly built Beethoven Hall or disreputably. There were now more than three hundred saloons, found on nearly every downtown block, from holes in the wall to ornate beer and liquor palaces. The various vaudeville theaters and gambling establishments still abounded, though most had changed locations. Since Main Plaza had become respectable with its courthouse and park, and Military Plaza had as well, with its city hall and the gardens surrounding it, the majority were now found nearer to the fifteen-block area of increasingly opulent bordellos south and west of Military Plaza. The less affluent flocked to the cheap saloons, inexpensive shows, and Mexican and Chinese restaurants west of San Pedro Creek.[62] What were once small dry goods establishments had grown into grand department stores, brimming with goods from all over the country and beyond. Besides Wolfson's and Joske Brothers, these included Wolff and Marx on east Commerce Street. All offered specials and incentives for those shopping during festival times.

All and all, by the turn of the twentieth century, manifest destiny had triumphed. San Antonio's downtown had transformed itself into a typical American city, with all the typical goods, conveniences, and services. It carefully preserved its Hispanic heritage on its fringes but retained only those monuments in its center worthy of the name: San Fernando Cathedral and the "Alamo Chapel."

The venerable Veramendi Palace, on Soledad Street, once the home of Jim Bowie's beloved wife, Ursula, had degenerated into a saloon. And the Alamo probably didn't count. The original, uncompleted, Spanish mission site had been co-opted by Anglo-Americans, for the famous battle of 1836 had piqued America's imagination almost from the moment it was fought. The Alamo became the city's dominant myth. In reality, little of its physical space and structures of 1836 remained intact. The *convento* remains were now masked by Hugo and Schmeltzer, and most of the mission land had been absorbed by Alamo Plaza. The church's never-completed main facade had been transformed by the ideas of two German architects in 1849. In this form, the former church in particular became the city's icon and shrine, with Bowie, Travis, and Crockett its canonized saints.[63] By the mid-1890s, it would become the object of concern of the first historic-preservation movement in San Antonio, championed by female descendants of settlers of the Republic of Texas. During the same years, the Alamo facade would be decorated and illuminated with electric ornamentation during festivals.

Not only were parades and festivals bigger and more elaborate during this last decade of the century, but the attending crowds continued to increase. Contemporary observers commented on elaborate street decorations lining the route and crowds of spectators so dense that they occupied every available space and foothold on the facades of surrounding buildings, surging off sidewalks onto streets, leaving precious little space for the processions themselves.[64]

Taller buildings did help, but by this date, parade planners also set up a special viewing stand in Alamo Plaza and sometimes in Main Plaza to accommodate special guests in comfort. Otherwise, the parades were still free, but street viewers mostly had to stand and crane their necks. The final fillip of sophistication arrived with the new century, when, for a new festival entitled "Spring Carnival," Commerce Street would be sensationally illuminated by a series of specially erected electric arches. Before this date, nighttime illumination had grown from torchlight in the 1870s, to portable calcium lights on the plazas in the 1880s, to the existing electric street lighting in the 1890s. What better way to advertise progress in the metropolis?

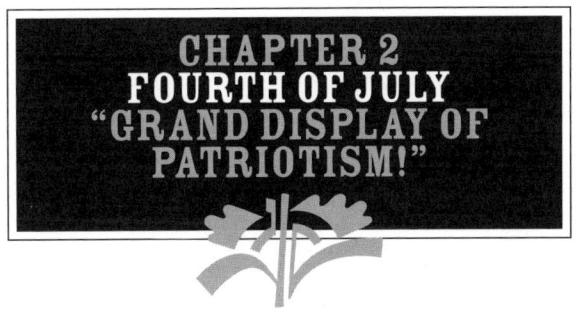

CHAPTER 2
FOURTH OF JULY
"GRAND DISPLAY OF PATRIOTISM!"

Upon the coming Fourth of July [of 1877], as upon all preceding fourths as far back as memory reverts, the remembrance of the anniversary of our [San Antonio's] nationality rests and has rested upon our fire department. This department is composed principally of our German citizens, and while Americans have often wondered why this especial observance of the day, the reason is plain. The Germans discharge their duties as citizens and as men. . . . It is the day when the proclamation of American liberty from British thralldom went forth from Philadelphia.. It is a day the fire companies have set apart to remember, and they will do it so long as the bonds of association remain intact.
—*San Antonio Express*, June 21, 1877

When we think of the most patriotic of American holidays, we think of the Fourth of July. As the seminal American symbol of independence, it has been celebrated in various cities and towns in the United States since the post-Revolution years. At first, it was a rowdy occasion for excessive drinking, but by 1825 it had become more genteel, with civic parades.[1] Its pattern as an organized American festival was set by 1850: a parade through city streets generally consisted of militia units, trade associations, political parties, reform associations, ethnic brotherhoods, and simple revelers.[2] The parade was frequently followed by a reading of the "Declaration of Independence" and then long-winded sermonlike orations that served to reinforce the authority of historical narratives as common ground among diverse groups.[3] In San Antonio, as we have already seen, the Fourth of July was duly celebrated in the nineteenth century, but it was to have a very checkered history indeed.

FOURTH OF JULY CELEBRATIONS IN SAN ANTONIO BEFORE AND DURING THE CIVIL WAR

The Fourth of July was San Antonio's second-oldest civic holiday.[4] The earliest account of its celebration dates to 1846, the year after Texas joined the Union. It consisted of a large barbecue on the Alameda (the section of the future Commerce Street east of the river), with horse, foot, and sack races; a greased-pig contest; horseshoe pitching; and orations. Many people from the surrounding countryside came into town to join in the festivities.[5]

The lack of regularly published newspapers before the 1850s precludes documentation of subsequent celebrations, but they may well have occurred. The *San Antonio Herald* reported that in 1859, the Alamo City Rifles, a militia and drill group, assembled in Alamo Plaza at 7:30 A.M. There they held a dress parade at 9 A.M. that consisted of a "march through the principal streets of the city in connection with the San Antonio Fire Company."[6] At 3 P.M., the Alamo Rifles reassembled at their armory and marched to San Pedro Springs Park, where later a dinner was held, presumably with patriotic speeches.

This parade was hardly extensive or glorious. Since Fourth of July and Washington's Birthday parades of the day were of similar components and size, we can imagine what it must have been like from the account by a young visitor to San Antonio from Boston, Harold Elisha Scudder, who wryly described the city's Washington's Birthday parade of 1859: "The [Alamo] Rifles, twenty-four guns, marched round the Military Plaza, followed by the San Antonio Fire Company with the engine drawn by four horses who raced off in every direction but the right one, and accompanied by a very rabble of Mexicans and Germans of all ages and sexes, but chiefly little boys. The procession was led by two bands, one for the Militia and one for the Fire Company, which played opposition tunes."[7]

Volunteer militia and fire companies, the principal participants of the 1859 Fourth of July and Washington's Birthday parades, would form the backbone of many Independence Day celebration processions to come.[8] Volunteer militia groups began to appear in San Antonio, as they already had in other cities, in the 1850s. In times of peace, they did precision military drills in uniform. In times of war, they volunteered for combat, serving in their own units. The Alamo Rifles were formed in 1857 under the command of Capt. John Wilcox, and its sixty members later fought for the Confederacy under Gen. George E. Deats.[9] It survived into the 1870s, only to be replaced in the next decade by various newer companies.[10]

The volunteer fire companies became the most permanent fixture in Fourth of July and other, later civic parades. Their form-fitting dress uniforms (trousers and matching shirt with a contrasting blazer and identical hats or helmets) admirably showed off their (mostly) athletic physiques. Their hand-drawn apparatuses (in 1859 no more than modest hand pumps, hose reels, and a two-wheeled hook and ladder truck) provided a ready-made festive note to any procession.[11] From the founding of Company 1 (originally called the Ben Milam Company) as a bucket brigade in 1854 and Company 2 in 1859, most of the members were German Americans.[12] The first separate hook and ladder unit, made up entirely of well-built gymnasts of the German American Turnverein, followed in 1869. This was just a year after the advent of Company 1's first steam pumper, the *William Menger*.

During the Civil War, most of the volunteer firemen of Companies 1 and 2 were occupied with military pursuits. To keep fires at bay, African American slaves of local citizens were mobilized into a fire company under the direction of Confederate military officers. After the war, these black firefighters, now free, reorganized themselves into two volunteer fire units: Company 3, in 1865, and Company 4, one year later. They served the African American community and had to be content with hand-me-down equipment from the white companies, for they received no financial aid from the city, as their white counterparts did. For many years they operated with only two hand pumpers.[13]

As the city expanded, the total number of hook and ladder and hose companies rose to eight before they were replaced by a professional organization in 1891. For reasons that are not very clear, their statutes from the beginning specified that "Washington's birthday and the 4th of July in each year shall be celebrated in such manner as the directory may agree." Though a parade was not mandated, they were obligated to offer "a celebration of some kind" for each holiday.[14]

The volunteer firemen came from all sorts of occupations. Ed Braden, Fire Company 1's first captain, served in the Confederate army, ran a livery service, and was a county commissioner in the 1880s. Candy manufacturer Gustav A. Duerler succeeded his father in leasing and improving San Pedro Springs Park. Ben Mauermann had a gun store and later became a founder and president of Alamo Cement Company. William Hoefling Sr. was a sausage maker, a county commissioner in the 1880s, and an alderman from Ward 2 in 1892–93. Hans Degener, who owned a lumberyard, also served several alderman's terms. Among the non–German Americans, Antonio P. Rivas came from a prominent Mexican American family and was active in politics, while Henry B. Andrews was vice president of the Sunset Railroad and later a director of the Texas National Bank.

For the African American firemen, the situation was somewhat different. Their civilian jobs were far more modest in scale. Zachariah Irvin, foreman of Company 3, was a driver for Erastus Reed Furniture Store. William Logwood worked as a porter for John Twohig. Solomon Bradfield was a janitor at the county courthouse. For these gentlemen, being a volunteer fireman was a key to earning prestige and recognition both within the African American community and beyond it. In the case of both African American and German American volunteer companies, their members had a close camaraderie that bound them together as tightly as the members of any fraternal organization.

Firemen and militia companies continued to celebrate the Fourth of July in 1860. The *San Antonio Daily Ledger and Texan* reported that all stores closed; that there was an artillery discharge in Military Plaza, where the procession formed; and that flags were hoisted at various places around the city. The Alamo Rifles and the volunteer firemen were nearly joined by nonfiremen Turnverein athletes, but the latter group started their parade on Soledad Street and arrived in Main Plaza just as the others were leaving it.[15] Patriotic speeches were given at two places, in front of the Menger Hotel and just down the street in front of the Alamo. The "Declaration" was read, and M. G. Anderson delivered the oration, in which, according to the *Daily Ledger and Texan,* "it was impossible to refrain entirely from the allusions common to the occasion, but the speaker showed his good taste in avoiding the usual highfalutin strain."[16]

By the time the next Fourth of July was reached, the Civil War had begun, and Texas had been absorbed into the Confederacy. Nevertheless, the day was celebrated. The fire companies and the Alamo Rifles this time were joined by officers of the Confederate Army, along with state, county, and city officials and citizens. The route was long for the day, starting with the circling of Military and Main Plazas, followed by a journey up Commerce Street to Alamo Plaza, where the procession paused for a reading of the "Declaration of Independence." The marching then resumed, returning up Commerce Street to Military Plaza. Everyone subsequently repaired to San Pedro Springs Park for a reading of the constitution of the Confederate States of America, orations, and then a picnic.[17]

SAN ANTONIO'S FOURTH OF JULY PARADES DURING THE PERIOD OF RECONSTRUCTION

It is unclear if the Fourth of July was celebrated during the rest of the war, but in the years just after the defeat of the Confederacy, its character, though similar in program, took on a very different face. Ironically, though it had been a Southern custom for plantation owners to force their slaves to celebrate the Fourth of July in antebellum days—a custom happily appropriated by the Confederacy in 1861—the victorious Union used the holiday as a symbol of Reconstruction in the South after 1865.[18]

The first of the postwar parades in 1866 was similar in makeup to the one of 1860—only much of the specific personnel had changed.[19] Fire Companies 1 and 2 marched, as always, and members of the Turnverein were there to start the parade on time. Gone (for the moment) were the Alamo Rifles, and the military officers who marched were the Union victors. The mayor and city officials appeared, but now they were members of a new, Reconstruction-appointed administration. There were also two new features. The first consisted of the liberal German members of the Laborer's Association (later renamed the Arbeiter Verein), founded in 1865.[20] This group occasionally included African American members.[21] The second was the appearance of a young girl dressed to represent the Goddess of Liberty. The goddess reflected a trend toward such allegorical figures that had been developing since the 1840s in Northern American cities, which would provide the impetus for later pageant floats full of visual historical rhetoric. Now it had also spread to the South.[22]

The procession started and ended at Military Plaza. It began at 7:30 A.M. and included a pause in front of the Menger Hotel for a reading of the "Declaration." There were no other events afterward.

Not all parade viewers in that first postwar year were celebrating. The memoirs of Vinton James, a San Antonio resident and Confederate sympathizer, describe the bitterness of the defeated Southerner toward the Union-sympathizing marchers in 1866. He noted the large presence of U.S. troops in the procession, as well as the conspicuous participation of Samuel Bell, a Union sympathizer who waved an enormous Union flag from a carriage. James remarked, "the people of southern persuasion viewed this 1866 4th of July celebration with sullen looks and silence and utter helplessness and bitter disappointment, as they had fought so hard and lost everything and all in vain. There were many good citizens who enjoyed the return of the Stars and Stripes, especially the Germans, many of whom were Northern sympathizers."[23]

On the other hand, Fred Mosebach (like Vinton James writing seventy years after the event) recalled the festival of the following year on a far more positive note, pointing out that among the participants were seven hundred African American members of the Loyal Union League.[24]

The 1867 parade circled the downtown streets and plazas, starting and ending in Alamo Plaza. The chief marshal, S. W. McAllister, was a prominent political figure of the day, serving both as a justice of the peace and as Bexar County judge. Marshals were usually chosen from among prominent community members, and aside from the ceremonial "honorary marshals," they were an indispensable feature in parades. It was up to them to maintain order within the line of march and to keep the disparate groups of marchers moving at a reasonable pace.

In Alamo Plaza, right after the parade ended, judge and lawyer Theodore G. Anderson read the "Declaration of Independence." He was followed by James Pearson Newcomb, journalist, Republican party politician, and at that time champion of the African American cause, who read the Emancipation Proclamation (a clear message of the festival's tone). Then Judge Thomas H. Stribling delivered an oration. The viewers and marchers alike then repaired to San Pedro Springs for an all-day picnic, and grand balls (presumably for the white population only) were held in the evening at the Menger Hotel and the Casino Club.

The members of the Loyal Union League (organized by the Unionist Republican Party), who marched so proudly in 1867, had an uneven history as far as the postwar Fourth of July celebrations were concerned. They were not permitted to participate in the 1869 parade but did so in 1870, along with members of the newly formed Colored Laborer's Association. Whether or not they marched during this period, African Americans generally held their own picnics, usually at a venue some distance from the main celebration at San Pedro Springs.[25] African American inclusion in Independence Day parades was at the whim of the white population. This was apparently also the case with Fire Companies 3 and 4. Presumably they were also organized under the existing volunteer firemen's statutes. They were not a part of the 1867 parade, though they did participate in several others, notably in 1875, 1876, and 1884.

The celebrations of 1869 and 1870 also had Mexican American participation in the form of the Club Mexicano-Texano. This was a Republican political club of Mexican American citizens, organized in 1868. Several of its members, notably Antonio P. Rivas (the volunteer fireman) and Juan E. Barrera, had fought for the Union, and part of the club's platform included racial equality.[26]

The military appeared in force in the form of local federal troops from the post. It was these troops that enraged Vinton James in the 1866 procession, but they would be a pivotal part of many San Antonio parades of different sorts throughout the nineteenth century, and their smart uniforms added to the spectacle.

In spite of the predominant Republican/Union tone, it should be noted that a number of the prominent participants in the Fourth of July festivals during these years were Confederate veterans, including the 1870 parade marshal, policeman Alejo Perez, and orator Gen. William H. Young. It is doubtful that such a mix would have been found in more diehard Southern cities.

Municipal validation in these processions was provided by the presence of city and county officials, who rode in the parades in carriages. In the immediate postwar years, the mayor of the Reconstruction administration was William C. A. Thielepape, so his presence would have reflected the Republican party character of the parades at that time. In general, the presence of these officials was nonpartisan. Thielepape's non-Reconstruction successor, François Giraud, also rode in Fourth of July parades, as did subsequent mayors right up to the end of the century. In the larger civic sense, parades provided the advertisement of city officials doing their job, whatever their political affiliation.

There was little in the way of allegorical display in the Fourth of July festivals of 1866–70, beyond the presence of patriotic uniforms and flags. The only exceptions were the girl impersonating the Goddess of Liberty in 1866 and thirty-eight girls who appeared as representatives of the states of the union (another popular theme of the day) in two subsequent celebrations.[27] In 1869, the *San Antonio Herald* printed a request for volunteers for this purpose among the young ladies of the community.[28] They are not listed in the marching roster published by the newspaper, though they were directed to report to the chief marshal in Alamo Plaza at 7:30 A.M. on parade day. In 1870, there was a mention of thirty-eight young ladies representing the United States again, this time marching at San Pedro Springs after the delivery there of the "Declaration of Independence."[29] The only other striking visual feature was the decoration of the Turnverein's hook and ladder truck, probably with evergreens and/or bunting, in 1870.[30] The size of the fire apparatuses, which would only grow larger over the years, provided ready-made floats, both decorated and undecorated, in many San Antonio parades in the later nineteenth century. When horses began to draw the fire engines, they would often be decorated too.

Though Reconstruction officially lasted until 1877, it lost its punch in 1872 with Giraud's mayoral triumph and basically disappeared entirely after the 1875 election of independent James H. French—who would hold the office for a decade.[31] It appears that even by 1871, San Antonio's Fourth of July parades were fast losing their pro-Reconstruction stance. Indeed, there *was* no parade in 1871, as the *San Antonio Express* lugubriously reported: "We learn with extreme regret that the Fire companies and societies generally feel indisposed to parade this coming fourth of July. . . . The patriotism of those city fathers who let the day go by without aiding its observance is questionable."[32]

Though there was a parade in 1872, it was relatively small. It consisted of the city administration in carriages, the city band, and the white firemen. Fire Company 1 sported red and white uniforms. Fire Company 2 and the Turner Hook and Ladder Company both wore blue and white. Though the hook and ladder truck was "cleaned and trimmed," it remained undecorated.[33] The parade ended in Alamo Plaza, where the mayor made a speech and the "Declaration" was read.

Patriotic apathy was to continue. The only actions in 1874 were the flying of a large green Irish flag alongside the American one by the city's Irish citizens and a celebration meeting hosted by the same group in the evening.[34]

Things picked up temporarily in 1875 and 1876. All four fire companies marched in the 1875 parade, and the Turner Hook and Ladder Company was augmented by the Turnverein band and a full contingent of their gymnasts. The death of Reconstruction was clear that year in the presence of the Alamo Rifles and marching veterans from both sides of the late conflict. On the other hand, racism was not rampant, since the African American fire companies participated. The city band and the usual contingent of mayor and aldermen in carriages rounded out the procession.

The parade was somewhat more elaborate in 1876: this was the year of the U.S. Centennial, which in many American cities was elaborately celebrated with grand parades, tableaux, orations, and activities.[35] In San Antonio, elaboration was modest. The procession was described as a whopping "600 yards long[!]" It consisted of the 1875 participants, including the Alamo Rifles in smart new gray cloth uniforms, with tall plumes on their helmets and polished weapons. These participants were augmented by the Eighth U.S. Calvary Band, from the military post; Russi's Band (one of a number of local short-lived municipal bands); various veterans' groups; and women of the African Methodist Episcopal (AME) church.[36] The presence of these ladies was noteworthy, not only because they were women of color but because at this time it was still unusual to find contingents of marching women in American parades.[37] Each organization carried colorful identifying banners. Surprisingly, though there was the usual series of events at San Pedro Springs in 1875, the official Centennial festival ended with a reading of the "Declaration of Independence" in Alamo Plaza right after the parade.

It appears, though, that once the Centennial had passed, there was a problem in drumming up enthusiasm to parade at all. In 1877, only Fire Company 2 and the Turner Hook and Ladder Company marched, along with a contingent of the military, the Alamo Rifles, and the usual city officials. Mother Nature did not cooperate, either. The original plan was to march from Alamo Plaza, along Commerce Street, and ultimately to San Pedro Springs, but the parade had to be aborted at Flores Street because of the early-morning heat and heavily blowing dust on the unpaved streets. Participants and viewers had to get to San Pedro Springs as best they could. For those who managed the journey, there were the usual orations, headlined by Joseph E. Dwyer, followed by a 5 P.M. dance.[38] These events must have been rather sedate, for many Anglo-Americans and German Americans went instead to Guenther's Mill. This was where the African Americans were holding their own event, with their own speakers on a flag-decorated speaker's platform, two bands playing throughout the day, and "a very large crowd [having] a very large time."[39]

DIVERSE CELEBRATIONS OR NO CELEBRATIONS:
THE FOURTH OF JULY, 1878–97

It might be thought that with the coming of the railroad in 1877, which brought an increasing number of Anglo-Americans to settle in San Antonio, Fourth of July festivals in the late 1870s and early 1880s would become more inclusive and elaborate. But the truth is that between 1878 and 1883, almost nothing went on. Certainly parades were virtually nonexistent, except for the fire companies and Maverick's band marching from Alamo Plaza to San Pedro Springs in 1879. There were firemen-sponsored picnics at San Pedro Springs during this period, an oration or two, and occasionally some fireworks, but little more. Otherwise, celebrations seem to have been restricted to private picnics or barbecues. The nadir apparently came in 1882, when most of the fire companies went to an organized parade in New Braunfels; only Company 1 intended to go to San Pedro Springs, but excessive mud from an all-day rainfall prevented even this. Rainfall would prove to be the nemesis of celebrations in later years as well: it forced cancellation of scheduled festivities in 1885 and again in 1889.

The only sizeable parade in the decade came in 1884. On July 1 of that year, the Confederate and Mexican War veterans' associations and the fire companies met and decided to plan a more ambitious procession. They invited participation from the military, various ethnic contingents (the Arbeiter Verein, the Sociedad Mutualista Mexicana, the Ancient Order of Hibernians), plus the Workingmen's Union and "all other societies."[40] It was short-range planning, but the parade ended up being of a considerable size. None of the invited ethnic societies involved themselves, but the military sent the Eighth Cavalry Band, which marched in two sections, plus mounted members of the Eighth Cavalry itself. Veterans of the Grand Army of the Republic (in new uniforms) joined the badge-wearing Mexican War and Confederate veterans. The fire companies, of course, came out in style. All the engines were decorated with flowers, evergreens, and flags, and the members of Fire Company 3 stood out in their red and white uniforms. These marchers included "a large number of citizens in carriages, buggies, farm wagons, donkey carts, on horseback and on foot," a spontaneous demonstration of popular patriotism.[41] New to the Fourth of July parades was the commercial element of five wagons from the Lone Star Brewery.

This was not the first appearance of commercial entries in a San Antonio parade, and it certainly would not be the last. By the mid-nineteenth century, American entrepreneurs were firmly committed to commercial advertisement in any form. Street banners, handbills, posters, cigar-store Indians, and newspaper advertisements abounded. Delivery wagons provided a convenient way to advertise a company by emblazoning names and logos on their sides. Sometimes, a firm would have a wagon permanently decorated to advertise their product, and these would simply be entered into a parade. The Lone Star Brewery was a little more ambitious in temporarily turning its wagons into floats in 1884. They displayed their machinery and ingredients on the wagons and decorated them for the occasion with bunting and the ubiquitous evergreens.

The veterans of the Mexican War appropriated the day for ceremonies in honor of themselves at the celebration held after the parade at San Pedro Springs. They received a handsome flag emblazoned with mottoes, an image of the Alamo, and a shield of the United States from James M. Carr, a local real estate mogul. Three young ladies, Alvina Klock, Sara Smith King, and Miss Seffel, made the flag presentation. Two of them, Misses Klocke and King, delivered patriotic addresses dealing with the veterans. U.S. marshal Hal Gosling gave a longer speech, as did former major T. Trevanian Teel, now an attorney (his was entitled "Texas, One and Indivisible"). Finally Capt. Charles Crawford eulogized those Mexicans "who had fought and died for Texas liberty."[42]

It was not unusual for young women to appear as patriotic orators and flag presenters during this period.[43] And it was probably also not unusual for Anglo-American veterans to recognize and praise those Hispanic residents who had fought alongside them (though Charles Crawford's wife was a Tejana, and he belonged to the Mexican Social Club and was to serve as a Sociedad Mutualista marshal in the Diez y Seis parade later that year).[44] While contemporary accounts of the 1884 exercises at San Pedro Springs do not report on the ethnic makeup of the attendees at these events, they were evidently not simply an Anglo-American preserve, even though the Mexican War had certainly marked an Anglo-American

Mexican War veterans gather at the speaker's platform, San Pedro Springs Park, July 4, 1884. *Courtesy Witte Museum, San Antonio, Texas*

victory over Texas's southern neighbor. The very fact that the Sociedad Mutualista and the Arbeiter Verein were invited to march, even though they chose not to, suggests an inclusive rather than exclusive definition of "American," an acknowledgment of the integrity of this diversity—a larger context for Independence Day.

But this attitude was not enough to ensure that such events would be repeated—on the Fourth of July, at least. During the rest of the 1880s (when it wasn't rained out), the celebration reverted to a firemen's festival. And when the volunteer fire companies yielded to a new, professional fire department in 1891—which evidently did not have any directives about celebrating this day, much less Washington's Birthday—the main impetus to publicly celebrate Independence Day disappeared with them, except for the big patriotic parades of 1898 and 1899 and the smaller one of 1900. Through the early and mid-1890s, what celebrations there were became small, scattered, and sometimes private. Concerts at beer gardens, gun-club shoots, and African American and other group picnics at local parks were the order of the day.

The one organized Fourth of July festival with a parade during this period was in 1895, but it was entirely different in its makeup from anything that had come before. It was sponsored by the Catholic Central Union, and its marchers were basically a roll-call of the members of Anglo-American and German American Catholic groups, including the Saint Joseph's Society (of the city's German Catholic parish), the Ancient Order of Hibernians, and other (unspecified) societies. Their parade had music by Carl Beck's Military Band (actually a private, not a military-affiliated, band). There was also one commercial venture, Captain Jesse Bennet's Dog and Horse Show. The route was also different from the customary one: it began and ended at Travis Square, circled Alamo and Main Plazas only, and returned via Houston Street to its starting point. The site for afternoon festivities was Riverside Park, and the program consisted of the requisite reading of the "Declaration of Independence" and speeches, rounded out by a performance by Captain Bennet's horses and dogs, athletic contests, and Beck's band in concert.

The Catholics held a similar celebration in 1896 (minus the parade), this time at San Pedro Springs, but it was somewhat marred by rain. However, the "Declaration" was read, and a series of lengthy orations were made, in spite of the inclement weather—and at least some people showed up to listen. Orations were the linchpin of nineteenth-century American festivals, whether political, ethnic, or patriotic, and individual speakers often went on for more than an hour.[45] There was a curious sameness to the hyperbolic declamatory style of speeches of the day, whatever the occasion. This is nicely illustrated by a small portion of an oration given at the 1896 festival by Joseph E. Dwyer.

> Revolutionary times bring forward great men. We cannot point to such a period without finding a cluster of them. The marked men of all times are usually connected with such events, and the magnitude of the events keeps their renown before the world. It takes a memorable period to try and develop men and heroes. Cromwell, Napoleon, Frederick and Washington were not less molded in such times as were John De Witt, Mirabeau, Castelar and our own Adams, Jefferson and Henry. What but such times could have handed down the names of Demosthenes and Cicero, as well as sturdy Brutus and Cato? Indeed, it requires an exigency to try the virtues and weaknesses of mankind, and for this reason all heroes and many statesmen are made by war. It requires an extraordinary genius to engrave his name in the records of nations so as to endure when wholly unconnected with the convulsions of the State, unless he be distinguished for science or letters alone. Bacon, Aristotle and Plato were not made great by convulsions any more than was Shakespeare, Racine or Corneille.[46]

And that was only part of the preamble. Such speeches required quite a high rate of literacy not only among the speakers but among the listeners too. A lot of this, of course, could have been attributable to the classical nature of nineteenth-century rhetoric and education. But it is hard not to wonder what sense this would have made to a working-class reveler who would have been fortunate to have finished grade school. On the other hand, such diverse allusions were such a ubiquitous (and even expected) part of nineteenth-century speeches that they would have made sense to many of the middle-class listeners at least.

Joseph E. Dwyer is a good example of the sort of public figure who was selected to deliver these flowery speeches. He began as a dry goods dealer and later joined his brother in operating a land and law office. During the Civil War, he was a major in the Confederate Army and later served as an alderman for Ward 1 in the 1880s. His father was an Irish pioneer and his mother Hispanic. He was a sought-after public orator of the day. He had already given a Fourth of July speech in 1877, and he would give an oration to the Mexican American community on the occasion of Diez y Seis in 1898. As such, he was representative of the multitextured fabric of San Antonio society of the period, but his rhetoric was typically and wholly American.

PATRIOTIC COMMUNITY-WIDE FOURTH OF JULY CELEBRATIONS IN 1898 AND 1899—AND A DECLINE AGAIN IN 1900

It is likely that without a war to rekindle the flames of patriotism, public Fourth of July celebrations in San Antonio would have fizzled. The needed impetus occurred in April, 1898, when the United States went to war with Spain. San Antonio, being a military center, was right in the middle of preparatory action. Teddy Roosevelt trained his Rough Riders at the city fairgrounds. Two militia companies of the period, the Belknap Rifles and the San Antonio Zouaves, enlisted en masse shortly after the declaration of war. By June, the city bristled with a patriotic zeal quite different from the divisive spirit that had pervaded it before and during the Civil War. By June 19, ambitious plans were underway to make a public display of this patriotism on the Fourth of July. Numerous organizational committees were manned by members of San Antonio's business and political community, enthusiastically headed by the mayor, Bryan Callaghan Jr.[47] Special railway rates were quickly arranged to accommodate viewers from outlying areas and cities; these extended from July 3 through July 5 in hopes of attracting out-of-town shoppers. Within three days, committeemen had secured cooperation not only of veterans but of troops still stationed at Fort Sam Houston and some field pieces and artillerists to fire the national salute.[48] A huge postparade barbecue was planned, with "fifteen heifers, twenty-five sheep, twenty-five goats and ten hogs provided, and a competent corps of cooks" in charge.[49]

The result was the enormous procession of three divisions cited in the prologue of this book. As we briefly examine the roster of participants again, it is easy to see how they differed from those in any of the previous Fourth of July parades. In the first division, the promised military troops (there were only twelve, but it was a credible number given their demand elsewhere) were augmented by both Union and Confederate veterans. Enough participating bands were there to satisfy everyone: Carl Beck's Military Band (divided into three units) was joined by the First Texas Volunteer United States Cavalry Band and the Alamo Band, which played one of this war's most popular tunes, "Hot Time in the Old Town Tonight." The city's small Cuban community marched, as did several fraternal organizations.[50] The second and third divisions were a celebration of the American nationalism of the ethnically diverse San Antonians. The second division was mainly made up of German American organizations, including *vereine* (mostly the militant hunters and athletes of the Krieger, Turner, Scheutzen, Jaegerlust, and Elsaaser Vereine) and two choirs, the Beethoven Männerchor and the Frohsinn Singing Society. There were several, mostly German, beer-related labor unions (Brewers, Coopers, and Drivers). German fraternal organizations also participated, including the eight lodges of the Sons of Hermann and fifty members of the Knights and Ladies of Honor, one of the few coed societies of the era (the men marched while the ladies rode in carriages). A commercial float from Joske Brothers' Department Store was included here, probably because the Joske family was of German origin.

The third division was an interesting mixture. The Irish and German Catholic societies, which had paraded in 1895, appeared here, along with mutual aid societies of various nationalities. These included the Christopher Columbus Society (which qualified as being both Catholic and Italian) and the French Mutual Aid Society (led by French consul P. E. Claudon), with two young girls of French descent representing the French and American Goddesses of Liberty. There were also seven Mexican mutual aid societies: La Unión, Mutualista, Benevolencia, Morales, Hidalgo, the Mexican Workingmen's Club, and the Sons of Mexico. This contingent was headed by Antonio P. Rivas as Uncle Sam. Cowboys on horseback followed. The now-professional fire department came in their decorated trucks and, as a tribute to Fourth of July parades past, with a marching contingent of ex–volunteer firemen. Citizens in carriages and on foot completed the ensemble.

Members of all divisions wore badges and uniforms, of course, and carried their organizational flags and banners, as well as American flags, all to show solidarity with their country. The shops en route were to have been decorated as well, but recent rains and a stormy-looking sky on parade day made shop owners leery of putting out their bunting and greens. There was, however, a large picture of George Washington displayed at the corner of Commerce and Alamo Streets.

The succeeding program was split into two venues: five thousand congregated at San Pedro Springs to hear orations both in English and Spanish, to be followed by athletic contests, while two thousand people, mostly German, went to Riverside Park, where there were equally patriotic speeches in English and German.

It was the first, last, and only Fourth of July parade in the nineteenth century where the entire city population participated as Americans. People from all walks of life marched with pride, from wealthy entrepreneurs to humble laborers, who made up most of the mutual aid societies. For once there was no agenda, no really dominant group in the parade.

The one contingent not mentioned in the 1898 press was the African Americans. On the other hand it is worth noting that African Americans did march in a San Antonio patriotic parade the following year. In that procession, four hundred members of the Tenth Cavalry ("the Black Demons of San Juan Hill" and rescuers of the Rough Riders) marched with their band in the patriotic parade the day after the Battle of Flowers and were roundly cheered as they reenacted their charge up San Juan Hill.[51]

The grand Independence Day parade of 1898 was not the beginning of a new trend. Though there was significant participation by both veterans and the military (including the triumphant San Antonio Zouaves, home from the war) in the procession held in 1899, community representation was much smaller. Two Mexican mutual aid societies (Hidalgo and Benevolencia) and carriages bearing the mayor, one alderman, and the city clerk made up a second division, and the third and last division consisted of seven undecorated fire engines preceded by the fire chief, William Tobin, riding in a buggy as marshal.

Fourth of July parades of the era in other American cities were becoming grand pageants featuring fancy floats where ladies garbed in reasonable imitations of classical robes represented such figures as "Columbia" or "Liberty and the Thirteen Colonies" or were featured in *tableaux-vivants* portraying famous scenes from American history (usually based on famous paintings of the day).[52] San Antonio's efforts from the 1870s right through the end of the century were curiously lacking in such rhetorical fare. Visual spectacle was instead provided by varying numbers of colorful and drab uniforms, banners and flags, gaudy badges worn by members of particular associations, and the shiny instruments and uniforms of band members. Even decorated fire engines were the exception, not the rule.

It was estimated by the *San Antonio Express* that in 1899, eight to ten thousand people showed up at San Pedro Springs after the parade for the orations, dancing, and fireworks, plus a drill by the Zouaves and a performance by African American cakewalkers.[53] This number appears impressive; it certainly strained the resources of San Pedro Springs, but it paled in comparison with the twenty-five thousand people estimated by the *Express* to have witnessed the earlier patriotic parade on April 22.[54]

By 1900, the celebration of the Fourth of July had subsided again to a parade of the fire department, the military and veterans, and city and county officials. There was more action afterward at three venues. Six thousand people turned up for a flag raising, speeches, a barbecue, athletic contests, a bonfire, and a dance that night at San Pedro Springs. One thousand Catholics attended a similar program at Riverside Park, while an undetermined number of African Americans heard orations and had their own athletic activities at Connor's Grove.[55] It should be noted that there were a sizeable number of black citizens at San Pedro Springs as well; the barbecue there was hosted by Lafayette Walker, a long-time African American political and social activist, whom we will meet at greater length in conjunction with Juneteenth festivals.[56]

The fact that the emphasis in 1900 was on the park festivals and not the parade is significant: as the Fourth of July was to continue to develop over the next century, its direction would continue to take it toward diverse group celebrations rather than a unified civic holiday centered on a parade. In this respect, the ground was already laid in the nineteenth century. Even then, it never appears to have been a holiday that had enough emotional appeal to the general public, except when it was driven by a specific surrounding event, such as Reconstruction (negative) or the Spanish-American War (positive). In San Antonio, the really big and enduring civic celebrations would be stimulated more by events that were truly local in origin and appeal than distant visions of George Washington and the American Revolution. There were other independences to be found closer to home.

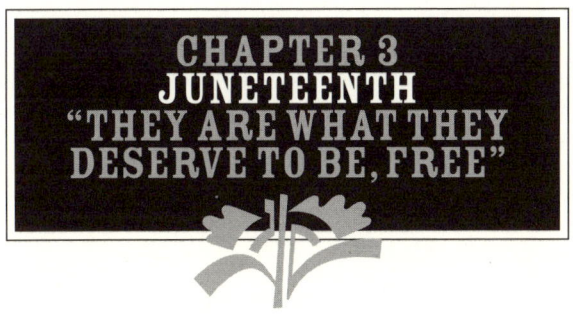

CHAPTER 3
JUNETEENTH
"THEY ARE WHAT THEY DESERVE TO BE, FREE"

> The people of Texas are informed in accordance with a Proclamation from the Executive of the United States, all slaves are free. This involves an absolute equality of rights of property between masters and slaves, and the connection heretofore existing between them becomes that between employer and free laborer. The freedmen are advised to remain at their present homes and work for wages. They are informed that they will not be allowed to collect at military posts, and that they will not be supported in idleness, either there or elsewhere.
> —Gen. Gordon Granger, in William H. Wiggins Jr., "Juneteenth: A Red Spot Day on the Texas Calendar"

Abraham Lincoln issued the Emancipation Proclamation on January 1, 1863. Slave owners in Texas were either unaware of it or blithely ignored it for another two and a half years, until Gen. Gordon Granger announced it in Galveston on June 19, 1865.[1] The spontaneous celebrations that erupted on that date in East Texas, western Louisiana, southwestern Arkansas, and southeastern Oklahoma were just the latest in a tradition of American emancipation festivals going back to 1808, first in the Northern United States, then in the West Indies, and later in the former Confederacy, the dates varying from July 4 (in New York) to April 16 (in Washington, D.C.) to diverse dates in May and August, depending on when slaves heard the news that they were free.[2] In many places in East Texas, these early celebrations had religious undertones and were based on the tradition of slave watch-night services. In other places (including other Texas towns), they were commemorated by barbecues, drinking, athletic contests, singing and dancing, and parading.[3] In San Antonio, Juneteenth (as it came to be known, an elision of "June" and "nineteenth") was mostly secular in nature and had much in common in structure with other local civic festivals.

One big difference existed between the vast majority of African Americans in the United States in the nineteenth century and any other nonnative group: they did not come voluntarily because old-country conditions were so unpromising that there was strong motivation to escape to where old rules no longer held and it was possible to make a fresh start. Voluntary immigrants were free to preserve those old-country customs that they saw as positive and drop the rest. In the case of African Americans, the situation was precisely the reverse. They were forcibly taken from their African homes and transported against their will under inhuman conditions to become slaves in a place where they had no rights. Their old-country customs were intentionally erased, their native languages and religions suppressed, and in many cases their family structures totally destroyed. Emancipation, whether earlier in the North or later in the South, may have freed them from being treated as subhuman, but that did not mean that they were readily absorbed into the "American melting pot." Their dark skins and non-European features marked them as easily distinguishable from Euro-American settlers. Texas was no exception—African Americans remained lowest on the social totem pole and in San Antonio were distinguished in nineteenth-century city directories by the mark © for "colored" after their names, so that there would be no doubt of the inferior status that the greater urban society (including Mexican Americans) accorded them.

Though African Americans in San Antonio were spared the epidemic of lynching that spread through the rest of the South and parts of the North at this time, their life in the city during the last third of the nineteenth century was far from comfortable. Partly because they were relatively few in number, and partly because white discrimination was so effective, they were intimidated into inferior jobs and living conditions.[4] In 1870, they constituted a mere 15 percent of the population and did not increase very much proportionally in the next thirty years. On top of that, 50 percent of the African Americans in the city showed a marked downward mobility during this time.[5] One of the best opportunities for Texas' African American men had been as cowboys. Many had been assigned ranching duties as slaves in West Texas, and after emancipation, they continued in the profession as free men. At the peak of the cattle drives, Texan men of color made up 25 percent of the cowboy population and prospered, for there was a far greater spirit of equality on the range than in town. Though few had command positions, and their wages were low, some earned and saved enough to buy their own ranches. With the end of the drives in the 1880s, this opportunity became a rarer option; indeed, they were excluded from the meat-packing industries that flourished in the city at this time. And in town, no matter what their status on the range, they were segregated and treated like all other African Americans.[6]

Cotton and other plantations were few in the area before the Civil War. Thus, most of San Antonio's slaves had been in urban and domestic servitude: they were porters, servants, janitors, hack and cart drivers; they occupied the most menial of hotel jobs and were teamsters in the freight-cart trade; and they engaged in manual and heavy labor.[7] After emancipation, they were relegated to the same occupations at very low wages, many of the hotel jobs paying only in tips. For women, who needed to work to help maintain their families, the main occupations were as laundresses and in domestic service—positions to which they would be consigned until well into the twentieth century. Jobs of higher status were those of owners of black businesses serving their own community, teachers in segregated schools, and community leaders in the role of pastors in their churches.

Though they acquired the right to vote with emancipation, African American voters were frequently manipulated—either by intimidation or by cleverness on the part of politicians. Their main white ally of the day was James Pearson Newcomb, whose support was at best a mixed blessing. Descending from a family of early Anglo-American settlers, he first made his mark as a newspaperman, publishing the pro-Union *Alamo Express* in 1856, when he was still in his teens. With the outbreak of the Civil War, his newspaper office was burned down by the Confederate Knights of the Golden Circle, forcing him to flee first to Mexico, then to California.[8] After the war, he returned and became a power in local politics as a Republican, initially under William Thielepape, San Antonio's first mayor under Reconstruction, and then as Texas' secretary of state. But Newcomb proved too radical even for Reconstruction politicians. Frustrated in his efforts to expedite the bringing of both a railroad and a street railway to San Antonio right after the war, he managed, in 1870, during his term as secretary of state, to bulldoze through a new San Antonio city charter that was so extreme that even many of his liberal German American colleagues were shocked (it was largely nullified in the following years by succeeding administrations). Among other things, it incorporated African American schools into the city's public school system under state administration.[9] The nullification, however, did not slow him down. Newcomb purchased property for subsistence housing for incoming African Americans west of Alazan Creek. He served as an alderman in 1878–79 and as secretary of the San Antonio Street Railway in 1877, was one of the founders of the Republican *San Antonio Light,* and became the city's postmaster in 1883.

But Newcomb's support for the black community was a double-edged sword.

Though publically campaigning for their rights, he privately considered African Americans racially inferior.[10] As long as they voted Republican, Newcomb was their advocate, even after his radical city charter failed. Along with James Brackenridge, he was responsible for constructing the first black public school building in the city in 1879, to supplement the already existing but woefully inadequate Rincon School, established eleven years earlier. But when African American Republican support began to erode toward the end of the 1880s, Newcomb abandoned them, becoming a member of the "Lily-Whites," an antiblack movement that led to what became basically an all-white Republican party in the 1890s.[11]

Newcomb aside, San Antonio institutions gradually developed the typical Jim Crow ordinances of most Southern cities, giving African Americans separate and unequal services and public facilities. They were virtually barred from white-owned hotels and restaurants. There were also more subtle forms of discrimination: black entertainers could and did play to white audiences but could not sit as spectators along with them. On the other hand, they had to endure Anglo-American caricatures of them in the black-face minstrel shows so popular during the nineteenth century—originally performed by whites only. It was only in the 1870s that "real," "genuine," or "bonafide Negro" minstrel troupes began touring in America with their own distinctive dance styles and cleaner humor but still within the white parameters set forth earlier.[12] Nevertheless, African Americans, forced to construct their own social life and institutions within their own boundaries, established a rich variety of community resources and activities. Because in Central Texas so many of their African roots had been expunged from their lives during the period of slavery, most of these institutions mirrored Anglo-American ones in name and organization but took on a character all their own.

The moral and spiritual mainstays of the community were its churches. One of the few institutions permitted them as slaves, churches continued the role of a central organization in the African American community after emancipation, and their number quickly multiplied after 1865, encouraged by Anglo-Americans who were eager to keep their own congregations to themselves.[13] African American counterparts to white denominations were founded. Earliest was Saint Paul's Methodist Episcopal Church in 1866.[14] The Green Chapel African Methodist Episcopal (AME) Church followed; it was organized with white help. It became so identified with Republican and Reconstruction causes under the Revs. Nance Duval and E. Hammitt that it led to the founding in 1867 of the less radical and ultimately more enduring Saint James AME Church with the aid of German American Democrats. More denominations soon followed. The Mount Zion

Baptist Church was established by freedmen in 1871, and the Macedonian (later Second) Baptist Church split off from Mount Zion in 1879. Others came later. An all-black Catholic mission, Saint Peter Claver, was built in 1888, and an African American Episcopal church was established soon after. Congregants tended to live near their churches, which led to more African Americans moving to eastern parts of the city after the establishment of Baptist churches there.

The churches were not only places of worship and the communal spirit generated by religious services; they also became community centers. Many social institutions emanated from them, of the variety associated with mutual aid societies in other communities. These provided financial assistance for the destitute, funerals, clothing and food distribution, and elderly and orphan aid.[15] Their Sunday school classes strengthened community and familial ties, and children and adults members alike would actively participate in Juneteenth celebrations.[16]

Many of the church pastors became important social forces. Activist African American pastors could act as liaisons to the larger San Antonio community as well. Some, such as teacher and pastor Rev. Nance Duval, became so celebrated as preachers that whites came to listen to their sermons (but only by invitation).[17] In daily life the owner of a prosperous bathhouse and barbershop (one of the few opportunities for black entrepreneurs right after the war), Duval used both his economic independence and his church status to help better his community, securing jobs for many and gaining the respect of Reconstruction Republicans and Democrats alike. When he died in 1869, members of the entire spectrum of the San Antonio community attended his funeral, and he was buried in a white cemetery.[18]

Henry Allen Boyd, a respected pastor at the Mount Zion Baptist Church in 1891, worked weekdays at a more menial position, as a porter at the post office.[19] Methodist ministers had no other occupation, and they were often transferred from one congregation to another in the course of their careers.[20] Though housing was provided for them, salaries were generally modest. Whether full-or parttime, clergymen were regarded as highly respected community leaders.

The other status occupations for African Americans were generally no more lucrative. The role of the African American volunteer firemen, who worked without compensation, has already been mentioned. Schooling was recognized, as in other segments of American society, as the key to both social and economic advancement, and teachers were esteemed. The earliest black school, the Rincon School, was modest at best, and its original teachers were white. The other eight schools added during the nineteenth century were not much better, though black community pressure brought a high school in the 1880s. An early effort by Anglo-

Americans to keep training in these schools mainly vocational was later augmented (again by community pressure) by stronger academic curricula. As African American teachers began to replace more patronizing white ones in the course of the later nineteenth century, they too became respected community leaders and, along with the ministers, powerful Juneteenth orators.

THE DEVELOPMENT OF JUNETEENTH FESTIVALS IN SAN ANTONIO

San Antonio's earliest Emancipation festival, if not exactly a "Juneteenth," was celebrated in 1866, occurring on June 11 rather than June 19. It had all of the earmarks of a typical San Antonio celebration, including a parade before a barbecue and a dance at San Pedro Springs.[21] Though the rather patronizing account chronicled in the *San Antonio Herald* does not mention it, there was probably a reading of the Emancipation Proclamation at San Pedro Springs before the barbecue began; this would have been in keeping with the manner in which subsequent Juneteenth celebrations developed.

Exactly when the African American population of the city began to have celebrations on June 19 is not clear.[22] The earliest full description of a local Juneteenth festival in a local newspaper did not come until 1879, but the article's tone suggests that they had already been taking place for some time.[23] In that year, there was a rather short parade, featuring a band, the two African American volunteer fire companies, the Order of the Golden Links (presumably a fraternal organization), and children of the AME church's Sabbath school.[24] The grand marshal, indeed the only marshal, was Lafayette Walker, mounted on "a large glossy animal."

Lafayette Walker, a blacksmith by trade, was heavily involved in Reconstruction politics, championing Republican candidates for office at that time and working to ensure African American voting rights then and later. He headed the Loyal Union League, a countrywide organization formed to guarantee these rights.[25] He was a friend of James Newcomb and also made friends among the German Democrats.[26] He survived Newcomb's defection and remained a spokesman for his community and was a frequent orator and parade marshal at Juneteenth festivals well into the 1890s.

The parade of 1879 began some time after 8 A.M. and had a short route—it commenced in Military Plaza and proceeded up Alamo Street, and then the marchers went to Maverick's Grove (on the river, just above the Alamo Mills). It is not clear whether there were orations that year, but picnics lasted until the afternoon, when a rainstorm ended the celebration.

A similar festival was held two years later, again with a downtown parade, but this time with two separate venues for the following celebrations. The larger of the two was held at San Pedro Springs; the second again took place at Maverick's Grove.[27] Though no reason for the split was given, it can be noted that James Pearson Newcomb was one of the orators at San Pedro Springs, along with African American bathhouse and barbershop owner Charles A. Johnson and Abram L. Grant, minister of Saint James's AME Church. Perhaps, then, the split had to do with pro- and anti-Newcomb factions. At least fifteen hundred people thronged San Pedro Springs, and quite a number of them came in by train from outlying towns and rural areas.[28]

A split occurred again in 1882. Lafayette Walker was once more grand marshal of the Newcomb/San Pedro Springs faction. James Newcomb again delivered an oration from a separate table marked "for whites only." It thus appears that although both Anglo- and African Americans attended the San Pedro Springs festival, they were not permitted to mingle. Rev. Elder Wright of the Macedonia Baptist Church delivered a second speech, while Rev. J. R. Carnes of Saint Paul's Church read the Emancipation Proclamation.[29]

Though Juneteenth commemorated the 1865 Texas announcement, Lincoln's previous proclamation was given full tribute in the festivities. In 1883, the year of the twentieth anniversary of the Emancipation Proclamation, San Antonio Juneteenth festivals hit their stride with enough clout that the parade was inaugurated with an eighteen-gun salute by the U.S. artillery at its starting point, the Alamo. Though the procession still did not circle all the plazas, it was considerably longer, with more varied participation, and important enough to make the front page of both the *Express* and the *Light*.[30] A cordon of city police led things off. Grand marshal William Dickey, treasurer of the festival's organizing committee, marched in front. He was followed by the Sunset Band; two African American militia companies; the Austin City Rifles and the Excelsior Guards; Fire Company 3, with its foreman, William Logwood; the Universal Joint Club; a baseball club; teachers and students of the Rincon School; a float featuring costumed girls representing "Columbia and the States of the Union"; and carriages containing orators and leading community citizens.

Black militia companies/drill teams were part of a flurry of such organizations, both black and white, that were founded in the 1880s. In 1884 alone, the

The Excelsior Guards, about eighteen years after their founding in 1884. *Courtesy Mrs. Vera Williams Young*

Belknap Rifles, the San Antonio Rifles, and the Excelsior Guards received their charters.[31] The Excelsiors would become a fixture of Juneteenth parades. They were precision marchers, competing against African American companies from other towns, much as their Anglo-American counterparts did with their own groups. The African American militia companies held encampments with competitive drills against other Texas groups in San Antonio in 1891 at Fest's Garden (on Alamo Street at East Commerce) and in 1893 at the fairgrounds, south of downtown. Besides these rigorous exercises, the two-day encampments featured dress parades, drills for children's auxiliaries, a "dairy maid" drill for lady participants, plenty of orations by African American community leaders, and nightly entertainments at the campgrounds.[32] In the Juneteenth parades, the Excelsior Guards' smart uniforms (blue with white facings and straw hats in 1883; blue blouses, white trousers, and helmets by the end of the century) excited much admiration from parade viewers. In fact there was a substantial crowd of these viewers in 1883, made up of spectators from all segments of the city's population.[33] A parade was a parade, after all, and available to everyone who cared to turn out; evidently many did.

The black baseball team in the 1883 parade marks the beginning of Juneteenth afternoon competitions in San Antonio, which would continue into the next century. By this period, baseball had truly become "America's pastime" all over the country, with all sorts of different groups fielding teams. It was considered a wholesome outlet for young men, both in and out of the African American community. The sport was already associated with Juneteenth celebrations in Texas, and it became a metaphor all over the region for African American integration into American culture.[34] In some regions, black teams would play white ones, though in San Antonio, this does not seem to have been the case. By the late 1880s and 1890s (depending on the year), participating African American teams included the Alamo Field Grays, the Rising Stars, the Mascots, the Early Birds, the Menger, the International Red Stockings, the Gray Mule Club, the Sunflowers, and the Browns. Of all of these, the Alamo Field Grays, later simply known as the Grays, were among the earliest and most enduring—in the following century, the team would provide several star players to the Negro League.[35] They always marched in uniform, adding to the color of the procession.

When examining the parade participants in 1883, it becomes evident that the African American community was forming counterparts to the most typical groups that made up other San Antonio parades of the era. At this point in time, even their allegorical presentations reflected this: the float of girls representing "Columbia" and the United States (all dressed, of course, in red, white, and blue) is startlingly similar in theme to the thirty-eight white girls representing the states in the 1869 and 1870 Fourth of July parades. The same allegory would appear again in other nineteenth-century parades—as it already had in many festival processions for decades throughout other American cities.

Fire Company 3 wore the red and white dress uniforms that they would wear just a few weeks later to celebrate the Fourth of July. These colorful firemen, the blue-and-white-garbed Excelsior Guards, and the girls on the float indicate that the prevailing motif of the U.S. national colors dominated the procession, as it did on Independence Day.

In 1883 postparade events took place entirely at San Pedro Springs and had many of the same players as the previous year. Once again, James Newcomb gave an address (this time entitled "The Progress of the Colored Race from Slavery and the Benefits Derived from Emancipation"), and Rev. J. R. Carnes read the Emancipation Proclamation and the Fourteenth and Fifteenth Amendments. Juneteenth was the only one of the six festivals treated here whose oration activities regularly opened with a prayer, reinforcing the role of the churches within the African American community. In 1883, the prayer was led by Rev. Joseph W. Womack, pastor of the Missionary Baptist Church.

Unlike the Fourth of July festivals of the late 1880s, which dwindled down to nearly nothing, Juneteenth celebrations continued to grow. The 1884 celebration was very similar to the one of the previous year. No artillery salute took place, but there was participation by the Eighth Cavalry Band, which also appeared two weeks later in the Fourth of July parade.[36] Though white groups did not customarily march in post-Reconstruction African American processions, the U.S. military continued to provide a contingent when asked. Also added this year was a second, apparently short-lived, local African American militia company, the Granger Guards, named in honor of the announcer of the Juneteenth message, Gen. Gordon Granger.[37] The route of march had expanded by this year to encompass all three of the downtown plazas, bringing it more in line with the city's other processions. The grand marshal for this parade was Zachariah Irvin, foreman of Fire Company 3. Three other marshals helped him out, including James Martin and Shed Porter, who had served on the Juneteenth organizing committee the previous year.[38]

The most remarkable thing about the 1884 celebration was the publication in the *Express* of the full text of the oration delivered at San Pedro Springs by Rev. Mack Henson, minister of Saint Paul's Methodist Church. Though it was common for nineteenth-century newspapers to publish the texts of orations (many of them extremely long), this is the only instance of a San Antonio daily doing so for the speech of an African American.[39] It is interesting to compare the tone of this speech to the more rose-colored pictures evoked by white speakers such as James P. Newcomb (who, in the previous year, had spoken "of the many benefits [African Americans] were enjoying in this locality").[40] Though some of Henson's speech is very topical (he comments on a plan to return all blacks to Africa and also upon the importance of nonpartisan voting), sections of it address far more timeless issues:

> Justice is often painted with bandaged eyes. She is described in forensic eloquence as utterly blind to wealth or poverty, high or low, white or black, but a mask of iron, however thick, could never blind American justice more than it does when a black man happens to be on trial. Here, even more than elsewhere, he will find all presumptions of law and evidence against him. The reasonable doubt which is usually interposed to save the life and liberty of a white man charged with crime, seldom has any force when a colored man is accused of crime, Indeed, color is a far better protection to the white criminal than anything else. . . .

... It is [the black man's] sad lot to live in a land where all presumptions are arrayed against him, unless we accept the presumption of inferiority and worthlessness. If his course is downward, he meets very little resistance. You can see that plainly by the meagre provisions made for his elevation. I mean for his education, which means his elevation and encouragement. But if upward, his way is disputed at every turn in the road.... [H]e excites resentment and calls forth stern and bitter opposition. If he offers himself to a builder as mechanic, to a client as a lawyer, to a patient as a physician, to a university as professor, or to a department as a clerk, no matter what may be his ability or attainments, there is a presumption, based upon his color or his previous condition, of incompetency, and if he succeeds at all, he has to do so against this most discouraging presumption.[41]

Such words would not have been out of place in civil rights speeches in the 1960s, and in the matter of unequal justice, they are still valid. Reverend Henson was part of a tradition of "race men," public orators who were proud of their origins, activists in the field of African American rights, and eloquent speakers in the general American nineteenth-century oratorical tradition.[42] In his tenure at Saint Paul's Church, which lasted from 1883 to 1886, Henson crusaded tirelessly for African American rights in San Antonio.[43] In 1883, he chaired the State Convention of Colored Men in Austin, and his continuing outspokenness for black and white equality would make himself and his congregation targets of white hostility. This led not only to vandalism of his church but to attempts on his life.[44] Though James P. Newcomb would continue to give his palliative speeches at Juneteenth festivals through 1886, Henson's orations inspired many others on similar topics, both secular and religious, in the years following his departure.

There is one final piece of evidence for the importance of the 1884 festival: the city's freight depot closed down on June 19. Virtually all of the men who worked at the depot were African American, and virtually all of them were at the Juneteenth festival.[45]

In 1887, marchers were joined by an African American union, the Colored Coachmen's Association, twenty of whose members rode on horseback. After tenuous beginnings in the 1870s, labor unions were finally being organized in San Antonio. Much of the impetus for this organization came from the Knights of Labor, whose influence peaked in 1886 with six assemblies in the city, one of which was African American.[46] Though the Knights ceased to wield much clout after 1891, unions continued to proliferate during the last decade of the century.

The Brotherhood of Coachmen would be proudly represented throughout the late 1880s and 1890s. One of their most active members was James Martin Jr., whom we have already met as a parade marshal. He was closely associated with the Juneteenth celebrations; he served on the organizing committee for the festival from 1883 to 1885 and was president of the general committee in 1890. He was also president of the committee to organize the San Pedro Springs celebrations in 1892 and 1893. He delivered an oration in 1895. In addition, he was active in the Junta Patriótica, a labor and political organization that became the voice of the Knights of Labor in the mid-1880s. In this capacity, Martin was one of the few men of color who participated in a nonblack celebration in San Antonio: in 1886 and in 1888, he delivered orations at Diez y Seis celebrations, first as a member of the Junta and then as a member of the equally prolabor San Pedro Club.

By 1890 the parades had become sizeable (the 1890 parade consisted of four separate divisions) and were as much a visual treat for spectators as other festival processions. The Excelsior Guards and baseball teams appeared in their snappy uniforms. Missing were the firemen, for Fire Company 4 had been disbanded in 1881 and Company 3 in 1888.[47] Other groups soon took up the slack. Juneteenth marchers in 1888 were joined by uniformly dressed members of the First Regiment of Texas Colored Veterans, as well as equestrian coachmen with banners and badges. Citizens fortunate enough to own or have access to carriages rode in the parade dressed in their best, and any available wagons (some decorated, some not) swelled the marchers' ranks further. Spectators from diverse populations of the city and beyond also increased as the parade route lengthened. The fame of San Antonio's Juneteenth festival increasingly attracted visitors from out of town: as in other celebrations of the period, special railroad rates were available on festival day. Some of the visitors came by special invitation. In 1890 there were two orators from Galveston, the politician N. Wright Cuney and Richard Nelson of the *Galveston Freemen's Journal*. In 1892, Professor A. H. Boyles of Houston and E. N. Martin of New Orleans were keynote speakers.[48]

There was apparently little correlation between the size of an organizing community and the elaborateness of a given festival. The African American population of San Antonio was never larger than its 15 percent of 1870 and began a slow proportional decline after that.[49] The number of attendees at any Juneteenth celebration was rarely more than two thousand, and that included out-of-town visitors from Houston and Galveston.[50] The elaborateness of the parades and festivals seemed to have more to do with city growth and urban pride than it did with absolute population ratios. The costs of staging these festivals were minimal: participating groups provided their own uniforms, if they were part of an organization that wore them, or badges and flags, if they were not. Floats, when they were used, were of the homemade variety until well into the 1890s, and any available flatbed wagon or coach could serve with proper decorations. Participating groups or individuals paid for tables that served as food booths where they sold homemade fried chicken, pies, and other dishes to raise money. Costs for whatever permits were needed were low, and the greatest expense would be to rent a celebration place, if it was a private venue like Fest's Garden. Most of the necessary money needed for handbills, advertisements, permits, and incidentals was generally raised by contributions within the community. Though the number of black merchants was small in comparison to, say, the number in the German American community, those who had money contributed, and the rest was literally raised by nickels and dimes. If anything could be said to represent a true American grassroots endeavor, it was a festival like Juneteenth that made up in enthusiasm whatever it lacked in sophistication.

Not only was the 1890 parade the biggest so far, but the festival that followed was bigger too; it lasted for two days, with different events planned for June 19 and 20. A detachment of U.S. artillery fired a twenty-five-gun salute at San Pedro Springs, in honor of Juneteenth's quarter-century anniversary. After the speeches, festival-goers could partake of victuals from over thirty food booths, thirteen melon wagons, and "any number of lemonade and ice cream stands."[51] The celebration was attended by a sizeable number of white citizens, who knew a good party when they saw it. It was at these postparade venues that various elements of San Antonio could mingle on a scale that was not practiced in everyday life. Though they still would not sit side by side, everyone was free to partake of food, view scheduled entertainments, hear speeches, and wander the festival grounds.

On the second day, the "colored baseball championship finals" were held for an enthusiastic crowd, and there were more orations and an exhibition drill by the Excelsior Guards. In the evening, a grand "calico ball" took place. Themed balls, luncheons, and parties were all the fashion in 1890 among elite members of society, and certainly not in the black community only. The basic premise was that all attending ladies were admitted only if their gowns were made of calico (or cotton, if it were a "cotton ball," or whatever type of fabric might be designated). The modest fabric was, in some ways, a societal leveler, though extravagance could still manifest itself in the elaborateness of the ball-gown design. At any rate, it gave the ladies a nice opportunity to show off and to assert their place in the community social hierarchy.[52]

A two-day festival was also staged in 1891 and featured two new parade participants, male and female members of the genteel Lawn Tennis and Croquet Club and members of African American fraternal organizations, including the Seven Stars of Consolidation, the Gate City Lodge, and two lodges of the Grand United Order of Odd Fellows (commonly known by their initials G.U.O.O.F.). It was at this time that fraternal orders reached their apex in America. The African Americans quickly formed their own lodges as counterparts to existing white orders (the first black Odd Fellows lodge being organized in New York in 1843). There were two chapters in San Antonio: Alamo Lodge 2142, established in 1880, and San Antonio Lodge 2522, formed in 1884.[53] They served both as mutual aid societies and as fraternal brotherhoods. The black members marched in their regalia (aprons stamped with the arms of the order) in many of the Juneteenth parades in the 1890s. They would eventually be joined by G.U.O.O.F members from other surrounding communities under an umbrella unit called the Sunset Lodge. They also established a ladies' auxiliary, known as the Household of Ruth, whose members marched on foot as well.[54]

THE GREAT SCHISM, 1892–97

Juneteenth continued its growth in the 1890s, but at the expense of unity. Beginning in 1892, two factions staged concurrent and often rival festivals. Unlike the split in venues for postparade activities ten years earlier, this included rival processions. The division appears to have been between the church-sponsored groups on the one hand and the fraternal, union, and sports factions on the other. Did the latter prove too rowdy for the family character of the church groups?

The church members staged their parade on a west-to-east route. They began by Main Plaza, proceeded up Commerce Street to Alamo Street, marched around Alamo Plaza, then headed further east, ultimately arriving at the corner of Commerce and Live Oak Streets. There a collection of vehicles conveyed marchers and spectators to the banks of Salado Creek, southeast, near Kampmann's Ranch. Besides Sunday school groups and members from both Methodist and Baptist churches, the parade included the Excelsior Guards and members of the Black Union Veterans.[55] The chief marshal was one of the few African American policemen of that era, J. M. Shelburn, who in 1898 would be in charge of the entire festival. Most of the orators were pastors.[56] The more uplifting character of this festival was reinforced by the presence of a float representing a

J. M. Shelburn, Juneteenth marshal and later festival chairman, ca. 1900. *Courtesy Mrs. Vera Williams Young*

"Negro Log Cabin," a reminder of slavery to those who had survived it and a lesson to all those participants and viewers born after 1865.

The other parade, organized by the Alamo Lodge of the G.U.O.O.F., was larger, containing two divisions. It also had its share of Union veterans, along with the ex-firemen's band and ex–volunteer fireman Zachariah Irvin as marshal. The balance of the procession was made up of nine lodges of the Odd Fellows from as far away as Corpus Christi and San Marcos and the local ladies' chapter of the Household of Ruth. There were also several baseball teams and lawn tennis clubs and one defecting Sunday school from the Saint James African Methodist Episcopal Church, who rode in decorated wagons. Their route and celebration venue were more familiar, the parade circling all three plazas, beginning at Franklin Street on the near west side and ending at Saint Mary's Street, where revelers rode the streetcars to San Pedro Springs. Two pastors of Saint James's Church served as orators (the Right Reverend Bishop Abram L. Grant and the Reverend Dr. D. E. Johnson), and baseball and tennis games were held. There was more white attendance at this festival than at Salado Creek, perhaps due in part to its San Pedro Springs location.

The split of 1892 was costly in terms of attendees. The *Light* reported that about eight hundred people went to each venue and that "at both places there was considerable lack of enthusiasm and the event seemed to be less infused with life than in former years."[57] Apparently things did not pick up the second day of either festival.

Evidence of bad feelings in the split can be seen not only in the rather lackluster spirit of the 1892 festivals but also by an 1893 excerpt from an African American newspaper of the period, the *Weekly Tonguelet*, which railed against such a schism, attributing its cause to political and commercial pressures, particularly by the owners of the streetcar line.[58]

The *Tonguelet* may well have been looking out for the image of the African American community in the eyes of San Antonio's other inhabitants—how would they view a group of people who they felt were inferior if this group couldn't agree enough to put on a unified show? Or perhaps the writer felt that it was a more powerful component of their society who wanted everyone to go to San Pedro Springs in order to benefit themselves. In any event, the appeal didn't work. The church faction in 1893 went to Riverside Park, this time augmented by some baseball teams, while the Excelsior Guards joined other ball teams and fraternal organizations in the parade to San Pedro Springs. Downtown must have been a confusing sight on the morning of June 19, 1893. The

Riverside Park people began their parade on the east side on South Center Street at 9 A.M., headed west over Crockett to Alamo Plaza, proceeded down Alamo Street to Commerce Street, and then went northward to Travis Square, where they boarded streetcars for the park. The San Pedro Springs procession started half an hour later from Military Plaza, proceeded along Commerce Street, also circling Alamo Plaza, and turned east on Houston Street to Soledad, where streetcars waited for the marchers and spectators. Since the parades started only half an hour apart and shared a common route on narrow Commerce Street—in opposite directions—did they collide somewhere? If they did, neither newspaper commented on it. However, there must have been some close calls, because the following year, the two processions followed more or less the same route, from Milam Square east over Commerce Street: "Each [procession] took the route.... [T]he San Pedro Park procession started second, but marched straight through Commerce Street to the Main Plaza and Commerce Street corner, but had to wait until the Riverside Park procession filed in, when they then followed and made one great procession down the street."[59]

What floats there were in these parades continued to be modest. The San Pedro Springs parade of 1894 featured "two German Day floats with school children." The German American Volksfests featured the most elaborate floats of the nineteenth century, as we will see in chapter 6. But those of 1893 were actually the simplest, being no more than decorated flatbed wagons with canopies. In the Volksfest parade, these had featured scenes from Grimm's fairy tales. By 1894, the German Americans had given up on plans for another Volksfest, but they still owned a certain number of flatbeds dedicated for floats. Perhaps they loaned or sold them to the African Americans. How they were decorated for Juneteenth is not known.[60]

Conflict among various factions continued over the next three years and appeared to take its toll: "Emancipation celebrations are easy enough to arrange, but a grand union celebration, without division or dissension is the hopeless task that confronts the arrangement committees at each recurring celebration," lamented the *Express* in 1896.[61] It appears as if the split was still church (at Riverside Park or Limburger's Garden, north of downtown on River Avenue—now Broadway) versus nonchurch (at San Pedro Springs) throughout the period. The San Pedro Springs parade of 1896 introduced one prominent new feature: it was the first in San Antonio to feature a queen, Miss Ella Belle Parker. She rode on her own decorated float, accompanied by her maids of honor. It is not clear who sponsored the royalty, but since the ladies were in the second division with the Brotherhood of Coachmen and the executive officers of the festival, it is probable that one of these two organizations was responsible.

In the following century festival royalty would become an obsession: by the late 1900s, every parade featured such a proliferation of queens, princesses, and duchesses, not to mention festival kings and the occasional prince, that it is fascinating to note that in the nineteenth century, the concept barely existed. This is true not only in San Antonio but in most urban festivals of the period.[62] In most cases, women riding or marching in secular urban parades were either allegorical representations (we've seen the Goddess of Liberty, "Columbia," and the states of the union so far) or were part of a women's organization, such as the Household of Ruth. To have a reigning female sovereign, even for a day, on public display in any procession was unknown in the city until this Juneteenth of 1896.[63] Miss Parker was the parade's finale, preceded by eight decorated floats with Sunday school children.

The "Great Schism" bottomed out in 1897, when there were three celebrations, each vying with similar programs for public attention; Juneteenth was beginning to rival the Fourth of July for the title of "most splintered celebration," but like the latter, it came roaring back as a united effort in 1898.

THE GLORIOUS JUNETEENTHS, 1898–1900

Was it the heightened patriotism inspired by the Spanish-American War that did it? Or was it simply that the African American community realized that factionalism was counterproductive? Whatever the reason, in 1898 the longest and grandest Juneteenth parade was mustered, and the most elaborate of united festivals was planned and carried out at San Pedro Springs. Both factions, which had marched in separate parades over the past several years, were there, united and in glory. The Excelsior Guards, now divided into two companies under Capt. Robert G. Ellis and Lieut. E. D. Sulski, were augmented by the Capital City Light Guards of Austin. Ministers and orators rode together in carriages. The baseball teams were out in force, in full uniform. The new sport of the day, cycling, was amply represented by numerous "wheels," decorated with greenery, and the queen for the occasion, Miss Clara McPherson, rode in a carriage with four maids of honor. There were five floats, including, once again, one with girls dressed as the Goddess of Liberty and each of the thirteen original states. Sunday school children marched with flags. The route of the procession was the

Miss Clara McPherson, queen of the Juneteenth festival, 1898.
Courtesy Mrs. Vera Williams Young

plazas-encircling one most favored by parading groups for all the city's festivals, with marchers and spectators boarding streetcars to San Pedro Springs at Soledad Street.

The San Pedro Springs opening program was also much more elaborate, combining traditional and new features and arranged to include people of all generations. It was beginning to resemble a patriotic pageant, then just coming into fashion, rather than a mere pretext for lengthy speeches. An opening chorus was sung by the Sunday school children, followed by traditional prayers. The queen and her court were ceremonially introduced, and then a solo was sung by a young girl, followed by *Columbia,* as sung by the Goddess of Liberty and the girls representing the thirteen original states. The goddess, Miss Ida Murray, delivered an oration based on a prize-winning patriotic essay she had written. The usual sequence of addresses and orations by pastors and other community leaders followed, punctuated by more patriotic songs sung by more young ladies.[64]

The balance of that day and the next was filled with baseball and tennis matches, a mock battle between the Austin Capital City Light Guards and the Excelsiors on the first afternoon, and balls in one of San Pedro Springs Park's pavilions each night. Something of the triumphal atmosphere can be evoked by a bit of verse appearing on posters announcing the event.

> Where the trees grow tall and the leaves are green
>   Where there's no sun to burn your face
> There's nothing but shade to be seen;
>   We cannot find a better place
> There will be no splits this year, of course
>   We've marshaled them from every source;
> The old, the young, the short, the thin
>   Will celebrate at San Pedro Springs
> There's Water, too to slack your thirst; the purest, coolest
>   ever found
> Everything you wish on earth can be had on San Pedro
>   grounds.[65]

Similarly grand parades and festivals took place in 1899 and 1900. The 1899 festival included cakewalkers, who attracted many white visitors to the grounds.[66] The cakewalk was a true African American invention that began during the period of slavery, danced by couples to a syncopated beat that became the precursor of ragtime and allowing for many improvisations. It was a competitive dance, deriving its name from the cake that was awarded to the winners. By the turn of

A possible Juneteenth parade in Alamo Plaza, ca. 1900.
Courtesy Daughters of the Republic of Texas Library

the twentieth century, it had reached the zenith of its popularity, now invading white ballrooms as well. But African American dancers were considered its peerless practitioners, and competitions took place in many American cities on a grand scale.[67] The cakewalk competition of the 1899 San Antonio Juneteenth festival attracted not only local competitors but couples from all over the state and caused a sensation.

The 1900 parade was the most elaborate of all. For reasons unknown, there were no baseball teams. Instead, the procession was augmented by a new African American union, the Restaurant and Bartenders' International League of America. Also new was the inclusion of the social clubs the Dew Drop and the Idlewild. These clubs offered a social alternative to church-organized groups, giving young people a safe environment in which to meet and mingle, and set the African American elite off from other members of black society. Police officers Hughes and North headed the marchers. The Goddess of Liberty appeared again, and the queen of 1900, Julia Travis, was accompanied by no fewer than eleven maids of honor. There were also two bands, the Twenty-fifth Infantry Band and the Hawkins Cornet Band. The slave's log cabin float appeared again—it was fast becoming an icon of past times as contrasted with the present. A commercial float was also entered by the community's largest and most successful business, the Pearl Steam Laundry (its manager, Lacy Robinson, served as secretary of the executive committee for the festival). It featured employees manning a large ironing machine and giving away collars and cuffs.[68] Such distribution of free samples was considered good advertising and was a common practice at the time in any procession that contained advertising floats. Two days of festivities followed the parade at Riverside Park.

On the threshold of the twentieth century, the Juneteenth festival had become a community institution. Celebrants could look on their festival with well-deserved pride. The components of the parade over the years—volunteer firemen, baseball teams, fraternal organizations and social clubs, cyclists, girls as American allegorical figures, unions, militia companies, and dignitaries in carriages—were all typical of any American parade of the period, and the introduction of "royalty" put this parade into the vanguard of what was to come.

In a period still far away from publicly defining a distinctive African American culture, only the cakewalk spoke a particularly ethnic language. The subjects of the orations presented after the parades, particularly from the mid-1880s onward, boldly addressed educational and social issues that were not to find solutions for another seventy to eighty years. If the African slaves had been robbed of their home cultures by slave owners, as free men and women in San Antonio they were (externally at least) enthusiastic practitioners of the progressive ideals of the nineteenth-century United States. In the nature of its participants and its activities, Juneteenth represents the most quintessentially American of all the city's festivals.

But celebrations, of course, are an illusion, the image that a community wishes to present of itself. It's true that the plazas and streets did belong to the African American community on parade days, as did San Pedro Springs or Riverside Park on festival days, but discrimination lurked just outside of the park boundaries. So the white community would view cakewalkers as exotic (and their own dancing as daring), something outside their lives. The normally tactful *Express* in 1900 would describe the African American parade viewers as "dusky spectators in lurid costumes," while comments abounded through the years about how much watermelon was consumed at the festivals. The newspapers would complement the Juneteenth festivals for maintaining order and decorous behavior—as if believing that the opposite was typically true of the black community.[69] It would take another century before much of this would be substantially changed, and even today the transformation is still not complete.

CHAPTER 4
DIEZ Y SEIS
"HOW THE SONS OF MEXICO & AMERICA ENJOY LIBERTY"

My friends and compatriots, neither the king nor tributes now exist for us. This shameful burden, only appropriate for slaves, we have borne for three centuries as a sign of tyranny and servitude; a terrible stain which we will know how to wash off with our courage. The moment of our emancipation has arrived, the hour of our liberty has sounded; and if I know your great valor, you will help me to defend it against the ambitious talons of the tyrants. In just a few hours you will see me march at the head of the men who boast of being free. I invite you to comply with this duty. For without fatherland or liberty we will always be distant from true happiness. It has been necessary to take that step that you already know, and begin for this reason what is necessary. The cause is holy and God will protect it. . . . Viva, then, the Virgin of Guadalupe! Viva America! For which we are going into battle!
—Father Miguel Hidalgo in a speech to his parishioners, September 16, 1810

At approximately 11 P.M. on the night of September 15, 1810, Father Miguel Hidalgo y Costilla, parish priest of the town of Dolores, exhorted his local followers to fight to end Spanish rule in Mexico.[1] After an impassioned speech, he issued his *grito,* or call for independence ("Viva América! Muera el mal gobierno!" to which the crowd replied, "Mueran los Gachupines!").

Though Father Hidalgo was apprehended and executed in the following year, and the struggle took another decade, Mexico achieved its independence from Spain on August 24, 1821. The *grito,* which started it all, became a symbol of Mexican independence just as the fall of the Bastille did for the establishment of a republic in France. In the city of San Antonio, Diez y Seis was officially declared a holiday in 1825, just a little over a year after Agustín Iturbide's attempt at establishing an empire in Mexico failed and the Mexican republican constitution was adopted.[2]

San Antonio, then better known as San Antonio de Bexar, had existed as part of New Spain since 1718. In that year, a presidio manned by a garrison was established to protect its first mission, San Antonio de Valero. Thirteen years later, fifty-five settlers from the Canary Islands were brought in by the Spanish government to augment this outpost. They founded the adjacent community, at first called the Villa de San Fernando, across the river from the mission. These settlers were induced to the make the voyage with promises of land grants and the status of *hidalguera,* or minor landed nobility—certainly more than had been given to the garrison soldiers or converted Native Americans already there.

Considering everything, it was probably a good deal. The Canary Islands were remote from Spain and therefore far from any center of action. They had been conquered by Spain in the early fifteenth century. The Spanish military had deported many of the native population, called Guanches, from the main island of Tenerife, selling them into slavery in Valencia in 1494.[3] But in the outlying islands, the conquerors intermarried with both the remaining Guanches and the African Berbers who had also settled there. In the process, all of these previous inhabitants converted to Catholicism. By the eighteenth century, they were considered to be Spanish, as were the other settlers in Mexico from Spain.

It probably took people from a hot, dry climate like the Canary Islands to accept the equally hot and remote location of South Texas as a place of settlement.[4] The good land nearest the river was given to them, and they settled in to form the fledgling community's urban elite, even though in the richer regions of central Mexico, they would have been considered poor country squires. They constituted the upper class of San Antonio's society and at first married within their group. Soon descendants of the garrison soldiers, as well as other ambitious settlers from New Spain who came north, gained status by marrying into these landowner families. Thus by the end of the eighteenth century, most of the original islander families were no longer "pure," and the resultant population was eventually referred to as Tejanos.[5]

Through the period of Spanish domination and the Mexican republic (during which it formed part of the state of Coahuila), San Antonio remained on the northern frontier of things. Remote from more sophisticated Mexican cities, without good roads toward the south, prey to Indian raids, its residents developed their own insular society. This society was mainly based on a modest agrarian economy, ranching, a small artisan and merchant class, and freighting by oxcart and mule teams to and from Mexico and between San Antonio and the Gulf Coast.[6]

Gradually, during the early nineteenth century, other people joined the community. Laborers from Mexico, with no societal status, drifted back and forth, south to north and back again, depending on economic conditions. They were the inhabitants of the modest *jacales* at the town's peripheries. The more established population lived in solid adobe and stone structures as close as possible to the two central, adjacent plazas. The most prestigious residences were grouped around what was later called Main Plaza, where San Fernando Church, the spiritual center of the community, was located. The Tejano population of San Antonio de Bexar was thus composed of various settlers who came at various times, some directly from Spain, others from Mexico. While the Canary Islanders still were considered the top of society, it was getting more difficult to sort out differences, particularly as upwardly mobile mestizo artisans and merchants began to prosper though business and marriage connections.

During the period of the Mexican republic, Anglo-American settlers from the United States also began coming in, beginning with Moses and Stephen Austin's colony along the Brazos River and increasing from there. They saw Mexican rule as repressive and found natural allies among the landed Tejano elite, who suffered the most from the economic pressures of the distant government of the day. In addition, a small number of the Tejanos, as well as a somewhat larger number of Anglo-Americans, were slave owners, which was outlawed by the central government. This dissatisfaction would eventually lead to the battle for a separate Republic of Texas in 1836.

This is not the place to deal at length with the history and myths of the "Texas Struggle for Independence," well chronicled from both sides. Suffice it to say that the establishment of the Republic of Texas, and the Republic's subsequent absorption into the United States in 1845, set the stage for a flood of Anglo-American immigration, augmented by the influx of settlers from Germany. The manners, customs, and value systems of these immigrants were the diametric opposite of the more relaxed lifestyle of the Tejanos, particularly those of the working class. The newcomers saw bullfights and cockfights as barbaric, gambling as sinful (though the Anglo-Americans certainly indulged in it themselves), the *fandangos* as immoral, and the propensity for working-class Mexican ladies to bathe naked in the river and shun corsets as shocking. *Jacales*, put together of mud, poles, and thatch, were considered to be no more than flimsy, unsanitary dumps and their inhabitants to be at best quaint and exotic, at worst the lowest of the low. In denigrating the *jacales* Anglo-Americans conveniently forgot the far more squalid jerry-built dwellings of the period along the rivers in Manhattan, where, in true European peasant fashion, animals lived on the ground floor and humans in the loft above. Clashes were bound to happen, and the ultimate outcome resulted in the tipping of the political and economic balance and land

An example of a Mexican American *jacal*, built from handy materials. Anglo-American photographers of the day considered them "quaint," and, along with images of alfresco food vendors and bird vendors, they were hot sellers as examples of San Antonio's exotic "third world" ambiance. These photographs thus give a rather lop-sided image of the city's complex and rich Tejano society. *Courtesy Witte Museum, San Antonio, Texas*

ownership to the Anglo-Americans, particularly in the wake of the imposition of American land laws and their manipulation by the newcomers. In 1850, there was a three-way population split among Germans, Anglo-Americans and Tejanos. By 1865, the Tejanos were in the minority, and, during the rest of the nineteenth century, this minority status would be strongly reinforced by the even bigger tide of Anglo-American immigration that arrived with the railroads after 1877. From then on, the value system of manifest destiny ruled.

This is not to say that society was totally ethnically segregated. Anglo and German Catholics often intermarried with the more prestigious Tejano families over the course of the nineteenth century. Jim Bowie (who converted to Catholicism) and Ursula Veramendi are perhaps the most famous couple, but intermarriage continued at least until the 1880s. A few of the other notable alliances included Edward Dwyer Sr. and Mariana Leal, Bryan Callaghan Sr. and Concepción Ramon, Friedrich Groos and Gertrudis Rodriguez of Eagle Pass, Wilhelm Marx and Elena Yturri, and Thad W. Smith and Gertrudis Mateu. Though it was most

A squatter's shack in Manhattan, along the Hudson River, ca.1875.
Copyright © Collection of the New-York Historical Society, 46150

frequent to find Anglo-American males marrying Tejanas, there were also instances of Tejano men marrying non-Hispanic women. Two examples are Lorenzo de Zavala and his second wife, Emily West, of New York, and the alliance of José María Olivarri and Georgie Cupples Smith. There were also cases in which those who were subsequently thought of as "old Mexican or Spanish families" actually came from somewhere else: the eighteenth-century settler Angel Navarro was born in Ajaccio, Corsica, gaining his Tejano status via marriage to the heiress of two San Antonio ranching families. José Fermín Cassiano, born Giuseppe Cassini of San Remo, Italy, married Gertrudis Pérez Cordero, widow of the last Spanish governor of Texas.

The upper class of Tejano descent became even more flexible in definition by the end of the century. This can be seen in the membership of the elite Club Social Mexicano, established in 1883. By the 1890s, its members included various Cassianos and Navarros, as well as the ancient scions Juan E. Barrera, Antonio

P. Rivas, Narciso Leal, Fortunato Villareal, and Juan T. Cardenas, plus Mexican consul Plutarco Ornelas. Also among its rolls were Lucien Lacoste and Leopold Guerguin (French); Antonio Bruni (Italian); Ferdinand Herff, A. T. Wulff, and Ed Froboese (German); and Thad W. Smith, Charles Crawford, and Edward Dwyer Jr.[7] Some of the latter gentlemen had Tejana wives (Froboese, Crawford, and Bruni, for example), but others did not.

On a day-to-day level, there was also considerable interaction. Most of the Military Plaza produce and market vendors were Mexican American, and they were patronized by everyone.[8] The observation has already been made of the Spanish cadence that had crept into San Antonio's English speech by the 1870s.[9] Customs had a way of being borrowed back and forth and refashioned into something distinctly hybrid.

On the other hand, the political role of Mexican Americans had shifted considerably from movers and shakers to subordinates. After 1845, Tejanos generally no longer occupied power positions such as mayor, judge, or alderman, though they did serve frequently in the lower echelons of government and civil service. During and after Reconstruction, they held such positions as market masters, deputy sheriffs, tax assessors, policemen, and notaries. The men who held these subordinate roles were strategic for garnering Mexican American votes; they were often Tejanos who held considerable power in their own barrios. They carefully cultivated votes from among the people in their neighborhoods. In exchange, they could successfully lobby for local interests.

This patronage system reached its apogee under the various nineteenth-century administrations of Mayor Bryan Callaghan Jr. (1885–93 and 1897–99).[10] Callaghan was an expert at the courting of various ethnic groups to maintain his political power. He himself was of mixed ethnic descent. His mother was from one of the old Tejano families; his Irish-born father had served as mayor before the Civil War; and his wealthy wife, Adele Guilbeau, was the daughter of a Frenchman. He had a privileged education that included a law degree from the University of Virginia and was fluent in English, Spanish, French, and German. The well-oiled political organization that he perfected during his nineteenth-century terms as mayor attempted to address problems among the various ethnic constituencies as a canny way to impose power.[11] Adept at public relations, he rode in the civic parades of every group except African Americans from the 1880s through the end of the century, even when he was out of office.

Callaghan gave Tejanos the illusion of recognition, even if they were never top players. The same policy was roughly followed under interim mayors George

Paschal (1893–95) and Henry Elmendorff (1895–97). The reality was that the Tejano population was steadily dwindling and losing their century-old land grants throughout the period as more and more Anglo-Americans established themselves in San Antonio. It would not be until the era of the Mexican Revolution (beginning in 1910) that large numbers of Mexican refugees of many political stripes and social levels would arrive to change the population ratios. Even then the struggle to return to the status and recognition that they had enjoyed in pre-1845 San Antonio would take much, much longer.

EARLY DIEZ Y SEIS FESTIVALS IN SAN ANTONIO

Commemoration of the anniversary of Mexican independence in San Antonio came within a year of the establishment of the Mexican Republic. It was first held in 1825, making it the oldest mostly civic festival in the city. And it sprang into existence full-blown as a three-day celebration. On the evening of September 15, a torchlight parade wound through the city's principal streets, culminating in a cannonade and a ringing of bells at 11 P.M., the very hour of Father Hidalgo's *grito* fifteen years earlier. The next day two parades were held, one civilian, the other military. Then a Te Deum Mass was said at San Fernando church, followed by a reenactment of the *grito* and several flowery orations. In addition, prisoners were set at liberty. In the evening, debutantes were officially welcomed at a grand ball. The following day, citizens dressed in mourning attended a Mass of the Departed.[12] Similar celebrations organized by a *junta patriótica* (municipal patriotic committee) took place in 1829 and 1830, with the same activities.[13]

With the changes of government after San Antonio's absorption into the Republic of Texas, and later into the United States, the celebrations became less structured. Tejano citizens congregated in the plazas, ate holiday foods, drank wine and liquor, and held *fandangos*.[14] The wealthier among them attended private balls.

The revival of Diez y Seis as an organized street holiday in San Antonio had to await the development of civic celebrations after the Civil War. Although the general outlines of San Antonio's postwar festivals were seen as early as the Fourth of July celebration in 1866, it would be about a decade before Diez y Seis and other civic fetes reached their final nineteenth-century formats. From the first, Diez y Seis would be the San Antonio festival most influenced by politics. Just after the war, the Tejanos had formed their own two political clubs, since members of the community had fought on both sides in the late conflict. The Democratic (conservative) club was called Los Bexareños Democráticos, while the Club Mexicano-Texano served the radicals (later Republicans). Over the next few years, particularly as the lingering passions of the war began to fade, membership in these two clubs would fluctuate according to issues of the day. Both of them joined to celebrate Mexican independence in 1868. There was no parade that year, but at the hour of the *grito,* slumbering members of the community were awakened by guns being fired in the air, music, and "hurrahing." In front of the French Building, American and Mexican flags were displayed, and Epitacio Mondragón, a radical and a journalist, delivered the *grito.* Afterward, members of the two clubs split up, the Bexareños Democráticos repairing to Dryden's Hall with their friends and families, where patriotic addresses were delivered by club members Angel Navarro and Juan Barrera, as well as by "a very beautiful girl of thirteen."[15]

Juan E. Barrera and Angel Navarro were both from prominent, landed Tejano families, and both would be active figures in late nineteenth-century society and politics. Navarro, grandson and namesake of the hispanified Corsican, had already been active in prewar San Antonio politics: he had served as the representative of Bexar County in the Texas Legislature in 1857.[16] Juan E. Barrera's father was provisional governor of San Antonio in 1836 and was ousted from the post by General Santa Anna.[17] Barrera served as a constable in 1855 and would be deputy county clerk under Thad W. Smith in the late 1870s. He himself became county clerk in 1883.[18] Both men were frequent attendees of political meetings throughout the period, as well as members of the Mexican Social Club, founded at around this time, which served not only as an elite social club but as an active forum for community politics.

In 1869, the Club Mexicano-Texano members were the principal celebrators, and Mondragón again made a speech. There was even a short torchlight parade, which formed on Military Plaza and marched to the oration ceremony held once again at the French Building, then continued to circle both plazas for awhile after the ceremonies, finally breaking up at Soledad Street and Main Plaza. As well as members of the Club Mexicano-Texano, the procession featured the members of Fire Company 1. They probably participated because the lone Tejano member of the company (and its assistant captain in 1872) was Antonio P. Rivas, a member of the Club Mexicano-Texano.[19]

Rivas would also figure in the next organized celebration in 1876, which was apparently restricted to the upper class. It included a ball and ceremonies held at Wolfram's Central Gardens. Wolfram's at that time consisted of a spacious hall surrounded by extensive gardens and paths, with tall trees along the riverbanks. For the occasion, a speaker's platform was set up draped with a Mexican flag. The hall where the ball was held was decorated with evergreens. A patriotic note was sounded with portraits of famous heroes of the battle for Mexican independence: Father Hidalgo, General Zaragosa, General Morelos, and Colonel Garza. This was typical of such decorations of the time, and similar expressions were seen in other festivals. The organizers for the occasion were part of what can only be described as a "mixed Latin" upper class, including three men of French descent (Edward Guilbeau, Leopold Guerguin, and Louis Giraud). Also included was the policeman Alejo Perez, a member of Los Bexareños Democráticos who had also served as assistant marshal in the Fourth of July parade of 1870, and, once again, Antonio P. Rivas.[20]

Rivas is one of those figures who winds in and out of Diez y Seis and other San Antonio civic festivals, as well as other aspects of public life of the period. Born in 1842, he was descended on both sides from garrison families that had received land grants. The family had been around long enough that the westernmost part of Houston Street was originally known as Rivas Street.[21] Though he listed various professions in the city's directories over the years, including farmer, grocer, dry goods merchant, and real estate owner, Rivas was evidently of comfortable means and had a charismatic personality that enabled him to move freely within San Antonio's society. This is seen not only in his volunteer fire activities but in the fact that he would later serve as a Volksfest parade marshal in 1885, as a marshal in the 1896 Battle of Flowers parade, and on the executive committee for the huge 1898 Fourth of July celebration.[22] Rivas's presence, as one of the founders of the Club Mexicano-Texano, along with that of his rival, Bexareño Democrático Alejo Perez, on the organizing committee of Diez y Seis in 1876 is proof positive that political arguments were left at the ballroom door.

The *San Antonio Express* commented the following year on the sorts of Diez y Seis celebrations going on at that time: "As a general thing, the higher class has gathered, during the morning of the anniversary, and had speaking, patriotic in its character and allusions. [While] led by a brass band, about a dozen of [the] poorest class marched about the streets last evening, through rain and mud, bearing the American and Spanish [*sic*] standards. It seemed that the idea of this procession originated with the laborers in the rock quarries."[23]

EARLY DIEZ Y SEIS FESTIVALS OF THE SOCIEDAD BENEVOLENCIA AND THE SOCIEDAD MUTUALISTA

It was in 1878 that the festival portion of Diez y Seis as a public, civic-minded event began—following the time-honored city model. The impetus came not from the upper class but from the twenty-four members of the Sociedad Benevolencia Mexicana, whom the *Express* characterized as "basically day-laborers."[24] At 11 P.M., the hour of the *grito*, fifteen hundred people congregated at the speaker's stand in San Pedro Springs Park and inaugurated the festival with gun salutes, music, and cheers. The *grito* was delivered by Guillermo Sasas, a member of the Sociedad, and then "four beautiful Mexican maidens" sang the Mexican national anthem and were crowned with wreaths. An oration in Spanish was delivered by Juan Barrera. He was followed (also in Spanish) by Juan T. Cardenas, ex–deputy sheriff and a fellow founder of Los Bexareños Democráticos, after which attendees gorged themselves on Mexican food for sale at open-air booths. The following day, the celebration continued at San Pedro Springs, while in the evening, a ball was held at Krisch's Hall attended by "only the very best of our Mexican Citizens," many of the female contingent having their gowns trimmed with the red, white and green of the Mexican flag.[25] Antonio P. Rivas, Alejo Perez, and Leopold Guerguin again served on the ball committee, as did jeweler Manuel Pereida, another upper-class member of the Bexareños.

The Sociedad Benevolencia Mexicana, founded in 1875, was the earliest of the Mexican workers' mutual aid societies in San Antonio.[26] Mutual aid societies had been and were being organized among many different ethnic and other groups, not only in San Antonio but all over the United States and Mexico.[27] In a period when there were no social services to aid the poor when they were sick or had to be buried, the societies grew up as a way to cope with these expenses. They also fostered feelings of fraternity among their members. The Sociedad Benevolencia Mexicana was formed not solely of day laborers, as the *Express* suggested, but also included artisans and small shopkeepers, who met at the home of Máximo Martínez on May 1, 1875. Their statutes, drawn up shortly afterward and renewed in 1889, are worth discussing, since they were not only adapted from earlier models but themselves formed the basis for other Mexican mutual aid societies to follow.[28]

As with other mutual aid societies, the founders established initiation fees and monthly dues (at that time $1.50 and $.50, respectively). The aim was to protect and aid members at times of grave illness and death by dispensing fees collected by the treasury at rates fixed in the statutes. Secondarily, with their surplus funds, the Sociedad Benevolencia Mexicana intended to buy a press for the dissemination of society information and to set up a library for the use of members: literacy was recognized as a way for the members to better themselves. This society also worked for peace and harmony among its members and scrupulously avoided religious or political questions at its meetings. To be a member of the Sociedad Benevolencia, a person had to be between eighteen and fifty years of age, gainfully employed, and not suffering from a chronic illness (preexisting conditions being a reason for noncoverage then as now). Members had to approve all new applicants and were expected to appear at all funerals, visit the sick, attend all meetings, maintain decorum at all times, and be prompt with their dues. Meetings were strictly on the democratic model; all members had the right to voice their opinions, elect officers, and vote on all proposals. Everything was to be conducted with full parliamentary procedure. Only a third of existing funds could be disbursed at any time, to keep the organization solvent. The society had a flag, consisting of a star and a half moon and its motto on a white field, which was also on badges worn by the members for both solemn and festive occasions. The uniform for these occasions consisted of black suits and white gloves, with the badge worn on the left side. It was also stipulated that the members were obliged to observe their founder's day (May 1) and also Diez y Seis, "because it is when Mexico sanctioned its independence . . . [and is to be observed] with all possible pomp."[29]

The mutual aid societies thus became a forum not only for helping the sick and burying the dead but also for encouraging literacy and the bettering of the individual, following the American ideal of raising oneself up by one's bootstraps. They might also have been a way to give a group of fairly humble people greater clout; if politics were forbidden at meetings, the democratic process by which the meetings were conducted was an excellent way to hone political and oratorical skills.[30] Members of the Sociedad Benevolencia Mexicana would proudly march in many Diez y Seis parades to follow.

The 1878 Diez y Seis festival became the model for the festival of subsequent years. It lasted two days (later it would grow to three) and was held at San Pedro Springs. It commenced with the *grito* and proceeded to orations, after which four young girls sang the Mexican anthem. A salute was then fired in the air (sometimes by cannon, sometimes merely by rifle); succulent food was sold at decorated booths; and, in 1882, fireworks were set off. The two pavilions at San

Pedro Springs were the venues for popular balls, though the upper classes often held a more elegant ball somewhere else. (In 1881, for example, the ball was held at the white Odd Fellow's Hall; in the following year it was held at the newly constructed Maverick building.) The festival was augmented with an opening parade; in 1878 it consisted principally of Benevolencia members, in their black suits and badges, led by a band. The early processions generally took place in the afternoon, around 3 P.M., and then people slowly collected at San Pedro Springs, the crowd swelling until it was time for the *grito*. By 1882, the festival was attended by over five thousand people; around this time, the parades became evening torchlight affairs, leading up to the 11 P.M. *grito*.[31]

Though various classes danced separately, and the orators were generally drawn from the upper crust (Juan Barrera, for example, spoke again in 1880 and 1881), the Springs celebration itself was generally attended by members of both working and elite groups, who mingled amiably on what was not only a patriotic occasion but a good excuse for a party. It would, however, not always be totally harmonious. In 1880, the Benevolencia group decided to hold their postprocession celebration separately at Maverick's Grove, while the social set collected at San Pedro Springs. The four girls who sang the anthem over the years definitely came from the older families: for example, Antonita Peñaloza, one of the four in 1880, was the daughter of José M. Peñaloza, who delivered the oration the next day. Peñaloza was an alderman in the 1850s, a descendent of the landed Tejanos, and a member of Los Bexareños Democráticos who managed to have a career both as a politician and as a butcher, holding the municipal post of market master, a political plum, in 1873.

In the year 1883, about the same time that Juneteenth festivals became full-blown and the German American Volksfests were thriving, Diez y Seis celebrations also took a more elaborate turn. Two factors may have given it the impetus to do so: the establishment of an upper-class social club and the arrival of a new mutual aid society. The Mexican Social Club has already been discussed. Its members, as we have seen, were predictably more upper-class than strictly Mexican American, since many of its non-Tejano members had married women from the Tejano elite. A number of these gentlemen were prominent in politics of the day; others, like Ferdinand Herff, had become living icons in local society. Not only was Herff one of the original German settlers in Texas, but he had enjoyed a distinguished career as a physician and was universally loved for his selfless service to the entire San Antonio community. Virtually all of the members of the Club Social were enthusiastic participants in the celebration of Mexican independence.

At least one of these Social Club members, Charles Crawford, was instrumental in the formation of the Sociedad Mutualista Mexicana, the second Mexican American mutual aid society, organized in San Antonio in the early 1880s. The statutes for this group no longer exist, but from the beginning, this new society had a decided political slant. Most of its prominent members were hardly poor or in need of medical or burial expenses. They included Francisco N. Sanchez, who held the politically appointed post of public weigher at the market and would later jump to the Benevolencia; Lino Sanchez (no relation), who married a garrison descendent; José Garcia, who served as county tax assessor in the 1880s; José Cassiano and Eugenio Navarro, of venerable ancestry; and the club's president, Juan T. Cardenas. There were also non-Hispanic members aside from Crawford, among them the Honorable Oscar Bergstrom, a lawyer and judge who was active with many of the city's ethnic communities. There were lower- and lower- middle-class members too, but they held no power positions in the Sociedad Mutualista until well into the 1890s. The aforementioned gentlemen were all allies of the future mayor, Bryan Callaghan Jr., and most were enthusiastic Democrats.[32]

As Democrats and cronies of Callaghan, they also had considerable political clout. With the exception of Bergstrom, they organized a protest (along with Juan Barrera, who would shortly join the Mutualistas, and journalist Epitacio Mondragón) against Frederick Kerbel, who in 1883 was the proprietor of San Pedro Springs Park. In early August, Kerbel had expelled several respectable Mexican families from one of the park's dance platforms, at the insistence of some Anglo-Americans who refused to dance on the same floor with them and who threatened to withdraw their patronage of the park. By August 9, a large committee, headed by Juan T. Cardenas, met to make a formal protest to such discrimination. They drafted a petition to have Kerbel dismissed from his position at the park for bigoted behavior and threatened a lawsuit against the city if Mayor James French and the aldermen failed to act, since San Pedro Springs was a municipal park and therefore open to all. Many speeches were given at the protest meeting, all in Spanish, both by Hispanic/Tejano protestors and by sympathetic and influential Germans and Anglo-Americans. The attendees rallied all the newspapers behind them, including the *Express,* the *Light,* and the Spanish-language newspaper *El Hogar.*[33] The threat of so much publicity elicited a speedy apology by Kerbel and a vow to never again discriminate against minority groups, who had full equal rights to use the facilities.

Of all the people involved with the organization and activities of the Sociedad

Mutualista Mexicana, the most colorful and influential was Juan T. Cardenas. Not only was he involved with Diez y Seis festivals, but he was also an important political and social presence in San Antonio all through the last half of the nineteenth century. Captain Cardenas (as he preferred to be called) was born in nearby Seguin in 1844. His parents were both descended from garrison soldiers, and his maternal grandfather was French.[34]

Cardenas began his career as a printer in his hometown.[35] He was reputed to have been an Indian scout and/or Texas Ranger in his teens and to have fought in the Civil War for the Confederates in Sibley's Brigade. Since he was on the losing side of the war, he fled to Matamoros, Mexico, in 1865 and remained there until he was recruited as captain of police by Mayor J. H. Lyons in San Antonio to help deal with the 1866 cholera epidemic. He resigned a year later to become a journalist, first for the *San Antonio Herald,* then for the radical *El Mexicano de Texas.*[36] In 1872, he was appointed deputy sheriff, and after 1875, first deputy marshal. For the rest of the century, he would serve either in this capacity or as police captain under various San Antonio administrations. The highest political position he ever achieved was alderman of Ward 1 in 1884, the only Mexican American/Tejano on the city council during the later nineteenth century.[37]

From the 1880s onward, he was a true power behind the throne on the San Antonio political stage.[38] Much of his influence came from astutely playing the patronage game under Bryan Callaghan's administrations. The posts of police captain and marshal were precisely the sort of subordinate positions within the city government that allowed Cardenas to lobby behind the scenes and accrue power among the Mexican American community. He was a vocal figure, using his considerable connections and flawless bilingual oratorical skills in political campaigns and as a champion for municipal grievances. He continued to associate with the most prominent figures in San Antonio's Tejano and Anglo-American circles, first at political activities and later, in the 1890s, as a member and later vice president of the Mexican Social Club. Something of his social and political importance can be garnered from the fact that when he died in 1903, the flag over City Hall flew at half-mast.[39]

The Diez y Seis parade of 1883 was on a bigger scale than anything staged before, and much of that was due to the presence of the new Sociedad Mutualista Mexicana and its president, Juan T. Cardenas. Marshals included Francisco N. Sanchez and Bryan Callaghan Jr. (then at the beginning of his political career). Music was provided by U.S. Eighth Cavalry Band, a "hot item" that year.[40] The twenty-five-member executive committee (basically made up of Mutualista members) marched in force. Then came a carriage with the four young ladies who were to sing the anthem, dressed in starched, spotless white, followed by one occupied by Captain Cardenas as Mutualista president and Mexican consul Dr. Plutarco Ornelas. Rank-and file Sociedad Mutualista members marched dressed in black suits with insignias and black gloves.[41] The rear was brought up by Mexican American and Mexican citizens on foot and on horseback. It began at Military Plaza at 7:30 in the evening and ended at San Pedro Springs. At the Springs were numerous food booths draped with U.S. and Mexican bunting, many of their proprietors the same cooks who daily operated in Military Plaza. Lavish illumination was provided by festive colored Chinese lanterns typical of the period and by gas jets. This was augmented by a spectacular fireworks display after the *grito* and opening ceremonies, and many of the five thousand people at San Pedro Springs remained to dance late into the night.[42]

Cardenas would continue as a prominent Mutualista player in Diez y Seis festivities for the next decade. The 1884 parade, again Mutualista-sponsored, was similar but grander than that of the previous year, with Cardenas occupying a separate carriage in his role as alderman. The Mexican consul Dr. Ornelas again participated, as he would in most of the Diez y Seis celebrations through the end of the century. The ploy of featuring a diplomat from the "mother country" gave the festival more cachet among the non-Hispanic population and equally validated the humblest foot marchers. Antonio P. Rivas apparently joined the Mutualistas around this time, for he was one of the procession marshals. The otherwise incongruous participation of ex-Confederate members of the Albert Sydney Johnson Camp can perhaps be explained by the fact that Alderman Cardenas had served with the Confederates during the Civil War.[43] The parade route was extended to encompass all three plazas, basically conforming to the usual festival route. George Kalteyer, druggist and local pyrotechnical expert, graced the beginning of the parade with a fireworks display in the red, white, and green colors of Mexico, launched from his pharmacy in Military Plaza.

At San Pedro Springs, all the stops were pulled out. Over six thousand people "of all nationalities . . . gentlemen and ladies, both young and old" thronged the festival site.[44] Chinese lanterns, the parade torches, and "other lights" illuminated the richly festooned food booths, while the speaker's stand was draped with evergreens and bunting in U.S. and Mexican colors. Juan Barrera read the *grito,* a twenty-one-gun salute was fired by a platoon of U.S. artillery, and the usual Mutualista luminaries (including Cardenas, Barrera, and Ornelas) assembled on the speaker's stand. Of the four girls who sang the anthem, two were

The speaker's stand, San Pedro Springs Park, Diez y Seis celebration of 1883 or 1884, including the four young maidens who sang the anthem. Juan T. Cardenas is in the center back row. *Courtesy U.T. Institute of Texan Cultures*

daughters of Juan Barrera, the third was the offspring of Juan Cardenas, while the last was the child of tax assessor José E. Garcia, who was also on the stand. Besides singing, the girls also presented a silk banner bearing the colors and emblem of the Mexican flag to the Sociedad Mutualista (with a thank-you response from Alderman Cardenas).

The combined political and social influence of Dr. Ornelas and the Mutualista membership may account for the presence of Governor John Ireland and Major Tom Breckenridge, who both delivered speeches the next day. This was the first Diez y Seis festival at which speeches were delivered in both Spanish and English, evidently to appeal to a wider community audience. It also ensured the publication of the text of Breckenridge's speech, in the usual flowery style, in the *Express*. This oration managed to encompass Mexico, Texas, and the United States as "cradles of freedom."[45]

THE RIVAL CELEBRATIONS OF 1885 AND 1886

During the two years that the Mutualistas ran the show, the role of the Sociedad Benevolencia in Diez y Seis celebrations appears to have been completely shoved aside (unless the "Invited Societies" cited in the parade roster of 1884 included them—but this suggests subordination anyway).[46] In 1885, they were ready to fight back, and the result was two rival celebrations of the holiday. The *Light* announced planning meetings of the groups two days apart, the Mutualistas meeting on September 7, the Benevolencias on September 9.[47] At the former, Juan Cardenas of the Mutualistas declared that their organization was not a political one. However, the implications of who celebrated with which group resonated through the city, as reflected in an editorial in the *Express* on September 17, at the end of the festival: "It is true that there is nothing political in these celebrations . . . but the significant fact remains that the Mexican population is no longer a unit—a wedge has been entered, and there is a boding of downfall for those who have long made the solid Mexican vote, wielded as they directed, their stock in trade in political contests in this city."[48]

The Mutualistas still had more clout when it came to organization: they got the evening parade and San Pedro Springs as their festival venue. The Benevolencias had to settle for a parade at 3:30. They were also consigned to an alternate site for their festival, Fest's Garden (which Juneteenth celebrants would use in their split celebration of 1889).

There was evidently a good deal of animosity in the planning—and perhaps bullying too. The Military Plaza food vendors, counted on to provide freshly cooked dishes at the festivals, apparently would have preferred to have gone to Fest's Garden. There, booth space was free. At San Pedro Springs Park, booths had to be rented. Spanish-language newspaper publisher Santiago Warren, spokesman for the Benevolencias, accused the Mutualistas of making threats that if the vendors went to Fest's, "they would never be able to return to Military Plaza" afterward. In addition, the Mutualistas had also threatened that the Mexican theater company in town to perform for the Benevolencias would never be allowed to play in the city again.[49] The vendors eventually did work in both places without penalization, while the theater performances were finally scheduled at neutral Turner Hall, where they played to packed houses.[50]

Even if both celebrations were of similar size, the Mutualista parade was fancier, boasting three hundred torches and the Eighth Cavalry Band.[51] Antonio P. Rivas was grand marshal. This parade was enhanced by the Italian American mutual aid group the Società Italiano di Mutuo Soccorso (probably brought in by Mexican Social Club member Antonio Bruni).[52] Instead of Consul Ornelas riding in the parade, the procession stopped at his residence en route, where the doctor delivered an oration from his balcony and received an oratorical response from Mutualista president Cardenas. Juan Barrera read the *grito* at San Pedro Springs, and the U.S. artillery fired their twenty-one-gun salute, attended by "the elite of Mexican society in San Antonio," as well as "many of our leading citizens of the American and other nationalities."[53] The grounds were lavishly adorned with decorations supplied and put up by Frederick Kerbel, still the man in charge of San Pedro Springs (perhaps to atone for his expulsion of Mexican families from the dance floor and the consequent flap two years before?). Unfortunately, rain prevented the planned fireworks.

The Benevolencia parade formed in the afternoon on Washington Square, west of San Pedro Creek. It was more modest in scope. Officers and members of the society paraded in their black suits and white gloves, with Texas and Mexican Flags. The young ladies who were to sing the anthem rode in carriages (there were rival singers in the Mutualista parade), and policeman Francisco Galan was the chief marshal. An added attraction was the presence of assistant marshal Jacobo Coy, the moonlighting policeman who had participated in the shootout that killed King Fisher and Ben Thompson at the Vaudeville Theater the year before.[54]

Speeches at Fest's were delivered in Spanish by police officer Galan; Geronimo Perales, a clerk in the county clerk's office who gave an edifying sketch of

Mexican history; and Santiago (or James) Warren, who seems to have been the Benevolencias' community advocate.[55] Anglo-American attorney Tom Harrison and labor organizer and former alderman John H. Copeland also gave addresses in English. Dr. Ornelas attended a reception at Fest's the following day. This celebration was probably the more working-class of the two, but it also had status added by its Benevolencia and invited Anglo-American speakers, and the decorum of the dancing that followed the orations on both festival days was much commended (were the newspapers expecting a wild *fandango* at this location?).[56]

In spite of the animosity that so characterized the two rival festivals of the previous year, the Mutualistas and Benevolencias would bury the hatchet in 1886, mostly fueled by politics in the form of external pressure. In that year, the Knights of Labor, the first truly national labor union in the United States, attempted to become a political force in the city. Founded as a secret society in 1869, the Knights achieved growing influence ten years later under the leadership of Terence Powderly, when the group "went public." It dropped its mystical trappings and actively campaigned to recruit workers in all segments of the population to organize for their rights—including members of the petite bourgeoisie and farmers as well as workers. The Knights' peak year nationally was in 1886, when they had over seven hundred thousand members. A modest number of those were in San Antonio when representatives of the national organization started six assemblies in the city (put under the regional umbrella called District Assembly 78), which encompassed around two thousand citizens.[57] They swiftly moved to challenge what they called "the ring" in the coming county elections—in other words, Bryan Callaghan Jr. and his political allies in Bexar County—by forming a political organization known as the San Pedro Club. The Knights' greatest public manifestation, aside from a heavily attended meeting of the district assembly in the city during the same year, was its own appropriation of the celebration of Diez y Seis. This festival was probably chosen because it was only a few weeks away from the holding of county elections. "Ostensibly," said the *Express*, "both organizations [the benevolent societies and the Knights] are celebrating the independence of Mexico . . . though it has assumed much of a political nature in preparation for the coming contest at the county election, and the feeling over the affair has grown decidedly warm, particularly so among the leaders."[58]

Though the San Pedro Club and the other Knights of Labor assemblies (calling themselves by the venerable title Junta Patriótica) drew the afternoon slot for their procession and Fest's Garden for their festival, their parade had a markedly different character from the usual Diez y Seis procession. To begin with, it was ethnically mixed. The political arm of the San Pedro Club marched, of course, in the person of nineteen members, and the sixty members of the Mexican Assembly of the Knights were no surprise, either. The Anglo-American/German Travis Assembly and the Painter's Assembly were perhaps a little less typical, but the real innovation was the participation of the seventeen African American members of the Alamo Assembly of Knights. It was the only instance when blacks would march with nonblacks as equals in a parade in the period between the early Reconstruction processions and the Battle of Flowers patriotic parade of 1899. The political message this carried was delivered rather blatantly by the first marcher among the San Pedro Club members, who walked with a club over his shoulder and a banner displaying a broken ring, a motto repeated on all the assembly members' badges.

Whether or not it had any significance besides attention grabbing, the band that followed the mounted police and grand marshal/shoemaker Epifaneo Montes was from that dubious entertainment palace, the Fashion Theater, accompanied by its chorus girls in carriages. There were also several prominent anti-"ring" candidates in carriages (riding at the end of the parade, not right after the showgirls).

But the most unusual feature was a series of six allegorical floats, dealing with stirring moments in Mexican history, distributed in chronological order among the various assemblies. The first, according to descriptions in the *Express* and the *Light*, showed "Cortez weeping under the tree of Noche Triesti [sic] (sad night), when defeated by the Indians. His faithful Mallncho [sic] is with him, as interpreter."[59] The second float depicted "Guatamozín, the successor of Montezuma and his Indian casiques [sic] in pursuit of Cortez." The third showed the proclaiming of the *grito* at Dolores; the fourth an allegorical representation of the Mexican declaration of independence, with Father Hidalgo again; and the next the tragic execution of Hidalgo the following year by General Allende, General Collega, and their soldiers. The final float was of Iturbide's triumphal entry into Mexico City (obviously before he made his imperial pretensions known).

A few of the actors on the floats are documented. Cortez on the first float was played by Anglo-American Dick Tronson. José María Flores, future founder of another mutual aid society, La Unión, was the heroic Guatamozín on the second. Iturbide, on the last float, was impersonated by Cipriano Trinidad, who had defected from the Benevolencias, which he had helped found. Whether this casting reflected any political issues of the day is not known.

The Knights of Labor floats were the only other series to form a narrative pageant in nineteenth-century San Antonio parades (aside from earlier and later ones in the German Volksfests). They were probably very much of the homemade variety: no photographs survive, but the *Express* described them as "well presented, though probably not executed in the highest style of art." On the other hand, "the costumes, of the Indians and Mexicans, of that time, were realistic and elicited much admiration."[60] The very presence of these floats suggests either the influence of German members of the Knights (since Volksfest parades, as we will see, presented veritable pageants each year) or perhaps the sort of patriotic program favored by their national organization, tailored to fit the occasion. Each float was like a tableau (a popular pastime at this period), where people entertained each other by assuming frozen poses of appropriately costumed heroes and villains in memorable historic scenes.[61] It would, of course, have been difficult to maintain a frozen pose on a bumpy wagon for several miles (particularly with watchers waving and shouting), but the general idea would have been gotten across. If possible, the float and costume designers would have used as their source history-book illustrations or historical paintings; these references would have been known, if not well known, to the viewing audience of parade spectators.

At the bunting-and-evergreen-draped Fest's Garden, a crowd of twenty-five hundred was present to hear Miss Concepción Acosta recite "an original Spanish poem," presumably patriotic in nature. A bilingual oration was delivered by Charles (here styled "Carlos") Crawford, who had managed in the past to be a Mutualista marshal, then a Benevolencia marshal, and in 1886 switched his allegiance yet again. Other English-language orators included John H. Copeland (another prominent Benevolencia defector), the perennially radical John Pearson Newcomb, Gen. George W. Russ, and African American coachman and activist James W. Martin, all of whom spoke in English. Manuel Lopez, Master Workman of the Knights' Mexican Assembly, then delivered a speech in Spanish. Once again, however, a line was drawn as far as social mingling between people of color and everyone else was concerned. Though they had paraded together, segregated dancing took place in the two pavilions at the garden, African Americans in one, everyone else in the other. Even so, in its ethnic mix and unusual parade, the Knights of Labor's Diez y Seis was unique in San Antonio's nineteenth-century history. But it would have no follow-up—most of its candidates lost in the following election. The Knights' national reputation was itself tarnished by the end of 1886, the result of numerous, often violent strikes by its members. Though they would lurch along in San Antonio until 1891, the Knights of Labor would no longer have the presence they did five years earlier.[62]

Meanwhile, the united Mutualista/Benevolencia parade took place on the evening of September 15. It repeated the usual format of the past few years, once again augmented by the Italian American Società Italiano di Mutuo Soccorso, its own contingent of politicians, and members of both mutual aid societies in their black suits and badges. George Kalteyer once again provided fireworks on Military Plaza, where the procession began. The whole parade had a homey air, for much teasing took place between marchers and spectators along the entire route to San Pedro Springs. Juan Cardenas introduced orator Miguel Barrera (apparently no relation to Juan), and then Edward Dwyer followed with an speech in English. Dr. Ornelas diplomatically laid low that year.

THE GENERALLY UNITED BUT SOMETIMES DIVIDED MUTUAL AID SOCIETY PARADES

For the next seven years, The Mutualistas and Benevolencias paraded together (joined by the Società Italiano di Mutuo Soccorso), much as they did in 1886. The parades continued to grow in length and over this period were enhanced by a host of new mutual aid societies. There would eventually be eleven. The largest included La Unión, organized in 1887, which marched for the first time in 1890, and the Sociedad Marez in 1893. Three others, the Sociedad Benito Juarez, which arrived in 1891, the Sociedad Ignacio Zaragosa, and the Sociedad Miguel Hidalgo, which appeared in 1893, were branches of other South Texas mutual aid societies, the former two founded in Corpus Christi in 1881 and the Hidalgo in Brownsville in the same year.[63] These latter organizations were more authentically working-class than the Mutualistas and thus in spirit more like the Sociedad Benevolencia.[64] All of their members wore badges and sashes, usually in the Mexican national colors of green, white, and red, over black suits, and by 1891, all were supplied with dark blue uniforms, which gave the subsequent grand balls an intriguing pseudomilitary note. By 1893, the members of the general organizing committee wore silk, rosetted, gold-fringed badges proudly emblazoned with the motto "Comité General, 16 de Septiembre de 1893."[65] Dr. Ornelas appeared again each year, as did Brian Callaghan Jr. during his various terms as mayor. In 1891 a single allegorical float was included, depicting a time-honored theme: it represented "Mexico" and "America" in the persons of two pretty girls, appropriately costumed. In the foreground, in three dimensions, was the symbol seen on the Mexican flag: the Mexican eagle perched above a cactus with a snake in its beak. On a throne were seated, hand and hand, the two girls (in their respective national colors) as the two republics.[66] This was a variation on the representation of the various states of the union or the Goddess of Liberty, used in other festival parades. Unfortunately, the "America" float suffered a tragedy when it reached San Pedro Springs—it struck an electric wire over one of the small bridges, and one of the drivers of the horses pulling it was thrown off and badly burned.[67] Perhaps this is why no more floats appeared in Diez y Seis parades until later in the decade.

Visually, both the parade and San Pedro Springs were picturesque in appearance. Newspaper accounts had long been describing the impression that the flickering, reddish torchlight made on the spectators. The proliferation of society banners, sashes, and badges enhanced this visual effect, even more so when George Kalteyer set off his fireworks in Military Plaza at the start of each parade, most of them employing Mexican colors. The increasingly elaborate decorations at San Pedro Springs also inspired viewers: in 1887, for example, the "procession entered at the main entrance, above which was a brilliant star of gas illuminating the words 'Bien Venido.'. . . [T]he springs were surrounded by a necklace of Chinese lanterns, and everywhere around the grounds these lights threw their softened rays." The swirl of attendees was gaily dressed. More women were present than men: "Nearly all were dressed in white, but here and there flecks of color would stand out prominently." And all of this was surrounded by the dark foil of the tall trees in the park.[68] To complete the appeal to all senses, there was music by both marching and dance bands, the stirring words of oration, and the enticing aroma and taste of spicy foods, which came in more varieties each year. Indeed, some of the larger food booths had virtually expanded to temporary full-course restaurants, replete with extensive awnings, lit by Mexican tin lanterns, and ornamented by bunting and lace trim.

Juan T. Cardenas continued to be active in the parades and as a Spanish-language orator through 1891. He reappeared as a grand marshal several years later but apparently let his domination of the Mutualistas lapse after 1891. His health may have started to fail during the 1890s, or perhaps his more gentlemanly status as a member of the Mexican Social Club mellowed some of his combative spirit (or both). Many of the other Mutualista chiefs of the 1880s also disappeared around this time in Diez y Seis celebrations. Perhaps this had to do with the fact that the Mutualista members themselves began to be more authentically working-class, not only in their rank and file but in their officers as well. The 1886 Knights' parade did have one lasting impact, for if this early union soon vanished, local craft unions and workingmen's clubs (and not necessarily Hispanic ones) marched in parades through the end of the century.[69] The Spanish-language speakers came increasingly from less "establishment" elements, such as the president of La Unión, the laborer Guadalupe Bias (or Baez), who spoke in 1890. On the other hand, Asencio Lozano and the young, brilliant Antonio D. Flores, who orated in English and would soon begin a short but distinguished career as a lawyer (he was to die tragically at the young age of twenty-six in 1898), were both from the older, more elite tradition.

It was at the various grand balls that the society still remained stratified. San Pedro Park housed two dance pavilions. In most cases the lower, older, closed-in one near the park entrance was the home of a dance for anyone who wanted to attend, either for free or at a suitably modest cost. The upper, open-air one, north of the bandstand on a small hill, was generally reserved for the members of the various mutual aid societies and their invited guests. As the members of the Club Social Mexicano began to disassociate themselves from the Sociedad Mutualista, they sometimes reverted to their older tradition of an exclusive ball at a different venue, such as the one given at the Casino Club in 1892: "the fair and the wealthy and the courteous were all there, making the affair one of the most gorgeous events in the history of that organization."[70] Following a now-established tradition, all of the festivals started on the night of September 15 and continued for two days afterward at San Pedro Springs.

The shape of the celebration of Diez y Seis changed very little through 1899. The parades continued to get longer, and as more mutual aid societies were formed, they joined in. By the end of the century they included two for women, the Sociedad Beneficia de Señoras y Senoritas, and the Sociedad Benito Juarez de Señoras y Señoritas.[71] Perhaps it was the greater number of organizations that caused two rival celebrations to take place in 1894, 1896, and 1898, while in 1895, 1897, and 1899 everyone celebrated together. It appears that the impetus for splitting was again spats between Benevolencia and Mutualista factions. The Benevolencias usually celebrated during these divided years with the Sociedades Hidalgo, Morales, and Zaragosa, and the Mutualistas with the Italian Società Italiano di Mutuo Soccorso (and later also the Christopher Columbus Society). They were joined by the Gran Círculo de Obreros, plus the Anglo-American and Mexican workingmen's clubs, which had appropriated the name Junta Patriótica for themselves. In 1894, the Benevolencia procession included Mayor George Paschal and aides, plus county officials. The Mutualistas boasted four allegorical floats, representing a rather curious mixture of themes: "Hidalgo and

America," "Mexico," "San Pedro Springs," and the "United States." They were joined by the Mexican Opera Company, which performed at their festival at San Pedro Springs (the rivals held theirs at Limburger's Garden). In 1896, it was the Mutualistas' turn to have the mayor—this time Henry Elmendorff—plus the Belknap Rifles, while the Benevolencias had the Hispanic Masons and Carl Beck's Military Band.

In 1898 the split was different—the Mutualistas, the Benevolencias, and the other mutual aid societies marched in one parade, accompanying a float with thirty young ladies as the "Mexican emblem." This was a "living flag" display of a type that was popular at the end of the nineteenth century and would become even more so in the twentieth (it can still be seen today in football half-time shows). It featured the girls dressed in appropriate colors grouped to form the Mexican standard. Juan T. Cardenas reappeared for one last hurrah as the grand marshal. This faction held their festival at Wolfram's Central Gardens. The other parade was sponsored by the laborers of the Junta Patriótica and included the First Texas Cavalry Band and a "Group of Typical Cowboys under the leadership of Ed Pfefferling."[72] When the festivals split, Dr. Ornelas diplomatically refused to participate in them. In the other years, it had basically been all the groups marching together (including Consul Ornelas), with the festivities at San Pedro Springs. In 1897, not only did the Belknap Rifles participate, but so did the recently formed San Antonio Zouaves. Its captain, Eugene Hernandez, was from an old Tejano family, but the rest of its members were Anglo- and a few German Americans.[73]

The associated festivals continued in the same way, with the *grito* and the speeches. There was generally at least one English-speaking orator (the Mutualista festival of 1896 was the exception). The speakers now came from a broader social spectrum. Some were workingmen or craftsmen-activists like Andrés López Montalbo (1897), a printer and champion for Hispanic voting rights. Others were professionals like Manuel Gonzalez-Dena (1895). He was editor of the newspaper *El Mexico-Tejano* and later *La Frontizera*, as well as a member of the Gran Círculo de Obreros. Women Mutualistas such as Señorita Adele Hernandez (1898) also spoke, as did educators Manuel G. Treviño and Leonard Garza, the head of Spanish in the San Antonio public schools (1899). A few of the older elite sometimes still participated. Francisco N. Sanchez was a marshal in the Benevolencia parade of 1894. Antonio P. Rivas opened the Social Club ball in San Pedro Springs's upper pavilion in 1895. Lino Sanchez orated for the Mutualistas in 1896. Often there were also patriotic essays and poems. The girls in white who sang the anthem continued to do so, in growing numbers. In 1895, a chorus of thirty sang, and at the mutual aid festival in 1896, fifty girls sang. One new feature was the decoration of houses and stores within the Mexican American "trans–San Pedro" neighborhoods. Everyone who could (including the residents of many *jacales*) flew Mexican flags, and the houses and stores boasted bunting in Mexican colors, evergreens, and flowers. People from the entire San Antonio community, "including a few colored people," continued to come to the postparade festival to enjoy the food, fireworks, small games of chance, and other activities.[74] Dr. Ornelas also made a practice of receiving representatives of each participating mutual aid group at a formal reception on September 16, when they sent messages via the consul to officials in Mexico. The route for the various parades generally started from the near west side, often Washington Square, and circled Military and Main Plazas and sometimes Alamo Plaza as well. Participants in the parades ending in San Pedro Springs festivals always marched the entire route to the park (rather than catching streetcars, as other paraders did) because the entry of the participating marchers by torchlight was one of the best-loved features of the festival.

In general, despite the Mexican colors, trappings, and refreshments, the general profile of San Antonio's Diez y Seis celebrations followed that of other city festivals; their skin was ethnically distinctive, but their core was American. Toward the end of the century, this American core would become even more evident with the participation of such groups as the Belknap Rifles and Carl Beck's Military Band. This "Americanization" becomes even clearer when celebrations of Diez y Seis in Mexico are compared to San Antonio celebrations. The *Express* of 1896 describes village Diez y Seis festivals of the period, noting that sometimes they might go on for a week or more. They would begin with a parade on the evening of September 15, which would end at the town plaza: "Here a grand stand has been built, upon which sit the local dignitaries, literally covered with decorations, broad red sashes and gold lace. The orator of the day . . . reads the Mexican Declaration of Independence; [he] usually wears a general's uniform, though only a civilian."[75]

Afterward, the entire population would repair to the public hall, a salute would be fired by cannon at 11 P.M., and then there would be a dance. The dance described sounded very much like the *fandangos* popular in San Antonio earlier in the century, though perhaps more elegant in the ceremonial party dress of the participants. Instead of cakes being bought for the ladies, they were offered spangle-filled *cascarones* by the gentlemen, which they in turn cracked over their chosen beaux' heads.[76] Celebrations on ranches in rural areas were somewhat different: two- or three-day affairs with barbecues, horse racing, cockfighting, gambling, and always a dance at night.

In short, the paraders appear to have been exclusively members of the military in the urban festivals, and the character of the dances was in conformity to local Mexican tradition.

In the capital, Mexico City, the celebration took on a very different tone. During the later decades of the nineteenth century, Diez y Seis reflected a second significance beyond the simple anniversary of the *grito*. September 16 was also President Porfirio Díaz's birthday and was used accordingly by the ruling elite to give messages of order and progress and to reinforce the celebration of secular over religious events. The municipal government even had a substantial budget reserved for the celebration of this holiday, along with Cinco de Mayo and Constitution Day, on February 5.[77]

The buildings on the Mexico City parade route lay mostly along the recently built Paseo de la Reforma. They were generally owned by wealthy Mexicans, as well as British and American real estate firms, and were elaborately lit for the occasion with festoons of electric lights. The well-patrolled streets on the route were richly decorated with flower- and evergreen-draped triumphal arches, floral coats of arms, streamers, and Mexican flags, joined by evergreen and floral garlands.[78] At the same time spontaneous barrio celebrations of the day were suppressed, so that all focus was on the elegant parade of the elite through downtown. The spectacle was made richer by added financing besides the municipal funds, usually under the umbrella of a *junta patriótica* (in the traditional sense of the phrase, like those that sponsored the festivals in San Antonio in the 1820s and 1830s). The parade itself also looked very different from either the village military parades or the Mexican American ones, for that matter. It consisted of carriages in which rode ladies of high society. These vehicles were profusely covered with flowers, and the ladies in them threw flowers to admiring spectators (often male) on the balconies above, who also threw blossoms and bonbons back at them. The carriages were punctuated by flower-decorated floats, some organized by resident foreign colonies, others by elite schools and other organizations. The entire spectacle was witnessed by President Díaz and his wife from a prominent balcony. The organizers awarded prizes for the best carriages and floats later in the evening, at a private ball at the city's exclusive Jockey Club.[79]

This sort of "Díaz festival" was really reserved for the wealthy; the poorer population of the city was reduced to being spectators along the parade route.

This was essentially different from the democratic festivals of the villages. Both of the Mexican celebration styles were different from the even more democratic ones in San Antonio, where both workers and socialites marched and San Pedro Springs was open—and free—to all. In San Antonio, if there were Mexican Social Club balls, there were always also dances attended by everybody. And the essential American-ness of the festivals as the years progressed was evident not only in their multicultural attendance but in the fact that respected orations were given—and honored—in both Spanish and English.

The 1900 celebration was planned to be the best yet; it was to include all the societies marching together and the usual activities scheduled at San Pedro Springs but also to have participating delegations of officials from various Mexican states, as well as a well-known Mexican national military band. Thus the parade was to be given something of an international character.

But the parade was never held. Just a week before Diez y Seis was to begin, the most catastrophic hurricane the United States ever experienced hit the port of Galveston, its fifteen-foot-high storm surge virtually flattening the city and killing six thousand of its inhabitants, plus a large number on the adjacent mainland. Though there had been some warning, and people of the area were accustomed to tropical storms, this one was of such magnitude that the usual precautions proved futile.[80]

As news of the disaster was carried through the rest of the state, there was a rush to send aid in the form of durable goods, food, and money. The United Mexican Societies, now the organizers of San Antonio's Diez y Seis festival, felt that a parade was an inappropriate way to mark this particular season,. They canceled it, along with the invitations to the Mexican dignitaries and musicians. Homes remained undecorated as a mark of the disaster. A toned-down festival was held at San Pedro Springs, with Manuel Gonzalez-Dena delivering the *grito,* Professor Manuel Treviño giving the Spanish oration, and Edward Dwyer giving the English one. All proceeds from food sales, customarily divided among the cooks, were donated to Galveston relief via Mayor Marshall Hicks. When the chips were down, the American aspect of Mexican Americanism asserted itself within the community, with contributions from all social and economic levels. Civic pride ruled not only in celebrations but in common human concerns as the new century began.[81]

CHAPTER 5
COLUMBUS DAY
"SAN ANTONIO JOINS IN THE GREAT AMERICAN FESTIVITIES"

> In the grand and mighty chorus of honor to the memory of Christopher Columbus, which rolled heavenward from a thousand towns and city of this country yesterday, old San Antonio's voice rose clear and strong. Today from Maine to California the festivities will continue, and in this old city of the Alamo the people have donned their holiday attire and are doing their part.
> —*San Antonio Express,* October 22, 1891

Columbus Day is no longer the widely celebrated holiday it was in the late nineteenth century. It has lost popularity partly because Lief Eriksson is now acknowledged as the first named European to have reached America and partly because the superiority of European culture is far less accepted now than it was then. In San Antonio, it was indeed celebrated, at least in the last fifteen years of the nineteenth century. Its observation was both typical and atypical of other civic celebrations in the city, atypical in part because of constant shifts both in the makeup of the festival and in some of its details.

The principal impetus behind Columbus Day celebrations in San Antonio was the city's tiny Italian American citizenry. Columbus Day was appropriated by Italian Americans in the nineteenth-century United States as a day of celebration. They claimed Christopher Columbus as their own due to his possible Genoese origins, which would have made the first European man (so far as they knew) to set foot on New World soil an Italian.[1] There is evidence that it was celebrated in New York as early as the late 1840s or early 1850s by Italian Americans from Genoa and later by Italian Americans in general.[2]

The number of Italians who settled in San Antonio during the nineteenth century was very small—in the city directory of 1879–80 they numbered only twenty-five out of a total of over twenty-one thousand inhabitants.[3] This was in marked contrast to the thousands of Italian immigrants flocking to port cities such as New York, Boston, San Francisco, and New Orleans, the majority of whom came from Naples, Sicily, and Calabria. San Antonio's Italians trickled in independently and came from diverse Italian cities and towns; extended families tended to settle close to one another. The majority were of a modest mercantile bent. Most—among them Giocchur (later George) and Angelo Battaglia, Luigi Moglia, Antonio Saladino, Antonio Tommassi, Frank Talerico, and Clemente Molteni—dominated the fresh produce markets and fruit stands of the city. Some were craftsmen, notably Salvatore Lucchese, a shoemaker who founded a dynasty of boot makers. Darius M Quasso was a merchant tailor.

The most prominent of the Italian Americans during this time was undoubtedly Antonio Bruni. Bruni arrived in Texas from Villa Bosi, near Parma, in 1862. He began as a grocer in San Antonio, prospered as a dealer in dry goods, and then took to politics, serving as an alderman of Ward 1 in 1879 and as market master in the mid-1880s.[4] He married a Tejana, María Trinidad Arocha, in 1863 and quickly entered the circle of the more prominent Tejano politicians, so much so that some later historians considered him to be a Tejano, even though he would be proud of his Italian origins throughout his life.[5] He was among the founders of the Società Italiana di Mutuo Soccorso in 1884 (he had previously, by default, been a member of the French mutual aid society) and allied them with the Sociedad Mutualista.[6] We have already seen that the Mutuo Soccorso members marched in Diez y Seis parades alongside the Mutualistas in various years, and this seems to have had much to do with Bruni's influence. It is probably not surprising that Bruni also was an early member of the Mexican Social Club.

CELEBRATIONS OF COLUMBUS DAY, 1885–91

There is some evidence that in San Antonio the celebration of the anniversary of Columbus's landing superceded an earlier Italian festival commemorating the fall of Rome, but the latter apparently never had any great popular appeal.[7] The first mention of an Italian-generated celebration of Columbus Day in the city was in 1885. Since October 19, the first day of the two-day festival, brought cooler weather than the other festivals discussed so far, it is not surprising that its parade started at 3:30 P.M. It was a short procession, both in length and in number of participants. The small Italian colony gathered in front of City Hall, then still in the old "Bat Cave" in Military Plaza. They marched from there directly out Acequia Street to San Pedro Springs, their arrival accompanied by a twenty-one-gun salute. As usual, orators spoke at San Pedro Springs, this time in three languages: Bruni himself held forth in Italian, Juan T. Cardenas (his Mutualista ally) spoke in Spanish, and lawyer and judge James H. McLeary orated in English. Two grand balls followed. Most of San Antonio's Italian Americans made up both the reception and the ball committees, with Antonio Bruni serving as master of ceremonies at the more exclusive of the dances. The committees were augmented by several members of the greater community, including Antonio P. Rivas, Edward Froboese and his brother Hermann, and Edward Steves.[8] This is not surprising, since in order to have a critical mass to make the celebration work, the Italian Americans obviously needed extra help from their colleagues.

At first glance, this celebration appears very much in nature like the others, but it did have one distinctive feature: a lavish display of fireworks. There were, of course, fireworks at other festivals; however, the Italian ones, generally reserved for the grand finale of the last night of the park activities, were far more elaborate. They featured not only the usual star bursts and Roman candles but complex set-pieces. These were ground displays, in which whole tableaux of images appeared outlined in shimmering colors. The images themselves were made of frames of bamboo, which could be reused.[9] The set-pieces in 1885 included not only "Columbus and His Ship" but also an initial display spelling out "Welcome," a walking elephant, "Noah's Ark," a rainbow, and (of all things) Santa Claus. Fancy displays of this sort would grace subsequent Columbus Day festivities.

In the following years, the Italian contingent realized that if they wanted to hold a parade that would attract public attention, they would have to augment their small numbers with the addition of other groups. In 1887, they were able to secure participation from the military post. They were honored with the last appearance of the Eighth Cavalry Band, which had played in so many parades during their residence in San Antonio, just one day prior to their departure for Fort Davis. Two cavalry companies and one infantry company also participated. Keeping to a martial theme, the organizers also secured the participation of the Belknap Rifles and the uniform rank of the Knights of Pythias (a fraternal organization). Mayor Bryan Callaghan Jr. and other city officials also rode in carriages with the Società president, Darius M. Quasso, and the omnipresent Antonio Bruni. To enhance things even further, they also enlisted the City Band and included a float depicting "Columbus' First Voyage to the New World." This was colorfully described by the *San Antonio Light* under the headline "Chris' Advent": "[It represented] the ship of Columbus with the gallant discoverer at the prow and supported by his crew. On arrival at the Springs the scene of Columbus' landing was represented. Columbus and his crew descended. Then he claimed the country and planted the standard of the Spanish monarch on the soil while the Indians gazed in astonishment."[10]

Many speeches were scheduled that year, in four languages (including German); however, only the Italian one, by Col. Carlo A. Solero, was delivered due to the small turnout.[11] Other events were held, including military drills, games and sports, and two balls. It is not known if more people from the wider community turned out for these activities than for the orations, but the festival must have been deemed a success by its organizers, for it was to be repeated in subsequent years, following the same general format.

During the late 1880s and early 1890s, the processions followed the usual route encompassing all three plazas. They were generally augmented by the participation of the Sociedad Mutualista, whose presence evidently gave a more pan-Latin air to the procession, so that the *Light* could say in an 1889 headline that "Christopher's Discovery [is] to be celebrated like the Mexican Fiestas."[12] Actually, during this period, the Sociedad Mutualista and the Società Italiana di Mutuo Soccorso appear to have had a symbiotic relationship as far as celebrations were concerned, for the Società likewise marched in the Mutualistas' Diez y Seis parades. But Columbus Day processions also subsequently included other groups, such as the French mutual aid society and volunteer firemen. Whatever bands were available were engaged. These included the Firemen's Band and the Mexican National Zapadores Band in 1890 and the U.S. Infantry Band in 1891. Since there was no Italian consul in the city, Dr. Ornelas stood in to do the honors in 1890 and 1891. The 1889 parade apparently recycled the float depicting "Columbus' First Voyage to the New World" (now transformed into the landing of his third voyage), but whether there was a reenactment in the form of a tableau at San Pedro Springs afterward is not recorded.

More people from the city must have attended the Springs festivities during these years, since orations in various languages were indeed given. The speaker in English was usually a public official: Judge McLeary again delivered the English oration in 1890, while the year before, the English contributor had been the Honorable Oscar Bergstrom, businessman, politician, and Mutualista member. Not surprisingly, Juan T. Cardenas spoke several times during these years in Spanish. Colonel Solero was a regular in Italian, while Edgar Schramm did the honors in German. The other events scheduled included music, balls, and fireworks.[13]

One of the interesting features of Columbus Day celebrations was that the "day" was not fixed. Twentieth-century celebrations generally took place on October 12, the date of Columbus's first landing. In the later nineteenth century, the date was less precise. In 1887, the parade day was October 12; in 1889, 1890, and 1891, it was October 13; in 1892, 1893, and 1894 it was October 21; while in 1895, it was October 19.

CONFLICTING OR CONCURRENT CELEBRATIONS, 1891–92

It is clear that the commemoration of Columbus's landing was not the sole property of the Italian Americans, no matter how much augmentation they secured. On October 21, 1891, two other parades took place besides the Italian one, which was held in the evening. If anyone felt like devoting the entire day and evening to celebration, this was the best date of the century to do it.

Non-Italian Catholic societies appropriated the morning to have a procession through the city streets from Travis Park to the new hall of the Saint Joseph's Society on East Commerce Street. The Twenty-Second Regiment Infantry Band provided music, and the rest of the parade consisted primarily of gentlemen from various Catholic societies of many ethnicities, including the Ancient Order of Hibernians, the Cathedral Society, the Polish Society, Saint Michael's and Saint Joseph's parishes, and the Catholic Knights of America. All wore their regalia and waved banners. City officials and parochial schoolboys also joined in. The latter included students from Saint Mary's College, orphans from Saint John's, and twenty African American children from Saint Peter Claver's School. The Saint Mary's boys carried banners emblazoned with what the *San Antonio Express* described as "an alleged counterfeit presentment of Columbus, who must have been a very homely man if those pictures of him were correct likenesses."[14]

The procession encompassed Alamo and Main Plazas, making a detour up Dwyer Avenue to pass the bishop's residence. The men left the march to attend Mass at San Fernando Cathedral, whose facade was draped with a huge American flag. The boys went on to Saint Joseph's Hall (adorned, as customary, with bunting and evergreens), where a dedication ceremony was held after Mass was finished. It was presided over by Bishop Neraz and priests from the Catholic parishes.

The third celebration was an African American one, which was held later in the morning, led by the Excelsior Guards and the Brackner Lone Star Colored Brass Band. It circled the principal plazas, and then viewers and marchers caught streetcars to Riverside Park, where the festivities continued with orations, a band concert, and a sham battle staged by the Excelsior Guards. The speeches here were political in nature, as elections were only a month away, and were sponsored by the *Tonguelet* printing company and other local African American organizations.[15]

The year 1892 brought two celebrations of a rival sort. Whereas the three 1891 parades were spaced throughout the day, the following year brought the real possibility of conflict. The year 1892 marked the four hundredth anniversary of Columbus's first voyage, and by August 30, the Italian Americans were making plans to have a grandiose parade, particularly since the Società Italiana di Mutuo Soccorso had been joined since 1890 by a second Italian society named for Columbus himself.[16] Under the leadership of Antonio Bruni and other members of the organizing committee, they planned a large parade with several floats and the usual associated events at San Pedro Springs Park, which would last three days, beginning on October 21.

Unfortunately for Bruni and his fellow planners, the German American community, in the wake of a spectacular German Day parade held the previous year, had decided to make Columbus and American history the theme of their elaborate parade for 1892. They had scheduled the procession and opening festivities at Wolfram's Central Gardens for the same day in October. Each group had apparently been making preliminary plans without knowledge of the other, and last-minute attempts to have the two processions and festivals amalgamate ended in failure (probably because the Germans liked to charge admission to their festival, while events held at San Pedro Springs Park were, by city ordinance, free). In the end, the German Americans grudgingly changed their parade date to October 29 but retained their elaborate floats and Columbian commemorative theme. Since their community was far bigger and had considerably more economic and political clout within the now-Anglo-American-dominated city, they got the more glamorous parade.

Though they only had one float (Columbus's ship again—was it perennially recycled with minor modifications?), the Italian Americans retaliated by the sheer volume of parade participants.[17] Military of all types marched, from U.S. artillery and cavalry and an army band to both Confederate and Union veterans, with the Belknaps thrown in for good measure. Not only did the two Italian mutual aid societies march, but they were augmented by a third Italian American group, the Italiana Alpini, plus four Mexican American mutual aid societies, the Mexican Social Club, the French Workingmen's Society, the Farmer's Alliance, Mayor Callaghan, and city and county officials. In its makeup, then, this parade had little to distinguish it from Fourth of July and Diez y Seis processions of this era, except for the proliferation of Italian flags. If Italian Americans formed the organizing committees for their Columbus Day festivities, still, except for the fireworks (and perhaps Italian food at San Pedro Springs?), the result was a classic example of the "San Antonio festival model."[18]

The Italian Americans also piled it on at San Pedro Springs with a forty-four-gun salute, multilingual orators once again, and the usual two balls. The third and last day featured "the grandest display of fireworks ever witnessed in San Antonio," which included set-pieces of Columbus and also one of the buildings that graced the Columbian Exhibition in Chicago."[19]

Evidently, this celebration was declared a success even before it was over. The Italian Americans decided to hold a meeting to appoint a committee of a dozen prominent citizens to raise funds for the purpose of erecting a bust or statue of Columbus during the commemorative festivities of 1893. "The committee," they decided, would "include Americans, Germans, Italians, Mexicans and Frenchmen," thus emphasizing the American-ness of the festival.[20]

COLUMBUS DAY IN THE MID- TO LATE 1890S

Unfortunately, a sculpted tribute to Christopher Columbus would have to wait until 1957.[21] The fund-raising efforts for an image were at least partially successful, in spite of the economic depression hanging over the city in 1893. What the committee was able to afford at that time instead of a sculpture was "an elegant painting of Christopher Columbus by the Italian artist, Prof. G. Giovannetti," in return for which he received a "costly gold medal."[22] The afternoon presentation was staged with much ceremony at City Hall. Members of the Christopher Columbus Society, headed by Antonio Bruni and Darius Quasso, marched around the city-council chamber with the painting, accompanied by a band that played outside in the corridor. The artist was present to receive his medal, as were male and female members of the Italian American community, who filled every bit of vacant space in the room. Flowery speeches were made at the presentation ceremony, praising Columbus and George Washington as, respectively, discoverer of and giver of freedom to the United States. Nothing, however, is known about what the painting looked like or about its fate in subsequent years (it has long vanished from City Hall). As for the artist, nothing else is known of G. Giovannetti (although he could not have been so great or successful if he was willing to take payment in the form of a medal).[23]

Meanwhile, the parade was already forming on Military Plaza, outside City Hall. The artist and his entourage of officials placed themselves in hacks among the other marchers, and the parade wound through the plazas, which were profusely decorated with bunting in Italian and American colors. The makeup of the parade was similar to that of 1892, with the absence of the French mutual aid society and the added presence of the now-professional fire department with their vehicles. The grand marshal was Giocchur Battaglia, who had served terms as president of both the Mutuo Soccorso and the Christopher Columbus Society. Among the other marshals was "Federigo" Kerbel—the same proprietor at San Pedro Springs who had caused such grief to the Mexican American community ten years before, now totally reeducated and rehabilitated. By this time, the Columbus ship float, if it still existed, must have been in poor shape, for it was absent from the procession, to be replaced simply by a man wearing a Columbus costume and carrying a flag of Spain.[24] The activities at San Pedro Springs differed little from the year before, though an Italian note was struck by an operatic concert given the second day.

A similar festival with a similar parade, minus the military, was held the following year, but after that, parades were abandoned for the rest of the century. Had the non-Italian participants become so overwhelming in number in comparison to the Italian Americans that the latter decided that organizing a parade as a community was no longer worth it? Or was it simply that Columbus Day was not a holiday to generate much patriotic enthusiasm? Perhaps something of the lack of excitement is reflected in the headline of the *San Antonio Light* in 1895: "COLUMBUS DAY. Our Entire Country Should Celebrate. San Antonio Will Do So, Anyhow."[25] Since the *Light,* more so than the *San Antonio Express,* tended to call things as it saw them, this may indeed have been the case.

There was, however, and would continue to be until the end of the century, a two-day celebration at San Pedro Springs that followed the traditional pattern of speeches, food, and balls. The Italian Americans lavished the bulk of their limited budget on ever more spectacular fireworks displays. In 1895, spectators enjoyed thirty-two different displays—mostly rockets of many and elaborate types and colors but also several large set-pieces. These included the "Walking Elephant," "Noah's Ark," "Rainbow," and "Columbus and His Ship" (this time specified as the *Santa Maria*), seen in previous years upon recycled frames, and, in addition, the "Battle of the Alamo."[26] The expense for this display was lavish— around seven hundred dollars—and a pyrotechnical expert, Professor G. Grisaffi, was hired for the event. During the last five years of the century, the fireworks were the principal attraction.

The changing fortunes and faces of Columbus Day celebrations during the 1880s and 1890s are probably indicative of the lack of public enthusiasm for celebrating the holiday, as well as the limited means and numbers of the Italian American community. In a way, its waxing and waning were similar to the Fourth of July—whereas that holiday's importance peaked with the Spanish-American War in 1898, Columbus Day's brightest hour in nineteenth-century San Antonio came in the year of the four hundredth anniversary of the explorer's landing in 1892. But in the end, Columbus Day was not institutionalized in San Antonio even to the extent that the Fourth of July had been. There was not enough community support to keep it going as a full-blown civic celebration as the new century loomed. Twentieth-century celebrations of Columbus Day would only resume after a hiatus and would follow models of a later time.

CHAPTER 6
VOLKSFESTS
"GERMANIA AND COLUMBIA"

> In this country, the Volksfest is no longer characteristically German, except in name, for the advantages and pleasures of such a festival were so readily recognized by all nationalities, when introduced, that it has become nationalized, all nationalities taking as great a part, and as much interest in its success, as the Germans. What Mardi Gras is to New Orleans, the Orioles to Baltimore, and the Veiled Prophets to St. Louis, is the Volksfest to San Antonio.
> —*San Antonio Express,* October 22, 1885

The history of the German settlers in Texas is well documented. They were the largest single group to immigrate to the state directly from Europe in the nineteenth century. German settlers were in Texas as early as 1831, but large-scale immigration plans began in 1842 with the creation of the Verein zum Schutz Deutscher Einwandrer, better known by its popular name Adelsverein (literally "Noble's Association," named for its aristocratic sponsors), headquartered in the German cities of Mainz and Biebrich. The then–Republic of Texas was attractive as a destination for the *verein*'s immigrants, for there were no U.S. tariff barriers and the land was reputed to be fertile. Such enticements, they reasoned, would offer German settlers the chance to get into things on the ground floor.[1]

The German arrivals actually came in several waves. Between 1844 and 1848, farmers, skilled laborers, and small tradesmen arrived, many settling in the Hill Country, north of San Antonio, and others in southeast Texas, mainly between San Antonio and Houston. The majority of these immigrants came from German states that had connections with Adelsverein organizers: Hesse-Darmstadt, Nassau, Electoral Hesse, western Thuringia, and Alsace.[2] After the failed revolution of 1848, another wave of Germans came to Texas, this time from a wider variety of locations. Among them were the intellectual "forty-eighters." Many of this group were political and social idealists, and though small in number, their impact on Texas society would be disproportionately large. Some of them formed utopian colonies, the best known being the Free Thinkers, who founded the Hill Country towns of Comfort and Sisterdale.[3]

The majority of "forty-eighters" had been minor nobility and professionals in Germany and included doctors, teachers, scientists, musicians, lawyers, brewers, merchants, architects, and builders.[4] Though some of the earlier wave had settled in San Antonio, the professionals were even more attracted to an urban center, where they could pursue the sorts of occupations they brought with them. Some came to San Antonio directly, while others arrived later, after such utopian efforts as the Bettina and Latin colonies failed. Perhaps the most famous of these indirect arrivals was Dr. Ferdinand Herff Sr.[5] Trained as a surgeon in Bonn, he was one of the original members of the "Bettina forty." When the colony failed, he went back to Germany, married there, and returned to Texas in 1849, this time to settle in San Antonio.

Both country farmers and city professionals from the various German states put down strong roots in Texas and brought with them a European cultural stability that had been lacking in the region. Their culture, which they tried to retain as they settled into their new environment, led to the establishment of American branches of many of their traditional clubs (*vereine*) and civic organizations. The *vereine* included groups sharing common interests such as physical culture (*turnverein*), shooting and hunting (*scheutzen vereine*), military veterans (*krieger vereine*), and gardening (*garten vereine*). Many of the Free Thinkers soon formed book clubs, such as San Antonio's Alamo Literary Society. They also staged German dramas.[6] The most popular were plays by the early romantic poet and playwright Friedrich von Schiller, then in vogue on both sides of the Atlantic. Even more important was the proliferation of choirs, for both men and women. Three of these, the Beethoven Männerchor, the Catholic Liederkranz, and the Beethoven Damenchor (formed somewhat later), survive to this day in San Antonio, and others still operate in the Hill Country. The choirs sponsored *sängerfests,* or singing festivals, which brought choirs from all over the region together to sing and socialize. They also offered an opportunity to discuss local needs, particularly educational ones.[7] These activities kept social ties among the various German communities strong and lasting.

In the 1850s, San Antonio was still isolated from the rest of the United States, and Anglo-American culture as such barely existed. The new German Americans therefore felt free to preserve their own cultural values alongside those of their Anglo-American and Tejano neighbors.[8] They settled mostly along what became Commerce Street, east of the San Antonio River, and later on the near south side. At this point, it was common for enterprising German Americans to speak English and Spanish along with their own language, and shop signs were often in all three languages. Not satisfied with existing schools in San Antonio, the German American Free Thinkers established a German-English school in 1859 to teach their children both the German and the American languages and cultures in a secular setting; it was not unusual for literate Anglo-Americans seeking a high-quality education to send their children there too.[9]

Literacy was further reflected in the publication of several successive German-language newspapers, including the radically abolitionist *San Antonio Zeitung* before the Civil War and the *Freie Press Fuer San Antonio*, established in 1865, which flourished into the twentieth century.[10]

Cultural and social issues were further addressed with the establishment of the Casino Association in 1858. Though founded primarily as a social club, it sponsored other activities through the auspices of its clubhouse, Casino Hall. The hall became the site for plays, operas, and other performances open to the public. Many of these productions originated within the association's own theatrical *verein*.[11] This venue was later supplemented by Turner Hall, built in 1875 as headquarters of the Turnverein, which also offered concert, lecture, and theater space.[12] The Turnverein itself not only practiced physical culture and sponsored gymnastic contests but also staged their own plays and music and sponsored a volunteer hook and ladder company; indeed, as we've already seen, it was mostly German Americans who served as volunteer firemen.

There was one aspect in which becoming American would affect these immigrants—the way German Americans would be perceived as a group. During the first half of the nineteenth century, there was still no unified Germany. The arriving immigrants identified themselves with the particular German-speaking state where they had originated, for each had distinct customs, culture, and dialect. Non–German Americans simply saw them as a generic group, and particularly after the unification of Germany in 1871, German Americans would also perceive themselves that way.

One of the more interesting aspects of the German migration is that it consisted of Protestants, Catholics, Jews, and secular-minded Free Thinkers. Though each group naturally formed its own religious congregations or like-thinking groups and tended to marry within them (with the exception of some of the Catholics), the rigid social and religious divisions of the old country gradually began to disappear in the new land. The Free Thinkers, who had no religious bent, substituted secular institutions such as the *vereine* and were the moving force behind the Casino Association and the Beethoven Männerchor.[13] However, some of the *vereine*, thanks to their special interests, attracted non–Free Thinkers as well. So did some of the choirs. The San Antonio Liederkrantz may have been all-Catholic in membership, but the Beethoven Männerchor included both Jews and Christians. Eventually, membership in many of the *vereine*, choirs, volunteer fire departments, and the Casino Club was drawn from all the religious and secular groups and, in the case of some of them, included non–German American members.[14]

This steady progress in "civilizing" San Antonio had a setback with the coming of the Civil War. Many of the Free Thinkers, though small in number, had strong abolitionist sympathies, and life became difficult for them once Texas declared for the Confederacy. A group of German American Hill Country Unionists were killed in a conflict with Confederate troops on the Nueces River when they tried to flee to Mexico.[15] Though spared such an extreme fate, San Antonio's German Americans suffered for their antislavery views—and many who did not share this viewpoint were perceived to by their Anglo-American fellow citizens. Some went to Mexico for the duration of the war, where they made useful business contacts that would serve them well later. Others, such as the rabid abolitionist Adolph Douai (publisher of the *San Antonio Zeitung*), were run out of town by proslavery factions as early as 1854.[16] The newspaper itself and its building were wrecked by a secessionist mob in 1861.[17] But active abolitionists were apparently the exception. A substantial number of the German American middle class were against dissolving the Union, but this had more to do with the practical threat of disruption of business than concern for enslaved African Americans. Many of the blue-collar German Americans were indifferent to politics and resented the vociferousness of their antislavery neighbors. Others, including Hermann D. Kampmann, Gustav Schmeltzer, Adolph Dreiss, and William Hoefling Sr., fought for the Confederacy.

Not surprisingly, after the Civil War, many of the "forty-eighter" German Americans enthusiastically supported the Republican Reconstruction government. One of their number, Wilhelm Carl August Thielepape, a liberal progressive, was the Reconstruction-appointed mayor in 1867 and held the post until 1870. During the same period, half the city's aldermen were German American.[18] Civic involvement would, however, outlast Reconstruction. German Americans would continue to serve as aldermen through the century, representing the interests of the wards and their own businesses where they lived, predominantly on the city's near northeast and southeast sides.

Reconstruction politics and sympathies were not issues in the city for long, and the German Americans, along with the rest of the population, quickly returned to their prewar occupations and continued to prosper. The *vereine,* choirs, and other groups were revived; the Casino Club, the German-English school, and the *Freie Presse* all flourished. Saint John's Lutheran Church, whose construction began in 1860 and then was suspended during the war, reached completion by 1875.[19] The Catholic German Americans began construction of their own parish church, Saint Joseph's, in 1868, while six years later, the Jewish Reformed synagogue, Temple Beth-El, was built on Travis Square.

This is not to say, of course, that all the German American citizens of San Antonio were lions of culture and paragons of politics. There were healthy numbers of blue-collar workers, as well as tradesmen and others, who were more interested in beer and bowling than attending concerts and edifying lectures. There were a considerable number of German-owned saloons, which were generally male retreats.[20] On the other hand, German Americans viewed the consumption of beer as opposed to harder liquor in quite a different light. A good deal of family entertainment was centered around family-owned beer halls and beer gardens, which often featured music. Some were small, like Ruppersberg's on Garden (later Saint Mary's) Street. Others were more elaborate and could be rented out by groups for larger events. We have already seen Limburger's Garden and Fest's Garden used by various groups for postparade festivities when San Pedro Springs Park was unavailable.[21] Indeed, it was Mayor Bryan Callaghan's anti-temperance stand that gained him many supporters among the beer-loving German Americans.[22]

German American blue-collar workers also formed the backbone of San Antonio's short-lived labor-union movement. The Arbeiter Verein, which was first organized in New Braunfels in the 1850s, opened a local chapter in San Antonio around 1865, initially called the Laborer's Association. Occupational unions soon followed. The typographer's union local arrived in the mid-1870s. Others, including the carpenters, tinners, blacksmiths, butchers, painters, brewers, and beer-wagon drivers, followed during succeeding decades.[23] All would march in various Volksfest parades.

German Americans also prospered in the upper echelons of San Antonio's business world. Mention of the careers of Henry and Louis Berg and Hermann Kampmann has already been made.[24] A further example was Bernard J. (Ben) Mauermann, who began in the family's gun business and was a volunteer fireman with the Turnverein. He later served as an alderman in 1882, and by the early

1890s, he would become secretary and eventually president of the Alamo Cement Company. By the 1890s, a number of families who started in modest dry goods businesses had become bankers (the Oppenheimers), department-store magnates (the Joske brothers, the Wolfson brothers), or large-scale wholesalers (Charles Hugo—who later became a banker—and Gustav Schmeltzer). Gustav Duerler, volunteer fire chief, was also a prosperous candy manufacturer and had the dubious fame of establishing San Antonio's pecan-shelling industry. The number of very successful gentlemen was comparatively large; they formed the backbone of the Casino Club. It was not only the Casino Club members but also members of the unions and more modest *vereine* who collaborated on the most ambitious festival held during the nineteenth century: the Volksfest.

THE VOLKSFESTS OF THE 1880S AND THEIR GENESIS

On September 19, 1869, San Antonio German Americans as a community held their first public festival. It honored the one hundredth birthday of the German naturalist Alexander von Humboldt and was organized by Casino Club members to benefit the German-English school. The celebration had all the earmarks of later city festivals. On September 14 orators delivered edifying speeches in the evergreen-festooned Casino Hall. This was followed by the ceremonial presentation of a plaster bust of Humboldt by artist Carl von Iwonski (to match a plaster bust of Schiller already owned by the school), a theatrical performance by community members, and a dance.[25] On September 19 a downtown parade was held consisting of German schoolchildren, the white fire companies, the Laborer's Association, and city dignitaries, led by a band. They marched from Alamo Plaza to San Pedro Springs, circling Main and Military Plazas on the way. At the Springs, a band concert was held, Turnverein members made human pyramids, songs were sung by various local choirs, and orations were given in both German and English. There were also a play and two more dances, one for invited guests, another for the general populace. Admission to the festival was fifty cents (this was apparently before the ordinance that no event in San Pedro Springs Park could charge admission); all proceeds went to the Humboldt School fund.[26]

This was a one-shot celebration. It was ostensibly modeled on Schillerfieren (Schiller fairs) and other memorial festivals held in Germany during the nineteenth century. These were usually organized by *vereine*. They were characterized by orations and processions with floats to local market squares, as well as tableaux of Schiller's plays.[27] On the other hand, the lack of anything so elaborate as tableaux and floats in the San Antonio festival, the parade's route around the city's streets and plazas, and the placing of the activities at San Pedro Springs Park sound very much like contemporary accounts of local Fourth of July celebrations. The specialized purpose of the Humboldt festival precluded its development into an annual fete, but the scale on which it was organized as a multiday event was a herald of things to come.

Perhaps the reason that an annual German American–sponsored festival was not instituted in San Antonio until over a decade later was that until that point, celebrations within the German American community (such as the *sängerfests*) sufficed.[28] But after the advent of the railroad in 1877 and the great infusion of Anglo-American newcomers to the city, the German Americans may have been spurred to assert their culture even as they lost domination in the city's demographics. At any rate, no specific date or event was commemorated in the seven ambitious German American–sponsored festivals that were held in the 1880s and 1890s. However, they did represent an American adaptation of a different old-country institution than the Schillerfieren: the Volksfest.

In its German original, the Volksfest grew out of early nineteenth-century romanticism. Volksfests emphasized the simplicity and upright character of the national Germanic heritage. In a period when heightened national identity was sweeping Europe, the various European German states began to define their own identities. Following the fashions of the romanticism popular at the time, they looked to ancient and medieval sources in their quest for heroes. Resurrection of legends of ancient Germanic victories led to grandiose monuments to heroes such as Arminius (Hermann), the tribal general who defeated three Roman legions in the Teutoberger Forest in 9 A.D. There was also the exaltation of ancient German myths (Valhalla and the great god Wotan), as well as frequent allegorical incarnations of Germania, the equivalent to the American Goddess of Liberty.[29]

The first Volksfest was held in the town of Hambach-on-the-Rhine in May, 1832. It featured a parade with deputations from towns all over the various German states (some wearing "ancient" costumes); city militia companies with red, black, and gold emblems; and a band. They all marched to a nearby ancient ruined castle, where nineteen orations were given, lasting the entire day.[30] Inspired by this landmark celebration, smaller villages began holding their own Volksfests—true "people's festivals." By the 1860s, these featured enthusiastic participation by various *vereine* and singing societies, and with Germany's unification in 1871, many of these festivals were held on a national scale. In some cases, the contribution of these groups was elaborate. A good example is the 1896 monument to Emperor Frederick Barbarossa on Kyffhäuser Mountain, where the emperor purportedly slept since medieval times, only to be awakened when the ancient *reich* was restored. It was a massive construction, entirely paid for by funds raised by the consolidated *krieger vereine*.[31]

The German American Volksfests were on a much more modest scale. The earliest in Texas were held sporadically from 1854 to the 1870s in the Hill Country and in Houston.[32] Dr. Max Lindner, a young pharmacist, had lived in Houston for nine years before moving to San Antonio for relief from his malaria.[33] He was familiar with the Houston celebrations; by late 1881 he had the idea to stage one in San Antonio.[34] He floated this idea by some of the German American community leaders, and enthusiasm was such that a planning meeting was held on January 17, 1882, in Turner Hall. A steering committee was swiftly appointed. It included Lindner; Ben Mauermann; Dr. Berthold Hadra, a respected physician who had recently served a term as president of the Beethoven Männerchor; and William Hoefling Sr., a sausage magnate.[35]

By the next day, a date for the festival had been determined (June 2 and 3) and a celebration venue obtained. Wolfram's Central Gardens was chosen because of its location on "Bowen's Island." The "island," in reality a peninsula, had only one entrance, at Garden Street. It was a perfect choice since the committee had decided to charge an admission fee, which could not be done at San Pedro Springs.[36] The committee estimated that it would have to raise five thousand dollars—quite a sum in 1882—from subscribers in the community in order to hold a proper festival to rival Houston's. Since they envisioned their Volksfest as a true "people's festival," they planned to solicit these funds from "all classes participating."[37] It is obvious that the German American community was thinking on a far grander scale than the planners of any other municipal festival held at this period. Most of the other contemporary fetes were put together one or at most two months in advance. The Volksfest planners worked with a lead of five months. They were also counting on recouping their contributions—and making a profit—not only from the proceeds of admissions and food sales to locals but by attracting German Americans from outlying towns with the incentive of special rail and stagecoach rates. Every celebrating group did this, but these organizers, even in January, were thinking about an extensive advertising campaign.

The very fact that the planners had gotten this far was already a remarkable feat. The various *vereine* were fiercely independent of each other, and few, if any, members belonged to more than one.³⁸ The Volksfest was therefore to unite the German American community of San Antonio in a way it never had been before.

By the middle of April, they had achieved their financial goal, and most events were in place. There would be two parades: an all-male "Grand Burlesque Torchlight Parade" to be held on the night of June 1 and an elaborate day parade with appropriately costumed men and women populating the floats on the afternoon of June 2. The day parade would be followed by the Central Gardens events. All of this was announced in the *San Antonio Express* in advertisements that began running as early as April 11. They read:

> Friday and Saturday
> June 2nd and 3rd 1882
> First Grand
> **VOLKSFEST**
> Grand Parade, Orations, Promenade Concert and Dance,
> Tableaux and Pantomimes
> **Brilliant Fireworks Every Evening**
> The Volksfest will be inaugurated on Thursday Evening June 1st by a
> **Grand Burlesque Torchlight Procession**
> All Railroads Sell Round Trip Tickets at Reduced Rates
> FOR FURTHER INFORMATION AND PROGRAMME SEE
> **THE EXECUTIVE COMMITTEE**

The torchlight parade was the subject of several gleeful planning meetings. Dr. Lindner arranged to buy readymade costumes "originally imported from France, but . . . used in New Orleans in one of the grand displays of the city."³⁹ The theme was "Darwin's Theory," and the costumes included "impersonations of the animal kingdom: bats and fishes, crabs and other inhabitants of the briny deep, butterfly, sun, moon, &c." G. G. Tobey, a Chicago businessman who would be passing through San Antonio at the time of the parade, offered several more costumes: "Kek Kek La (running warrior from the Sandwich Islands); Wacoa-Koo, the medicine man of the North Pole, one hundred and sixty-four years old; Kow-Kow-To-To—The Man-Eater; Ha-Ha-Sing, the Great Chinaman, ten feet high; Scorpion Jim, the celebrated Indian chief; George Washington, the Great Dwarf, two feet in his stockings, the wonder of the age and Hoop-La, white and black, the man of two colors."⁴⁰ The parade would also include "transparencies," mobile flats embellished with satirical pictures or inscriptions.

If none of these particular themes makes sense to a twenty-first-century reader, that is understandable. The burlesque parade was extremely topical, relating to specific social and political events of the day. It followed a tradition initiated in New Orleans at Mardi Gras in 1873, when the Twelfth Night Revelers staged a parade entitled "The World of Audubon," in which birds represented satirical topics of the moment. Transparencies were featured the same year in another Mardi Gras parade, "The Missing Links to Darwin's Origins of Species," presented by the Comus Society.[41]

In order to understand all the nuances of the 1882 Volksfest torchlight parade, pages would have to be spent here explaining not only the issues of the moment but the broad humor of the time as well. Suffice it to say that it was a raucous procession, marching from Central Gardens around the downtown streets and back to Central Gardens again. It was duly appreciated by the crowd of "human beings of every description and nationality, big, little, old and young, ladies and gentlemen," along Houston and Commerce Streets and Alamo Plaza.[42] San Antonio was still small enough for most viewers to know many of the marchers personally. Even if all of the allusions weren't understood by all the watchers, it is easy to imagine Gus Hellborn's family's and friends' reactions to seeing the tailor and Turnverein member dressed as a wasp. Or, for that matter, to seeing Adolf Wagner, future director of the Casino Club, as a crocodile.[43] The rowdy night crowds typical of the 1880s in Main and Military Plazas must have loved the parade too. Still, there was nothing particularly German about it, except for the ethnic origin of the men who marched in the costumes.

The following afternoon, a more traditional Volksfest parade was held. One of the elements that was certainly translated from German Volksfests was the tableau-like floats that dominated the procession, depicting aspects of a uniform theme—a harbinger of public pageants to come. They were designed both to entertain and to instruct. Each float was sponsored by one of the *vereine,* the members assigned its theme and then constructing and decorating it themselves. They also served as its personnel (augmented, when necessary, by family and friends drafted for the occasion). The rest of the members marched, adorned with emblems and badges, after their float.

The overall theme was "Scenes from Texas History"—certainly different from processions of the Fatherland and already with American precedents. The best-known precedent was Mardi Gras in New Orleans and other Gulf Coast cities, but the tradition that drove these festivals had very different ethnic and cultural origins, and the "Fat Tuesday" climax of the carnival itself had religious undertones.[44] A better precedent for the Volksfest processions in some ways was the

Veiled Prophet celebration and parade in Saint Louis, begun there by prominent businessmen in 1878 and basically serving to glorify the capitalistic ambitions of its organizers.[45]

In both of these festivals, the parades featured unified themes, usually literary, historical, or allegorical in nature (or sometimes a combination of the three), and reflected the growing popularity of the pageant movement in America during the late nineteenth century. The pageant movement involved an increasingly elaborate display of linked themes, usually reflecting particular relevance to the group that staged a pageant.[46] In Saint Louis and New Orleans, costumes and floats were often made by professionals and were very elaborate and expensive to produce. In both cities, all characters, male or female, were generally portrayed by men.

Such was not the case with the floats in San Antonio's first Volksfest. Its "Scenes of Texas History" motif firmly placed the German American community in its adopted land (unlike, for example, a Volksfest parade in Houston held in the 1870s, with its wine wagons and other makeshift floats).[47] The floats spanned historical events from the "Landing of Lasalle" and continued through "an excellent representation of the battle of San Jacinto and the capture of Santa Anna in 1836, by the Texas army."[48] Judging from the sole surviving photograph of an entry from that parade, however, the floats appear to have been rustic at best. The float in the photograph—the parade's prizewinner, by the Arbeiter Verein—depicted the "First German Settlers on Texas Soil."[49] It appears to have been made up of actual live oak trees and a small log cabin laid on a flatbed wagon, replete with a bearded "pioneer" driver (other actors described in contemporary accounts of the float evidently vacated the premises before it was immortalized on film). But this still represented the most elaborate mobile display in a parade in the city up to this point.

There were other familiar San Antonio components in this procession: Mayor James French and other city officials rode in carriages, and music was provided by the Twenty-second Regiment Infantry Band. The display was further lengthened by the inclusion of commercial wagons, led by beer companies ranging from San Antonio brewers such as Tony Faust to the national firms of Anheuser's and Lemp's. Other advertising floats were of a more local nature and included Frederick's Longhorn Furniture and Sim Hart's fancy carriage, advertising his cigar store, located downstairs from the infamous Vaudeville Theater.[50] The final embellishment was assorted German Americans dressed as cowboys and Indians, who skirmished among the floats at intervals.

Lemp's beer wagon, a readymade commercial entry in the 1882 Volksfest parade. *Courtesy Daughters of the Republic of Texas Library*

Since it was June and already into the hot season, the parade was held at 10 A.M. and followed a short route from Alamo Plaza to Central Gardens via Commerce Street. Once at Central Gardens, Dr. Hadra, of the steering committee, gave a short opening welcome speech. This was followed by the awarding of a prize to the Arbeiter Verein for the best-decorated *verein* float. A sit-down lunch was served to invited guests, including many non–German American luminaries who had contributed to make the festival possible. The afternoon was occupied by children's games, supervised by Dr. Lindner. In the evening were two orations, one in English by Col. Henry B. Andrews. He was probably selected to

Wolfram's Central Gardens: decorated beer booths, 1882 Volksfest.
Courtesy Daughters of the Republic of Texas Library

speak because he was not only an Anglo-American member of volunteer Fire Company 2 but also president of the Sunset Railroad (which brought many out-of-town visitors to the festival). It was a lengthy speech in the flowery style of the day. An oration was also given in German by August H. Siemering, editor and publisher of the *Freie Presse Fuer San Antonio*. At around sundown, dancing commenced, followed by fireworks supervised by George Kalteyer, the pharmacist and amateur pyrotechnic expert who also supplied them to the Mexican American community for their Diez y Seis parades.[51]

The next afternoon, more children's games were held, including sack races and footraces. In the evening, a satirical pantomime was presented, with the actors apparently recycling some of the costumes from the torchlight parade (including an owl, a wasp, and a kangaroo). The pantomime was written expressly

The Arbeiter Verein's prize-winning and obviously homemade float, "First German Settlers on our Texas Soil," 1882 Volksfest.
Courtesy Daughters of the Republic of Texas Library

for the occasion and parodied local elections.[52] Also featured was a performance by a group of then-popular white minstrels in blackface. Later on, there was more dancing and more fireworks.

Like Volksfests in the Fatherland, the San Antonio edition did contain elements that were definitely in the old-country tradition. Perhaps most important was the involvement of the *vereine* and choirs, united for the occasion in a way that was unprecedented in San Antonio. Their members made up many of the festival's organizing committees. They also figured prominently in the parades, both in grotesque costumes in the torchlight procession and riding in historical raiment on floats or marching in the day parade. Orations at the festival site could be traced to German Volksfests, but they were equally popular in American festivals of the period.

The differences from the Volksfest's Germanic roots show how much the immigrant culture had changed. The torchlight parade and its satirical political subject matter could only have been American; the same can be said for the pantomime the following evening. Though the program of the floats was determined beforehand and followed a preordained unified theme, the subject matter referred to Germans in the New World and to episodes of American and Texas history. The truly homemade aspect of the floats was local as well, as was the nature of the parade through the city streets to a centrally located park, rather than to an outlying shrine. The orations lasted only about an hour instead of all day, and the sale of food and drink during the day and evening at Central Gardens, the stores on the parade route decorated with the familiar evergreens and bunting in both German and American colors, and the children's athletic contests were all closely related to other festivals being celebrated in San Antonio. At this point, the San Antonio Volksfest was really a "people's festival" in the sense that contributions to hold it had come from the entire German American community and some members of the greater community at large. Though the admission cost would have excluded the city's poorest residents, the parades were free, and everyone who could chipped in to make the events a success. Unlike many German festivals, San Antonio's Volksfest emanated from the German Americans themselves, not from any official controlling or governmental organization (as often happened in Germany after unification).[53]

No one was happier about the success of the first Volksfest than Dr. Max Lindner. The pharmacist and some of his associates from the initial festival swiftly began planning for a second one, to be held the following year. In spite of their enthusiasm, it took some time for the plans to get off the ground. Meetings announced for early January at Turner Hall were so poorly attended that future ones were postponed. It wasn't until June 21 that plans were set in motion. Obviously, the 1883 Volksfest would not be held in early June as the last one had been. Instead of facing the heat of the beginning of summer, Lindner wisely decided instead to hold it in October, a traditional time for German beer festivals that encompassed October 6, the accepted date for the founding of the first German settlement in the United States at Germantown, Pennsylvania.[54] By early July, officers had been elected. Dr. Lindner was president, Col. Augustus Belknap vice-president, and Carl Runge recording secretary.[55] Committees were organized by mid-July, including one for each parade (torchlight and day), fireworks, street illumination, music, decorations, an operetta, and tableaux. A goal of six thousand dollars was set, twenty-five hundred dollars having already been pledged.[56] Again, admission would be charged, at fifty cents per adult and twenty-five cents for children, with small children free.

By the beginning of August, two-thirds of the funds had been raised. The tableau committee added a Schillerfest touch with ambitious plans for fourteen tableaux illustrating episodes from the poet's *Elysium*. Meanwhile, the music chairman, Professor Gabriel Katzenberger, was preparing to start rehearsals for a popular operetta of the day entitled *The Twin Sisters*, utilizing a cast of local young singers. Both performances would be part of the Central Gardens festivities, now expanded to four days.[57]

The festival would be embellished by electricity. The city's first electric company had been founded just the year before, and the direct current it offered was only partially successful. Nevertheless, special arrangements were made with the company to string electric lights for the occasion in Main, Military, and Alamo Plazas on poles forty feet high.[58] There would also be temporary electric lighting in Central Gardens.[59] Posters and flyers were printed up to advertise the festival not only within the city but in towns all over South Texas. On top of this, special invitations to editors of country newspapers had been issued to attend the festival (fifty-seven accepted).

The chair of the day-procession committee, August Siemering, died unexpectedly on September 20, just two weeks before the festival was to begin. However, the show went on: the parade theme had long been chosen ("Commerce Rules the World"), the various subjects had been apportioned out to the *vereine*, and the floats and costumes were well on their way to completion.[60]

By the evening of October 4, everything was ready. Many of the German American–owned stores along the parade route, especially on Commerce Street, were again decorated profusely with the requisite evergreens and bunting. In 1883 many shops also featured elaborately festive window displays, several blazing with the new electric lights. The torchlight parade again opened the festivities on October 4. Its route was similar to the year before. Aside from the special electric illumination along the route, a huge (but controlled) bonfire also was lit in the middle of Military Plaza.

The night parade was similar to the one held the year before, only larger. Both the U.S. Eighth Cavalry Band and the City Band participated, and a German beer-garden float (with real beer and beer drinkers aboard) was one of the hits of the evening. Since this particular event was an all-male affair, the "ladies" on the beer-garden float were robust gentlemen in drag. The rest of the procession consisted of burlesque figures and transparencies similar to those used in 1882, again making pointedly topical references. The *San Antonio Light* reported on one transparency that had a truly local context: "There were the champion contributors in the *Volksfest*, bankers on one side standing on a nickle [*sic*], on the other side sitting firmly down on a nickel while the *Volksfest* committee try in vain to get it, alluding to a certain banking firm who refused to contribute."[61] To add drama to the parade, specially treated torches emitting colored fire were ignited at various places along the route.

Once the procession reached Central Gardens, both paraders and viewers were dazzled by the most elaborate grounds decorations so far of any local festival site. Visitors entered through "medieval," crenellated city gates. The site fairly bristled with symbols of both Anglo-American and German heritage. The gates were crowned by wreaths, a gilded American eagle, Texas Lone Stars, and a large image of a man drinking beer. German, American, and other flags fluttered from the "battlements," as well as quotations from Shakespeare and a German motto.[62]

The parade of the next day, which began at 10 A.M., was even longer and again circled all three plazas. It was split into two separate divisions. The first was again headed by the Eighth Cavalry Band and contained the usual contingent of Volksfest and city officials and orators. It was marshaled by volunteer fire chief Hermann Karber and his aides. All were attired in full-dress formal wear with red, white, and blue badges and rode "superb chargers." In this division was the "Commerce" group of floats, which featured such themes as "Commerce," "Stock Raising," and "Railroad Builders"—in other words, manifest destiny rampant.[63] No photographs of these have survived, but the float representing "Commerce" managed to cram symbols of progress (goddesses of commerce, art, and science; ships; railroads), America (the eagle), American achievement (the Brooklyn Bridge, completed that very year), and the old country (the castle of Hohenzollern), not to mention international unity (flags of "all nations"), on to a single flatbed wagon.[64] It is worth mentioning that the "goddesses" were portrayed by women.[65] Women had appeared as float actors in the parade of 1882 as well and would continue to do so, unlike their New Orleans and Saint Louis counterparts.

The second division, whose marshals included the future mayor Bryan

Callaghan Jr., featured decorated pumpers and hose carts from volunteer Fire Companies 1 and 2. Then came the McAllister City Band, followed by a large contingent of elaborate commercial floats of uneven taste. Aside from the inevitable collection of beer-company wagons, the most interesting of these entries were Holland's tea and coffee wagon, chock-full of sacks and chests of both products and a huge teapot, and Alamo Music's contribution, which featured performers on a piano and two organs plus six juvenile drummers. The most elaborate of all was the float sponsored by the music merchants Rhodius and Temsky. It featured an Austrian alp and the Tyrolean Sextet, wearing traditional *lederhosen*. Unfortunately, it broke down in Alamo Plaza at the start of the parade when a wheel caught on a streetcar rail.[66]

Activities at Central Gardens over the next three days encompassed a far greater variety of events than the year before. On the afternoon following the parade, Dr. Lindner made a speech in German; this was followed by two English-language orators, U.S. marshal Hal Gosling and attorney Columbus Upson, the latter the most celebrated local public speaker of his day. Both praised not only German contributions to San Antonio but those of other nationalities as well. Gosling invoked "the hardy German, the valorous, brave, impulsive son of the Emerald Isle, the sturdy Scotch and honest son of Britain, the brilliant children of France, our brothers of our sister republic of Mexico and the sons and daughters of all the nations of the earth."[67]

This might have been dismissed as overblown rhetoric, but there is evidence that San Antonians of diverse nationalities not only attended the Volksfest but actively participated in it. As far as attendees were concerned, the *San Antonio Light* commented: "The German residents and visitors were present in large numbers, because by experience they understand and appreciate the Volksfest, as a means of innocent pleasure and of profit to the city, but the American, Mexican, British, Jewish and other residents were there in large numbers."[68]

Among the many beer and food stands was one run by Madame Candelaria, reputed survivor of the Alamo, who cooked and served Mexican dishes. The roster of the City Band reads like a cross-section of the city's population: it boasted Herman Bruchner, Louis Eberhardt, Joe McAllister, Ygnacio and Fernando Chavez, and Augustin Gutierrez.[69]

The City Band and the Eighth Cavalry Band both performed during the afternoon and gave repeat concerts over the next two days. Their programs were combinations of German music (the march from Wagner's *Tannhauser*), dances of the day (including waltzes and polkas), and Professor Katzenberger's own

Alamo March.⁷⁰ A further international note was sounded by Col. D. D. Munro, who appeared in full Scottish regalia, performing Scottish dances.

The highlight of the first evening was supposed to be the tableaux. Twelve were planned, all allegories taken from Schiller's *Elysium* that ranged from a "Scene from the Stone Age," through "Ceres Appearing to Mankind," to the "Triumph of Agriculture." All were to be acted by local ladies and gentlemen from the German American community in rich costumes. Unfortunately the display was truncated when someone accidentally set off the fireworks planned for later in the evening after the ninth tableau, burning one young woman spectator in the process. This tragedy did not, however, halt the dancing, which finished off the evening.⁷¹

The second and third days of the celebration followed the program of the first, with children's games added during the afternoon. The second day also saw the premiere of the operetta *The Twin Sisters*. The cast, recruited by Professor Katzenberger, comprised mainly children from San Antonio's juvenile choirs, with all the principal soloists being female. The audience loved it, and it was repeated the next day with a slightly different cast. The evening activities mirrored those of the first day, except that the tableaux were not repeated.⁷²

If anything, the 1883 Volksfest surpassed that of the year before. At the end of the first day, the festival had recouped half of the money invested in it, and on the succeeding days the committee reduced the admission to twenty-five cents for everyone. The Volksfest ended in the black, with over five thousand dollars collected—a triumph when the twenty-nine-hundred-dollar surplus from the previous year was added in. As they had hoped, the committee was able to return half of the subscription money to the people who had donated it.⁷³ They were euphoric enough to declare that the Volksfests were now established as an annual event and could only grow bigger and more profitable.

Or so they thought. Several claims for expense reimbursements lagged over until November for settlement: money to pay one of the bands and denial of another claim by the Eighth Cavalry Band for payment for rehearsal time (which had been included in their contract). These skirmishes were quickly resolved by compromise, but one claim resulted in prolonged litigation and many bitter feelings.

Ludwig Mahncke, who had a bar stand at the Volksfest, also put in a claim of $139 for supplying the Volksfest committee with refreshments (including, as it turned out, champagne) for which no transaction record existed. The committee offered him the compromise amount of $78.95 after considerable agitation among its members as to who may have ordered what. Mahncke was not satisfied.⁷⁴ He demanded that Dr. Lindner, as Volksfest president, make up the difference of $61.05 personally. Lindner refused, and Mahncke sued him for the money. The court awarded Mahncke the sum. Dr. Lindner then appealed the award; wrangling continued about just who drank the offending champagne and how much of it and when, with the Volksfest committee backing Lindner.⁷⁵ The litigation dragged on through the spring of 1884. It was eventually settled, but the bad blood between Mahncke and Lindner and the Volksfest committee lingered, to the point that none of the 1883 executive committee wanted to continue in their positions the following year.

In June, a meeting was held to institute an official Volksfest Association, and on June 19, new officers were elected. The board was multiethnic. Col. Augustus Belknap was elected president. There were no less than seven vice presidents, among them Mayor James French, Col. Henry B. Andrews, and George Kalteyer. Standing committees were also set up to oversee advertising, music, processions, decoration, dancing, sports, the soliciting committee, and other matters. A committee was also appointed to draft a permanent charter.

Since Central Gardens was not available for the desired October dates, it was decided to hold the Volksfest at San Pedro Springs.⁷⁶ The Volksfest organizers wanted to charge admission, as usual. Frederick Kerbel, the proprietor of the Springs, was on the Volksfest charter committee, but not even his influence could change the city attorney's position that municipal ordinances forbade the charging of admission for San Pedro Springs events. Ironically, the "people's festival" was thwarted by the very laws that favored the people of the city, and the 1884 Volksfest was canceled.⁷⁷

It was just as well. In 1884, the Volksfest planners appear to have been halfhearted about the project anyway. The animosity of the Mahncke-Lindner dispute died hard, and there was evidently a problem in getting community support for the project at all.⁷⁸

Things were apparently better in 1885—somewhat better, that is. Planning got started rather late, on July 26, but a slate of officers was elected, different from the abortive board of the year before. The president was Ladislas M. Madarasz, a prosperous plant-nursery owner, while Augustus Belknap now assumed the role of first vice president.⁷⁹ The following day the charter framed in 1884 was adopted, and the "San Antonio Volksfest Association" was approved as the organization's official name. Plans were already underway by then, the dates being set for October 22 through October 26.

The whole project was far less ambitious than in 1883. The parade roster resembled far more a Fourth of July or other patriotic procession than a particularly German one. Though most of the marshals were German American (including the grand marshal, fire chief Duerler), Antonio P. Rivas and Juan T. Cardenas were among their number. The Eighth Cavalry Band was back, augmented by U.S. military officers from the army post and some artillery. The Belknap Rifles joined in, as well as the Weimar Prairie City Rifles, a visiting militia group. As usual, the mayor and city council rode in carriages along with the executives of the Volksfest committee. A band from Eagle Pass participated, and the Fashion Theater Band also marched, though without the showgirls who would grace the Knights of Labor parade during the 1886 Diez y Seis festivities. All of the German American–dominated volunteer fire companies were there, their various trucks decorated with bunting.[80]

The *vereine* had formed the backbones of the two earlier Volksfest parades. In 1885, they were conspicuously missing (except the Turnverein in their capacity as firemen). There was consequently no group of edifying *verein*-sponsored floats. Instead there were only commercial ones, and few appear to have been German American businesses, with the notable exceptions of the *Texas Vorwarts* German newspaper, Harry Baum's Wholesale Liquors, and Steves and Sons Lumber.[81] Sim Hart was back in his carriage, distributing cigars from his shop. The Lone Star Brewing Company featured Gambrinus—god of beer—seated under a canopy on a longhorn chair, disbursing samples. The distribution of alcoholic drinks and smokes from floats in parades was common in these pretemperance days. There were several other beer wagons and a combined float for Red Cross Whiskey and Opera Puff Cigarettes, from which samples of both were thrown to spectators by the local tuxedo-clad distributors. A large number of floats had to do with the lumber business. They reproduced entire rooms, a roundhouse, and a fence enclosing a live hog. A more elegant note was struck by the Singer Sewing Machine Company. Its float featured four "charming damsels" bent over four Singer machines, the rest of the float decorated with embroidery among evergreens and floral wreaths.[82] This was one of the few displays to match the tone of the *verein* floats of the two previous years. Again, stores were decorated along the parade route, exhibiting German, American, French, and Mexican flags. Perhaps these street decorations were more dignified than those in the parade!

The accompanying festival was held at San Pedro Springs, this year without a general admission fee.[83] Orations began in the afternoon: a short introduction was given in English by president Madarasz, and then a longer-winded one was delivered in the same language by the Honorable Charles W. Ogden. Professor Herman Seele of New Braunfels delivered a German speech. All listened "with rapt attention."⁸⁴ The real highlights of the day were horse racing, on the track at San Pedro Springs, and the very Texan contest of bull riding for a five-dollar prize. The program was rounded out by shooting contests, military drills, a military band concert, fireworks, and dancing. On the second day, similar activities took place, including a baseball game and various athletic contests. There was also a mini-*sängerfest* in which only two choirs, the Beethoven and San Antonio Männerchors, participated.⁸⁵ The third and fourth days repeated most of this program, with the addition of other contests. Some of them were definitely of the *volks* variety, including a race by four entrants who paddled tin bathtubs with broomsticks over the park's lake. Two of them tipped over, much to the hilarity of spectators and participants alike.

Although plenty was going on at San Pedro Springs over the three days, response was not particularly enthusiastic. Since there was no admission charge to enter the grounds, the committee charged for various activities: fifty cents for the dances, twenty-five cents for the baseball game and horse races, and elevated prices for food. The *San Antonio Light* reporters were particularly disgruntled and loudly complained of this and other problems (including the police's failure to remove vehicles from some parts of the park) as early as the first day. "San Antonio is eternally killed for another Volksfest. Universal opinion on the street, "big failure." San Antonio has turned out better processions for a funeral. The Italian procession would have laid over the so-called Volksfest. Take the Fire Department out of the procession, where would it have been? Where were all our societies, Casino, Turn-Verein, Arbeiter Verein, etc.?"⁸⁶

Even though they printed a half-hearted retraction the next day, the *Light* was right. This was the last Volksfest to be held in the 1880s, and it certainly was a far cry from the spectacle of the two previous years. Perhaps part of the problem was that little distinguished it from other city festivals, for the distinctive allegorical floats and tableaux were conspicuously missing. Another reason, cited by the *Light,* could have been that the first rousing Columbus Day festivity had immediately preceded the Volksfest at San Pedro Springs, with similar activities, more spectacular fireworks, and no inflated charges.

GERMAN DAY AND THE GERMAN
AMERICAN VOLKSFESTS, 1890–93

In the later 1880s, the Volksfests were gone but not forgotten. By 1889, memories of both the Lindner-Mahncke lawsuit and the disappointment of the 1885 celebration had faded enough that there was talk about staging some sort of festivities the following year.[87]

Interest there was, but initial momentum there was not. When serious meetings began at the end of August, 1890, the issue arose as to whether the organizers wanted a full-blown Volksfest or something more modest. The potential organizers included representatives from the *vereine*, the Mission Hose Company of firemen, several singing societies, and members of fraternal organizations—the Knights and Ladies of Honor, the Order of Chosen Friends, and several local lodges of the Sons of Hermann.[88] Committees were not formed nor officers elected until September 10, so time was short if anything was to be done in October.

It was decided that instead of staging an elaborate multiday celebration, the German Americans would field only a parade in conjunction with the San Antonio International Exhibition of Texas and Mexico (already scheduled for October). This was the third of such commercial trade fairs to be held, starting in 1888, at the fairgrounds adjacent to Riverside Park. The 1890 fair was to open on the last day of September and run through October 11. Ten of the fair days were dedicated to special groups, including firemen, laborers, traveling salesmen, secret societies, Mexicans, and Germans (on the last day of the fair). Many other events were scheduled at the fairgrounds during the International Exhibition besides commercial displays. Included was an opening parade, consisting of city and county officials, a military contingent of marchers, a band, Mexican consul Dr. Ornelas, and members of a circus. Succeeding days also saw a parade of fraternal orders, circus performances, horse races, rodeo-type contests, and evening concerts. For Mexican Day, the local community was content to throw a banquet for their Mexican trade visitors at the fairgrounds, presided over by Dr. Ornelas.[89] German Day, on the other hand, provided an excellent excuse for a German American parade without the community having to finance an additional festival (or so they initially thought).

By September 11, just one month prior to German Day, plans were in full swing. Capt. Edgar Schramm, the president of the newly formed celebration committee, noted that the date was close enough to October 6—the 207th anniversary of the first Germans landing on American soil—to stage a parade on the order of the 1882 and 1883 Volksfest processions. He enthusiastically outlined an overall theme: "a classical historical idea of a procession representing twelve important periods in the history of the German race" (it was later modified to include German contributions to the New World as well). Although some people at this meeting thought that four weeks was not enough time to put together such a complex street pageant, the majority consensus was that it could be done. A finance committee was immediately formed to raise the sum needed, estimated at three thousand dollars.[90]

Four days later nearly twenty-three hundred dollars of that amount had been raised, and many committees had been appointed.[91] Never content with something so simple as a mere parade, the celebration committee decided to extend things into at least a small celebration. This would begin the evening the fair closed on October 11, with an oration or two at San Pedro Springs Park, with dancing to follow, and similar activities the next day. The railroads, which had already set up special rates for fair attendance, consented to extend those rates to cover the extra day.

On September 22, Captain Schramm headed out to New Orleans to see about acquiring used Mardi Gras costumes for the pageant floats, an easy if expensive way to procure fancy dress on short notice.[92] Edgar Schramm was a worthy successor to Dr. Lindner in his passionate commitment to Volksfest planning. A former Texas Ranger (the origin of his title of captain), in 1890 he was engaged in real estate sales and also as a general commission agent. In 1892, he would briefly publish the German-language newspaper *Texas Staats-Zeitung*. At this moment—in September, 1890—he threw himself into the parade project, much as Max Lindner had seven years before.

While he was in New Orleans, Schramm engaged Harry Dressel, a German-born Mardi Gras float designer, to make the twelve pageant floats. This was an important departure from the earlier Volksfests. The earlier processions had featured floats and costumes made by the *vereine* to which they were assigned, with prizes given to the best ones. This year, the *vereine* would still raise money for the floats and their members would still ride on them in costume, but Dressel would come to San Antonio and build them with a professional crew. Schramm was also successful in securing "Parisian" costumes, which would be altered by an "expert costumer," also imported from New Orleans.[93]

By October 1, Dressel was busily constructing the floats in San Antonio, in donated space at Hans Degener's lumberyard. An expanded goal of four thousand dollars was essentially raised.[94] The larger sum enabled even greater plans to be made. Carl Beck's Band and various singing societies would give concerts at Muth's Garden on the afternoons of September 11 and 12. Advertisements in the form of handbills and posters were printed up and distributed statewide.

The parade itself was a sensation. Besides the twelve floats constructed by Dressel, it consisted of the grand marshal and two aides in full dress on horse-

1890 German Day float: "Teutons and Cimbri." Mardi-Gras costumes, furs, and union suits. *Courtesy Witte Museum, San Antonio, Texas*

back; mounted police; the mayor, city officials, and German Day officers in carriages; and Carl Beck's Band and the Mexican National Zapadores Band, both in uniform. Members of each *verein* that sponsored a pageant float marched behind their display, with several of their wives riding in carriages. At the procession's end were two additional floats sponsored and decorated by two San Antonio choirs (the Beethoven Männerchor and the Frohsinn Singing Society), their themes representing the groups that made them.

Judging from photographs of the floats from this procession, they were on a considerably slicker scale than the earlier, homemade efforts. Seven of them dealt with ancient and medieval German history. Typical of these was "Teutons and Cimbri," depicting two of the first Germanic tribes who crossed the Alps and defeated the Romans. To the rear of the float was a round wooden tower that, according to the *San Antonio Express*, represented a tribal dwelling.[95] Standing in front and on top of the building were a number of "tribesmen," lavishly bearded and dressed in an assortment of garments. Some of these look improvised from whatever the costumers could scrounge up (including, perhaps, a white union suit). Others wore wooly furs—perhaps part of the New Orleans purchase, if not supplemented by locally killed hides. Most were wear-

1890 German Day float: "Alaric Conquers Rome," with triumphal arch. *Courtesy Witte Museum, San Antonio, Texas*

ing the horned helmets that were then popularly associated with ancient Germany (to which any contemporary photograph of Wagner's *Ring Cycle* operas will attest).

Additional horned helmets and furs were to be found in other entries, for example, "Alaric Conquers Rome." Rome was represented by a triumphal arch, replete with columns, pilasters, and frieze. Two "Roman" senators wore togas, and a priest was garbed in what appeared to be a modern choir robe with a colored border. In the case of the floats with medieval themes, there was a similar mix of costumes, with all the ladies having fashionable corseted figures, regardless of the period portrayed.[96]

How much would spectators have understood about the content of these floats? Perhaps German Americans who had attended the German-English school would have been familiar with this history. But to aid everyone else, the *Express* and the *Light* both printed synopses of the floats' content and their historical background before the actual parade day.[97] This marks a change from the more easily comprehended parades of 1882 and 1883, when the floats were described after the fact.

1890 German Day float: "The Kaiser Triumphant, 1870." Contemporary history. *Courtesy Witte Museum, San Antonio, Texas*

Spectators would have probably recognized at least one entry, though. It showed the surrender of the French to Kaiser Wilhelm I at Versailles after the latter's victory in the Franco-Prussian War in 1871. In current German mythology, this represented not only a victory but a symbol of German unification under a single ruler, which had happened the year before. This was thus a startlingly modern inclusion, but San Antonio's German American community had held a celebration with a torchlight parade, ball, and orations at the Casino Club to commemorate the event just a month after the capture of Paris in January, 1871.[98] On the float, the Kaiser stood in white uniform and spiked helmet. He was placed under a canopied dais. Kaiser Wilhelm was surrounded by various troops in very recognizable contemporary German military uniforms, hats, and helmets.[99]

The earlier fair parades had assembled in Alamo Plaza and marched directly down Commerce Street, then south to the fairgrounds. The German parade began and ended on Alamo Plaza and circled the others. The streets were jammed with spectators, and the parade itself stretched almost a mile long. So successful was this afternoon procession that it was repeated the next evening, illuminated by red and blue electric lights. This was fortunate, since the "Teutons and Cimbri" float had broken an axle as the parade started the previous afternoon and had to sit out the procession on a side street. This float was resurrected in all its glory the next evening.[100]

The events at San Pedro Springs were, for once, free. There was a short address by Captain Schramm the first day and dances on both evenings. After the night parade, the Zapadores Band played a concert in Alamo Plaza, to the glee of several thousand leftover spectators.

The parade organizers had reason to be gleeful themselves: they had raised over $4,600 and spent only $4,360.12. They immediately decided to hold an even bigger parade the next year.[101]

This time they envisioned the grandest San Antonio spectacle yet and began planning it early. On January 3, the planners reorganized themselves into the German-American Volksfest Association and wrote a new charter.[102] The name in itself is important, because it indicated a different conception and goal. In the 1880s, the association had simply been referred to as the San Antonio Volksfest Association, suggesting that the planning and sponsorship stemmed from a German tradition, even if it encompassed other groups. By calling itself "German-American," the association was now affiliated not only with its old-country roots but with its adopted country in a more formal way. Within two weeks of the first meeting, committees had been formed, and $4,251 of an initial $5,000 goal had been pledged (though the actual amount collected would lag quite a bit behind the initial declarations). The majority of these pledges came from members of the twenty-six German American organizations in the city, including *vereine,* choirs, ex–volunteer firemen, predominantly German craft unions and fraternal orders, and some private donors.[103]

On February 7, Captain Schramm, reelected president of the organization, was deputized to go to New Orleans again to contract with Harry Dressel and look for suitable costumes. He had to wait a few days before departing, since he was running as a token reform candidate for mayor against the still-popular Bryan Callaghan Jr. and elections were held February 8. He was trounced, of course, and thus free to leave.

The search for costumes was a bit more difficult than the year before. The original plan was for Schramm to view Mardi Gras parades while in New Orleans and to try to secure used costumes right after the festival. The theme that the committee had chosen was depictions of masterpieces by famous German poets—a throwback to old-country Schillerfieren. Schramm could find nothing suitable for this idea, but he was finally able to secure costumes worn during the Rex Ball by the Atlantis Society during the 1890 Mardi Gras. The costumes illustrated a tableau of the *Nieblungenleid*. Ready-made garments depicting such archetypal representations of ancient German mythology were irresistible. Shramm sent back an ecstatic description of the goods: "These costumes were used but a single time, and then only for fifteen minutes for a tableaux [*sic*] presentation at the Rex ball. They are specimens of most lavish elegance and grandeur, everything about them being solid and extra fine."[104]

Even to purchase used costumes, Schramm had to lay out three thousand dollars. Consequently, the fund-raising goal had to be elevated considerably—to nine thousand dollars. The Volksfest committee approved the amount, and soliciting efforts were intensified. The magnitude of this level of funds is hard to gauge in twenty-first-century dollars, but no such amount was ever raised—or needed—for any other festival in the city during the nineteenth century. The average event discussed up to this point was executed for but a fraction of this amount; the first Battle of Flowers parade, staged earlier in 1891, had been put together for under two hundred dollars.

There were other indulgences in planning. Professor Nolte, an artist, was employed to conceive and draw the sixteen float designs. Harry Dressel charged two thousand dollars to come for a month and cast some of the papier-mâché figures and structural elements on site.[105] The German-American Volksfest Association also bought a piece of property on Milam Square and erected a shed there to be used as a permanent float construction site.[106] Costs mounted up, and increasing pressure was put on fund-raising, still four thousand dollars short in mid-August. No International Fair took place that year, so organizers decided to augment the parade with a three-day festival at Central Gardens, to encompass October 9–11. The celebrations at the gardens were envisioned much along the lines of the 1882 and 1883 Volksfests, featuring band concerts, dancing—though at Krisch's Hall, there being no dance pavilion at Central Gardens at that time—and fireworks, but apparently no orations or sports. Some of the funds would thus be recouped by admission fees of fifty cents per person (the tickets were different colors on different days to keep track). Hoping to attract great crowds via special travel rates, the committee set up a tourist bureau at J. Jacobson's establishment on Houston Street in the beginning of October. The bureau acted as a clearing-house for hotel rooms and other Volksfest information for visitors and local citizens alike. By this point in time, it thus appears that the organization of the tourist industry in San Antonio was in full flower.[107]

Events opened on the evening of October 8 with a parade of cyclists. Bicycling was all the rage at this time, and several clubs had formed to bring enthusiasts of the sport together, the largest of which was the Alamo Wheelmen (there were "wheelwomen" as well).[108] Experienced with parades, having participated in the Battle of Flowers procession six months earlier, the cyclists were enthusiastically received, since they decorated their wheels with both flowers and lanterns and rode on a route that began and ended in Alamo Plaza and included the residential areas of Travis Park and King William Street. It was a far more genteel affair than the old torchlight parades.

The spectacular parade held the next afternoon had four divisions. Each division held four of the sixteen floats, again followed by marching members of the sponsoring organizations in badges and regalia. The sponsors had expanded from the *vereine* to include diverse German American organizations. The first division featured a military band, ex–volunteer firemen, and float sponsors—members of the Grand Army of the Republic, the Krieger Verein, the San Antonio Deutscher Männerchor, and the Frohsinn Singing Society, with marshals for each organization and carriages holding children of members of each group. The other divisions were composed in a similar manner. The second division featured the Alamo Band, members of the Sons of Hermann fraternal organization, the Garten Verein, the Order of Chosen Friends, and the Saint Joseph's Catholic Society. The third had the Fire Company Band, the Schleicher and Schiller Lodges of the Knights of Honor, the Jaegerlust shooting club, and the Beethoven Männerchor. The last included the Washington Band, the Turnverein, and the last floats, sponsored jointly by the painters, blacksmiths, tinners, and carpenters unions.

The floats were complex enough that supplements appeared in both the *Express* and the *Light* as a special pullout, with elaborate explanations and color chromo-lithographs of all sixteen, so that viewers could understand them. The style of the lavish images echoed the colored newspaper supplements of the elaborate Crewe floats from Mardi Gras, which were included in the *New Orleans Picayune* of the period (indeed, the pullout for the *Light* was printed in New Orleans).[109] These pullouts were actually reproductions of the artist's sketches for the float designs, so what we have are Professor Nolte's renditions.

The opening and closing floats represented allegories. The first featured the paired figures of "Germania and Columbia." This was a popular theme in the 1890s, and it was often found in German American parades in surrounding Hill Country towns. Barely a month before, in the 1891 Diez y Seis parade, there had been a float featuring "Mexico" and "America." In this float, the two girls portraying the nations had been surrounded with flags and emblems of both countries.[110] The German American ladies rode in a chariot drawn by four winged

1891 German American Volksfest color newspaper foldout.
Courtesy Daughters of the Republic of Texas Library

horses. Both women wore classical robes and tall diadems. Papier-mâché clouds billowed around them, somehow looking, in the lithograph at least, more like giant bubbles than anything else. The last float, which featured an enormous papier-mâché image of "Father Rhine," was over thirty-three feet long. Father Rhine was represented as a reclining river god in the classical manner, with a rock throne, his arm resting on an urn from which poured forth the river waters. To the front of the float and to the side were six Rhine maidens, shown nude in the illustration. In reality they were played by six boys, doubtlessly dressed.[111]

These two floats were relatively easy to figure out, but the rest of the fourteen would have been a stretch for viewers of the day. They featured four scenes from *Beowulf* and four from the *Lay of Nieblungen* (the same source that Wagner used for his operas). There were also three depicting the *Legend of Hagen and Gudrun* and one each of *Tannheuser, Percival,* and *Hueon at the Caliph's Court* (the last taken from a nineteenth-century poem by Cristolph Martin Wieland entitled *Oberon*).

Judging from the chromo-lithograph, these floats were pretentious and grand. At least five of them featured men (or boys) with varying armaments and armor,

1891 German American Volksfest float: "Germania and Columbia."
Courtesy U.T. Institute of Texan Cultures

battling various oversized mythic monsters. By the end of the spectacle they were perhaps a little less grand; freeze-action tableau poses were difficult to sustain. A float depicting "Hagen Killing Griffins" featured Captain Schramm's son, Milton, in the role of Hagen. An *Express* reporter observed that "the route was rather long for Hagen, who soon tired out and made peace with one of the young griffins, leaning upon her for support in the most affectionate manner."[112]

How much did spectators really understand of the floats' content? How many people really studied the long recitations about them published in the papers? The *Light* did make these comments after the parade: "The richness and elegance of the display was in keeping with the character and intelligence of the German Americans of our city. The sixteen magnificent floats were each a poem, appealing more to sentiment than to the enthusiasm of the crowd."[113] Perhaps it was overkill as well as overpriced, but everyone was dazzled by the glitter the day of parade, even more so when the floats made an encore the following evening, the glittering armor, rich fabrics, and glass "jewels" gleaming under artificial light.

The parade followed a slightly different route than the usual one. It was originally scheduled to begin and end in Main Plaza, circling Alamo Plaza in the process; it actually had to be altered to extend its starting and ending point to Military Plaza, due to its extreme length.[114] An even larger crowd witnessed the

"Germania and Columbia" float, New Braunfels Founder's Day Parade, 1895.
Courtesy Daughters of the Republic of Texas Library

night procession, crowding the sidewalks, windows, balconies, and any flat roof to capacity. While many then repaired to Central Gardens for music, food, and fireworks each night, more people than the Volksfest planners had hoped flocked to the city's saloons, which did a booming business. However, no rowdiness appeared to spill into the streets; Military and Main Plazas were somewhat more refined places in the 1890s than they had been a decade before, the less savory elements having been pushed further west.[115] As for the parade and the Central Gardens festival, the *San Antonio Light* had no reason to complain, as it had six years earlier. At last a San Antonio group had produced a parade to rival those of New Orleans and Saint Louis.

Unfortunately, the German-American Volksfest Association was not quite so happy. Somewhere along the line the ancient kings and heroes had preempted the *volks* at the *fest*. Though five thousand visitors allegedly came to town for

1891 German American Volksfest float: "Father Rhine," a classical river god in his paper-mâché glory. *Courtesy Daughters of the Republic of Texas Library*

the occasion, this was far less than the hoped-for number. As they went over their accounts after the festival, the association's members found that they had expended $11,377 and that donations of subscribers had only reached $4,308. Though they did make up more of the deficit by collecting on promised pledges and from Central Gardens receipts, by the beginning of the new year, they were still nearly $3,000 in the hole.[116]

Still, by early January, Captain Schramm and the Volksfest Association decided to plan for the 1892 Volksfest, even though they were still in the red. The sobering fact of debt did govern the fact that the parade concept was considerably scaled down. There was much debate through January as to whether to seek recycled costumes from New Orleans again, as the association's treasurer, William Hoefling Sr., had only budgeted $1,000 for them.[117] This matter continued to be discussed through the beginning of March. Apparently no agreement could be reached, and all plans were temporarily scrapped; there would not be another planning meeting until July.[118]

At the July meeting, Schramm was as disillusioned with the rest of the committee and its officers as they were with him. He resigned. A new organizing committee was formed, with former treasurer William Hoefling Sr. now the president. Hoefling had considerable economic and administrative experience. Besides being the city's most successful sausage maker, he had served terms as

1891 German American Volksfest float: "Hagen Killing Griffons."
Courtesy Daughters of the Republic of Texas Library

county commissioner, alderman, and longtime foreman of volunteer Fire Company 2. Under his more fiscally conservative leadership, a budget was fixed at $3,800 (last year's debt having finally been paid off principally by the cancellation of a mortgage held on the extravagant floats of 1891 by the Alamo, Lone Star, and City Breweries).[119] By August, the association had $2,000 in its treasury, plus flatbed wagons for the floats worth $250.

The committee again decided to have pageant floats. Since 1892 was the four hundredth anniversary of Columbus's arrival in America, they decided that Columbus and American history would be a suitable theme. They set their parade for October 21. It never seems to have occurred to the German Americans that San Antonio's Italian Americans, who had been identified with Columbus Day in San Antonio for the past seven years, might want to make a special commemoration of the anniversary in 1892. The latter had already set their parade for the same date.[120] The association was about halfway into the planning stage when they were informed of the "rival" festival and immediately sent a delegation to the Italians demanding a change in the date of their celebration so as not to conflict with the Volksfest.[121] The Italians were miffed, to say the least. The arrogant behavior of the Volksfest people killed any idea of combining the two festivals, but after a week or so of negotiations, a compromise was reached. The German Americans could have their pageant if they changed the date of their

1892 German American Volksfest *San Antonio Light* pullout.
Courtesy U.T. Institute of Texan Cultures

parade and festival to October 29. The Volksfest Association grudgingly agreed and invited the Christopher Columbus Society to march in their parade.

Central Gardens was again engaged, and the usual special railroad rates were arranged. Advertisements were sent out, and chromo-lithographs of the pageant floats were printed up to be included with the newspapers. The floats depicted twelve scenes from American history; two of them dealt with Columbus, nine with subsequent historical events, and the last with an allegory of the "United States." This year, there were no imported costumes or float makers; instead, the planners returned to the construction of the floats and the provision of costumes by the sponsoring *verein*, union, or other group.[122]

The balance of the procession was organized as it had been the two previous years, with members of the sponsoring organizations marching behind their floats, but in only three divisions instead of four. Three bands and troops of U.S. cavalry marched in each division. Also in the first division were uniformed members of the Knights of Columbus.

Additional sponsors in the first division included the Christopher Columbus

1892 German American Volksfest float: "Landing of Columbus."
Courtesy U.T. Institute of Texan Cultures

Society and the local chapters of the typographical, carpenters, and tinners unions. The second division had the usual contingent of city officials, county officials, association officers, and members of the San Antonio Football Club in carriages. The float sponsors were the Garten Verein, the San Antonio Deutscher Männerchor, the Krieger Verein, the Beethoven Männerchor, and the Belknap Rifles. The third division's sponsors were the Grand Army of the Republic, the carpenters union, a group of amalgamated societies, and the Sons of Hermann. The sponsors—veterans, *vereine*, unions, choirs, a militia company, and an Italian society—were even more varied than in the previous year and more inclusive of San Antonio's non-German middle-class groups.

Judging from the surviving chromo-lithograph of the 1892 floats, they would have been much easier for the average viewer understand. The "Landing of Columbus," for example, had already been presented as a playlet in the Columbus Day festival of 1887.[123] At least two, "Washington Crossing the Delaware" and "Santa Anna before Sam Houston," were based on well-known paintings of the period, the former by Emil Luetze (1851) and the latter by William Huddle. Huddle's work, now in the state capitol in Austin, was painted in 1886, but it had

1892 German American Volksfest float: "Presentation of Pocahontas at the English Court" (also called "Pocahontas' Wedding"). She is shown meeting Queen Elizabeth, who had unfortunately died thirteen years before her arrival. *Courtesy U.T. Institute of Texan Cultures*

already assumed the status of an icon.[124] It would be interesting to compare this float with one of the same theme in the 1882 Volksfest, but no photograph or drawing of the latter has surfaced.

A second float also related to Texas in 1836: one depicting "Alamo Heroes," with the familiar, bell-shaped facade. Davy Crockett (on a platform), Bowie, Bonham, and Travis stood before the Alamo, surrounded by a clutter of shields, flags, and arms. A group of adoring women and children offered the heroes laurel wreaths. Two of the ladies were in classical dress, no doubt representing allegories of "Victory" or something of the sort.

The most improbable entry, however, depicted the "Presentation of Pocahontas at the Court of Queen Elizabeth," an unusual piece of sorcery considering that Pocahontas did not reach England until 1616, thirteen years after the queen's demise. By that point, the real Pocahontas had become thoroughly anglicized—in her only known portrait, she is dressed at the height of Stuart fashion. Viewers of 1892 would certainly have been skeptical: many of the older generation could

1892 German American Volksfest float: "Washington Crossing the Delaware" (based on Emil Leutze's well-known painting). *Courtesy U.T. Institute of Texan Cultures*

well remember Comanche raids, and younger ones might have gone to gape at Geronimo, Chief Natchez, and other members of the Chiricahua tribe when they were temporarily interned at Fort Sam Houston on their way to deportation to Florida in 1886.[125] Even the usually uncritical *San Antonio Express* was skeptical, remarking that "the story of John Smith as he is taken into an Indian camp and saved by the fair Pocahontas like the hero in a Bowery drama, just at the last moment, is . . . well known, [but] San Antonians who saw Geronimo's band of noble red men in captivity at the government headquarters here, are of the opinion that the wrinkled-visaged bucks [*sic*] and the stupid-featured faces of the 14-year-old Indian mothers were not quite as stately, as dignified, nor as lovely as meek poets and other Ananiases had portrayed them."[126] More hackneyed—and familiar—would have been "The United States and All Nations," a familiar theme in many parade floats through the last third of the century.

The activities at Central Gardens were also more inclusive, though there was still an admission charge. Those excluded were the poorer African and Mexican Americans, who were reported as viewing the festivities in Central Gardens

1892 German American Volksfest float: "Alamo Heroes." The "famous four," Crockett, Travis, Bowie, and Bonham, fully integrated into a mythological allegory. *Courtesy U.T. Institute of Texan Cultures*

"from the hill opposite the river."[127] The decorations were nice but less elaborate. The entrance featured a triple arch, each arch lit by "thirty-two incandescents," and twenty-five torches along the main path in the gardens.[128] Orations were once again given in German and English, band concerts were played over the two days, and dances were held each night.

The more economical measures taken by Hoefling and his committee worked this time. When all accounts were rendered, the association had a surplus of $437.60 in the bank, plus the continuing ownership of their flatbed wagons for future festival parades.[129]

It wasn't decided whether to hold another Volksfest until June, 1893. That year, an economic depression swept the country, and members of the German American business community in San Antonio suffered along with the rest. Under Hoefling, a modest festival was projected, though the association optimistically voiced "the intention . . . to make this celebration a grand affair" and stated that "every effort . . . [had been] made to make it surpass anything of the kind ever intended."[130]

1892 German American Volksfest float: "Santa Anna before Sam Houston." This float is also based on a historical painting, this time by William Huddle. *Courtesy U.T. Institute of Texan Cultures*

The float theme this year would be ten episodes from Grimm's fairy tales (they would include episodes from *Cinderella, Snow White, Red Riding Hood, Hansel and Gretel,* and the *Frog Prince*).[131] To save money, the association decided to buy back used Volksfest costumes from previous years that were now owned by Frederick Hensel, a local artist and Beethoven Männerchor member.[132] Hensel let them have all of them for fifteen hundred dollars—half of their original cost.

By August 22, plans had once again been made to rent Central Gardens and to schedule most of the traditional festival events there, including concerts, sports and games, choir performances, and dances. The satiric torchlight parade was resurrected. These activities made this festival closest of all to the celebrations of the early 1880s.

The torchlight parade was held on October 6, with its typical outlandish costumes (including someone costumed as the "Parvenue of Castroville" and several human beer kegs). There were many satiric transparencies. One of these represented "Our Texas Exhibit at the [Chicago] World's Fair" (which was being held

1892 German American Volksfest float: "The United States and All Nations." A favorite nineteenth-century festival and pageant theme. The nations depicted were those most recognizable and popular in 1892. No South Americans or Australians, few Asians, and no Africans except for African Americans—and those were lampooned at that. *Courtesy U.T. Institute of Texan Cultures*

with much fanfare at the time): it depicted the bust of a large hog. The parade was filled out with two bands and with advertising floats and featured a large contingent of cyclists and *verein*, union, choir, and Christopher Columbus Society members. It was further enlivened by colored lights, torches, and fireworks along the route, which began to the west, at Milam Square, and circled all three plazas before arriving at Central Gardens.[133] Except for some electric lights, decorations at the gardens were limited to the economical bunting and evergreens, and admission was kept low, at twenty-five cents for adults, ten cents for children.

The pageant parade on October 7 had fairy-tale floats, which because of the hard economic times were kept simple. Because there had evidently been some confusion in spectators identifying floats in previous years, each one was preceded by a herald who announced its title at intervals, though the fairy-tale themes were perhaps the most easily recognized of all. The float "Cinderella Tries on the Glass Slipper," for example, would be equally clear to twenty-first-

1893 German American Volksfest float: "Cinderella [Ashenbroedel] Tries on the Glass Slipper." *Courtesy U.T. Institute of Texan Cultures, Laura Long*

century viewers. Compared to the glitz of earlier years, the floats were reduced to the basics—canopies and a few prop chairs providing the ambiance. Only the recycled and converted costumes of the actors relieved the sparseness.

There were three divisions, but because most of the *vereine*, clubs, and unions had marched the night before, all but the painters union, the Christopher Columbus Society, and the Krieger Verein sat the day parade out. But other groups participated, padding the parade's length to a mile long. These included the Belknap Rifles and the Knights of Pythias, both in uniform; three hundred members of the U.S. infantry; three companies of U.S. cavalry; the Twenty-third Infantry Band; and the fire department—in other words, the city's perennial parade participants.[134]

An estimated two thousand visitors came from out of town during the three days of the festival, and an additional five thousand locals showed up. Fireworks ended the program each night, but a particularly spectacular display was staged the last evening to close things out.

The 1893 Volksfest was deemed a success, but the economic difficulties of the period made it the last. Though some German American organizations would contribute floats to a few Battle of Flowers parades after 1900, there would be no more raucous torchlight processions or ambitious pageants with unified float themes given again by any group during the rest of the nineteenth century. Unlike Mardi Gras and the Veiled Prophet parade, the Volksfest parades flowered only briefly, then declined and finally expired. As second-generation German Americans were increasingly absorbed into the general "Anglo-American" population of the city and new German immigration slowed to a comparative trickle, German Americans ultimately lacked the separate civic force to continue staging an independent festival. Also, the community lacked the solid number of rich businessmen who could bankroll an increasingly elaborate festival such as Saint Louis's Veiled Prophet celebration, which continued to grow on an even grander scale as the century ended. The epigraph at the beginning of this chapter was therefore wishful thinking, as far as the city's grandiose symbolic aspirations went. Perhaps the 1893 Volksfest was a good way to finish the German American efforts off, for in this last festival they had finally come full-cycle, back to the populist spirit of the first one.

CHAPTER 7
BATTLE OF FLOWERS PARADE
"FUN WITH FAIR FLORA"

> What the carnival fetes are to Nice, the Veiled Prophets are to St. Louis and Mardi Gras is to New Orleans, the Battle of the Flowers is to San Antonio. It is an annual floral festival commemorative of the struggle for Texas independence from Mexico in the war of 1836 and usually takes place on April 21, the anniversary of the battle of San Jacinto in which Gen. Sam Houston's army triumphed over the Mexicans. . . . The festival was first suggested by Mr. J. S. Alexander as an appropriate fete with which to entertain President Harrison during his visit to the city in 1891.
> —*San Antonio Express,* April 22, 1894, June 4, 1895

The Battle of Flowers parade was a child of the 1890s. It developed so quickly into an annual tradition that myths were already circulating about its founding within three years of the first parade. Much of this had to do with the group that initiated and staged this parade and their social and economic connections. They were upper-middle-class women, mainly Anglo-American but also German American, the wives and daughters of the members of the business and professional class in San Antonio. They belonged, in other words, to the power structure of the city in the 1890s. They thus had direct access to local civic-organization leaders and publicity agents.

There was a "tradition" established by 1894 that the ladies had planned the parade to entertain President Benjamin Harrison on his visit to San Antonio in 1891. Since his visit, scheduled for April 20, was just one day before the anniversary of the Battle of San Jacinto (when General Santa Anna was at last defeated by the Texians), it was thought convenient to celebrate both events together. A meeting was held, and as the official history of the Battle of Flowers Association, written in 1931 by Mrs. Helene von Phul, recounts:

> It was suggested by Mrs. [James L.] Slayden that April 21st, the anniversary of the Battle of San Jacinto, be celebrated by this parade; however, as Pres-

ident Harrison was to be here on April 20th, it was decided that for that one year the parade would be held on that day. The rain came down in such torrents, however, that it was impossible to hold the parade and President Harrison was not even able to leave his car. Four days afterwards the parade was held and natural flowers were used entirely. It was such a success that in 1892 the organization was called together again and Mrs. John J. Stevens was elected President. From that date until 1909 it had many successes and vicissitudes.[1]

The actual story of the first Battle of Flowers and the subsequent parades is not exactly as the 1894 *Express* and Mrs. van Phul related it. The real story is even better.

THE FIRST BATTLE OF FLOWERS PARADE, 1891: GENESIS AND OUTCOME

The exact sequence of who had the original idea for this parade and for what purpose it was intended is now clouded. It does appear that the idea was in the air before the visit of President Harrison became a factor. The wife of banker and cattleman John J. Stevens, Bettie Stevens, had seen at least one of the flower festivals held by high society in Mexico City for Diez y Seis/President Diaz's birthday and for Cinco de Mayo.[2] A gentleman of her acquaintance, banker John S. Alexander, had seen an even more famous flower festival while on the European grand tour.[3] This was the flower battle associated with Carnival in Nice. The southern French city had celebrated a rowdy carnival on Fat Tuesday since the early nineteenth century. With the influx of tourists, particularly wealthy ones from the mid-1870s onward, the festival was gentrified. In 1876, loosely basing their actions on a medieval tradition, the city fathers instituted an official flower battle in which fashionable ladies rode along the Promenade des Anglais in carriages richly decorated with flowers and bombarded each other with bouquets. As the century wore on, this festival became an ever more elaborate tourist attraction, with the carriages literally becoming bowers of fresh blooms. Added to this were intricate, professionally constructed floats, liberally adorned with fresh flowers.[4]

The idea of holding such a celebration in San Antonio was apparently in the air during the early months of 1891, but nothing had as yet come of it.[5] There had also been a proposal to celebrate San Jacinto Day in a formal way. Up to 1891, few had thought to celebrate it at all. Futile exhortations to commemorate the day had been made as early as 1882, when the *San Antonio Express* suggested that at least the volunteer firemen do something about it, as they did for the Fourth of July and Washington's Birthday.[6] By the last decade of the century, there was increasing consciousness of the shrine possibilities of the "Alamo Chapel," now the focal point of the newly beautified Alamo Plaza. No one would want to celebrate the tragedy of its fall, but the battle of San Jacinto was, after all, a fitting tribute to its vindication. Mrs. Stevens and her friends evidently began to think of celebrating the anniversary of Texas' triumph in another battle, but now with flowers instead of bullets. And there was one additional incentive: the year 1891, according to Thad. W. Smith and other local history buffs of the day, marked the two hundreth anniversary of the settling of San Antonio by several Native American tribes. W. J. Ballard, a visitor from Chicago, suggested that this important anniversary be celebrated with some kind of festival (even though the original tribes were certainly long gone).[7]

In spite of these vague plans, however, no concrete arrangements were made until the announcement of the impending visit of President Benjamin Harrison. It would be the first such visit to San Antonio by a sitting U.S. chief executive. Harrison was apparently not originally scheduled to stop in the city at all, but since he was coming to Galveston, San Antonio's movers and shakers began as early as April 7 to lobby that he stop on his route west.[8] By April 13, the plans were solidified. If San Antonio could not get Harrison to stay overnight as he would in Galveston, they would at least have him for something longer than a whistle-stop: he would arrive in the city on April 20 at 9 A.M. and depart at noon. A Committee on Arrangements, made up of business and civic leaders, was quickly assembled, and within five days, the three-hour visit was fully planned. The president would arrive at Sunset Depot to be greeted by a reception committee of city luminaries, local and state officials, and the governor. He would ride in a procession with these greeters through the streets of San Antonio in a long and complex route to visit as many neighborhoods as possible within the limited time. Stores and houses along the way were asked to decorate, and plans were made to dismiss all schoolchildren so that they would see the event. The procession would end at Alamo Plaza, where the president would mount a specially constructed reviewing stand, deliver a short speech, and receive a group of schoolchildren with floral tributes. He would then be escorted back to the depot for his midday departure.[9]

It was the impending visit of the president that galvanized the flower-battle enthusiasts to organize their own procession. On April 13, a large group of ladies and a few gentlemen met at the San Antonio Club, on the second floor of the Grand Opera House in Alamo Plaza, under the gavel of Col. Henry B. Andrews. Concrete plans were swiftly made. First, it was decided to hold the parade at 5 P.M. and to hold it on April 20 rather than on San Jacinto Day itself, in honor of Harrison's visit. This would be long after the president's departure, but his schedule was too tight at any rate to permit him to witness such an entertainment in the first place.[10] The planners were counting on many visitors flocking to San Antonio that day and staying around to shop, so that the parade would have a large audience when the stores closed.

Since the planners intended for this parade to become an annual event, they decreed that in following years, it would be held on April 21 to properly commemorate the victory at San Jacinto. They also decided that "the celebration will be after the manner of the flower carnival at Nice and Cannes, and the scene [of the flower battle itself] will be on Alamo Plaza, near the historic Alamo Building."[11] Anyone who wished to decorate a carriage of any kind with flowers was invited to participate. It was determined that a donkey brigade and a bicycle contingent would be asked to join as well. Committees of ladies were appointed. Their businessmen husbands and friends were drafted to take charge of the finances, while the matters of decorations, the battle itself, and parade organization would be handled by the women.[12]

There is quite a bit of evidence to help us envision what the planners had in mind if we look at the women themselves. The fact that the initial meeting was held at the San Antonio Club tells us a lot about them. This club was similar to many other American men's social clubs of the period. The majority of its members were Anglo-Americans, though membership appeared to be determined more by economic or political status than anything else. Thus, the membership included German Americans like Drs. Berthold Hadra and Ferdinand Herff, George Kalteyer, Hermann D. Kampmann, and Louis Berg, as well as Tejanos José Cassiano and Jesus Hernandez, not to mention Mexican consul Plutarco Ornelas—and Bryan Callaghan Jr.[13]

Since it was a men-only club, several resident gentlemen were disconcerted to be invaded on the occasion by so many ladies. The women involved with the planning were hardly delicate, idle butterflies, either. Like so many of their counterparts in other American cities of the time, ladies of this class were firmly encouraged by the Judeo-Christian ethic to volunteer their time in community organizations and charities. Many served on the boards of such organizations. On the planning committee, to give just a few examples, Mrs. E. A. Fry served on the Women's Parsonage and Home Ministry Society of the Travis Methodist Episcopal Church. Mrs. H. D. Kampmann (see the illustration of her carriage later in chap. 7) was director of the Protestant Home for Destitute Children, as well as serving on the boards of three different ladies' aid societies. Mrs. John J. Stevens was president of the Ladies' Aid Society of the Travis Methodist Episcopal Church, served on Saint Mark's Parish Aid Society, was first vice president of the Protestant Home for Destitute Children, and was a member of the San Antonio Library and Women's Exchange, as were Mrs. James Slayden and many others. And this was just for starters, for many more women who were also community activists in one way or another would throw themselves into future Battle of Flowers efforts. In short, though male members of the San Antonio Club were skeptical of women being able to organize anything, these ladies were perfectly capable of successfully planning and running large events.

The Battle of Flowers idea, with its parade of carriages, was not too different from one of the ladies' habitual pastimes, a favorite recreational and social activity of this period before the wide use of telephones: visiting each other on their "days." Each lady set aside a few hours one specific afternoon every week when she let it be known that she would remain "at home" and receive visitors. These visitors, of course, came in their carriages. Parading around on urban streets was also nothing new: it was an American and European custom of the period for ladies to dress up and ride in open vehicles or on horseback around the most fashionable thoroughfares for an hour or so in the late afternoon during the summer.[14] Those participating in the parade would thus be doing what they always did—only in a fancier way.

Once the idea of a parade of decorated carriages and a flower battle was decided on, the ladies had only a week to organize and prepare for their procession. Events thus moved quickly. By April 17, they had appointed Gustav Duerler and Capt. G. F. Chase from Fort Sam Houston as marshals and had gratefully accepted the use of two ox-drawn wagons to decorate with flowers as floats on which children and young girls would ride. Several ladies volunteered for this task. Others secured the donation of a lot on Houston Street for the purpose of preparing the carriages before parade time. They arranged for Alamo Plaza to be cleared of vehicles and streetcars from 5 until 7 P.M. The committee again begged "every citizen having a vehicle and flowers [to] participate."[15] The next day the simple route was announced. The parade would form just off Alamo Plaza, pass through the plaza to Commerce Street, circle Main Plaza, and then return to Alamo Plaza. There, the marshals would divide the carriages into two columns, which would circle the plaza in opposite directions so that their occupants could throw flowers at each other. The battle's beginning and ending would be signaled by a bugle call. The Alamo facade would also be decorated with donated flowers.[16]

By the afternoon of April 19, all preparations were complete. On April 20 it rained in torrents all day. A sodden President Harrison arrived on time and was driven around the city in a closed carriage. He delivered a speech in Alamo Plaza in the downpour to a drenched audience, while aides held umbrellas over him, and then retreated to a reception in the Grand Opera House until it was time to depart. The flower battle was postponed, much to the disappointment of late-afternoon soaked viewers who were assembling on Commerce Street and Alamo Plaza in spite of the rain.[17]

It was not postponed for long. The next day the parade organizers met at the Menger Hotel, and the spectacle was rescheduled for April 24. Unfortunately, many of the flowers had wilted in the four-day delay. Most of the local supply (both commercial and from gardens) had already been appropriated, so everyone decorated as best they could, and the idea to adorn the Alamo facade was scrapped. This explains why artificial flowers would begin to be employed as early as the next year—which would immediately differentiate this flower battle from the one in Nice, with its fetish of real flowers.

On the day of the parade, the weather was fine, and everyone, viewers and participants alike, was very excited. When first the military band and the marshals and then the decorated equestrians hove into view, spectators began cheering. When the carriages and flowery floats made their appearance, they broke into applause.[18] Many of the ladies wore dresses to match the color of their vehicle decorations. The parade was a gorgeous and colorful spectacle, quite different from the profusion of symbols and uniforms or pretentious "educational" floats of the city's other parades. Here delicacy and feminine charm reigned, both in the flower-decorated carriages of various shapes and sizes and in the floral wagon floats, filled with children. Participating cyclists decorated their wheels with flowers and greens, while equestrians adorned their mounts. Even the donkey brigade featured flower-festooned animals. A large portion of the participants were women—as was true in the Mexico City and Nice parades—but the Battle of Flowers was the only procession entirely planned and staged by women. It was a civic and feminine triumph of public spectacle. Almost.

Battle of Flowers parade. This photograph dates to 1898, but the aerial view gives a good idea of the disposition of crowds, vehicles, and marchers in Alamo Plaza during the procession. *Courtesy U.T. Institute of Texan Cultures, Vic Fritze*

The following article by an observant but anonymous *San Antonio Light* reporter is quoted here almost in its entirety to evoke both the parade and what happened afterward during the battle.

The plaza was one dense mass of humanity and a close estimate made places the number of sight-seers and participants at 15,000. The parade started about 5:30 o'clock . . . [and] contained over 100 carriages and other vehicles, all gaily decorated and many containing decorations of real artistic merit. . . .

. . . On arriving at the plaza the police divided the procession into two lines, each half going in opposite directions and passing around the park were brought face to face with each other. The crowd on foot pressed the carriages closely and the fight begun [*sic*] and raged furiously for nearly an hour. The occupants of the carriages had all the ammunition while those on foot had

An example of a decorated carriage in the Battle of Flowers parade of 1897, with ladies in garments to match the flowers trimming their carriage, their horses, and the tack of their youthful outriders. Unlike in the initial parade, artificial flowers can clearly be seen on the wheel spokes and the carriage itself. *Courtesy San Antonio Conservation Society*

none. They began picking the fallen roses from the pavement and even tore off the trimmings of the carriages, and soon had the best of the fight. Heavy bunches of laurel thrown soon had their effect, and many ladies lost their temper and used their whips indiscriminately on the crowd. One lady struck Mr. Doc Fitzgerald, a passive spectator, a severe blow on the face with her whip, but did not see fit to apologise for her mistake. Mr. H. P. Drought made an ugly cut with his whip into the crowd, struck a negro, and the boy ran into a carriage horse in front of the Menger and nearly caused a runaway. A negro driving in a phaeton by himself in the procession, struck Louis Glaser, a white boy, in the right eye with the end of his reins. The buckle on the straps made a cruel wound and the boy was taken to a drug store by sympathetic bystanders. One young angel with white wings appealed to the crowd for protection from the missiles saying, "I wish you men would make them quit."

A fakir on the north end of the plaza began selling his goods on top of his

C. M. McAmis on his decorated bicycle—but in a studio shot, not in the parade itself. *Courtesy Daughters of the Republic of Texas Library*

C. A. Goeth (*center*) and his friends with their decorated mounts, awaiting formation of the equestrian section in the Battle of Flowers, 1893. *Courtesy U.T. Institute of Texan Cultures*

stand. His green handkerchiefs were stolen and used to throw at the crowd and he soon concluded to quit.

The police were powerless to keep the people off the park beds, and prevent them from tearing off the flowers.

One outright fight occurred. Mr. Phil Shook, one of the horseback party, lost his temper, and cutting a man with a riding whip, was assaulted, and a fist fight on the pavement resulted. Both combatants were arrested by the police. Mr. Charley Baker used his umbrella as a defense.

While the crowd was very dense on the plaza, waiting for the procession to come along, Mr. Cristoph Pfeuffer's splendid team and carriage took fright on South Alamo street, at an electric car. The carriage was decorated and contained several ladies, a child and the driver. Dashing into Alamo street, past and into the crowd of people, it overturned a buggy and horse at the corner, and its driver jumped out and was dragged under the carriage by the lines. The lady on the first seat caught one of the lines and held it, but the horses made straight for the crowd of women and children in the park and struck a very deep mass of them, it being impossible for them to move out of the way. The ladies were thrown out and their clothing was badly torn. One little boy was knocked senseless, another was bruised, and one little girl had her apron torn off. Other children were trampled by frightened people. The plunging horses were secured and the carriage was taken to a side street. . . .

. . . The battle was a success, but if it is given next year, more police will be needed, carriages [not in the parade] must not be allowed on the plaza at all, and participants must not lose their temper.

In short, the flower battle itself turned into a free-for-all rather than the decorous pelting of Mexico City and Nice, spectators even harvesting the newly planted flowers of the plaza in their search for ammunition. As genteel as the planners had hoped it would be, a large portion of both spectators and participants were only a generation away from the frontier and less than a decade away from the era of the Vaudeville Theater and its infamous shoot-outs. Nevertheless, the idea was good, and the parade and battle were pronounced successful by participants and viewers alike.

Looking more closely at the newspaper accounts of this first Battle of Flowers, some interesting details emerge. There were over one hundred carriages in the parade, of which about a dozen were described in the papers—those mentioned were the rigs of prominent citizens.[19] This established a pattern that would color reports until the end of the century and would constantly lead to accusations that only the elite could be involved in this procession. The reportage did include a comic dilapidated carriage labeled "Poor But In It," but that was the work of four young Belknap Rifle members, who were hardly part of San Antonio's impoverished proletariat.[20] On the other hand, it is very possible that some of the other entries belonged to entrants of more modest means, so participation may have been broader than the specific examples cited. The ladies, after all, did invite anyone in the city to take part, if they had at their disposal a vehicle and decorations. There are some who may truly have been "poor but in it." There is also that tantalizing reference to the African American man who hit the boy with his reins during the melee. The *Light* describes him as riding by himself in a phaeton—a lightweight vehicle. Though African American servants certainly drove some of the ladies' carriages (much as they did every day), the fact that this man was alone raises the question of whether African Americans rode as independent participants in their own decorated turnouts. Several members of the black community were hack drivers; it is possible that they could have had access to their hacks for the parade. If this is so, the first Battle of Flowers parade, and perhaps later ones as well, may have been the most truly integrated procession in the nineteenth century—but the true facts will probably never be known.

The Battle of Flowers was unique in that no additional festival was attached to it. This differentiated it from its Mexico City counterpart, which was tied into Diez y Seis or Cinco de Mayo events, or the procession in Nice, which was part of a larger Carnival celebration. This singularity would be important for the local flower parade's development. All the other nineteenth-century San Antonio festivals generally used their parades as preludes and "come-ons" to the park celebrations. Even the 1890 German Day parade was part of the larger International Fair and added on a couple of extra events afterward. In the case of the Battle of Flowers, there would indeed later be a significant festival attached to it (it became the nucleus for the twentieth-century Fiesta San Jacinto), but the parade would remain the centerpiece, not a precursor, and the patriotic excuse for it, the Battle of San Jacinto, would only become prominent in subsequent processions in order to promote the idea of having the parade every year.

The ladies certainly realized that their lack of foresight in mustering sufficient police for crowd control was nearly catastrophic.[21] They did not as yet have the experience of the gentlemen who put together other parades of the period, and it is interesting that none of these gentlemen saw fit to advise them in this department. Of course, no other procession of the time featured a staged battle (unless an "attack" of a German immigrant wagon by "cowboys and Indians" in the 1892 German American Volksfest parade is counted).[22] Whatever the problems of the first Battle of Flowers, everyone considered the idea of the parade terrific and vowed to continue it as an annual event and to learn from their initial experience.

THE BATTLE OF FLOWERS ACQUIRES A "TRADITION," 1892–94

In 1892, the ladies made good their vows of the previous year and met a full month in advance of the parade date to make plans. In contrast to the year before, with its slapdash "we can put on a show" attitude, a whole series of committees was formed by March 23, with the proviso that any other women who wished to work would be enthusiastically welcomed to join in. Mrs. John J. Stevens was elected president; by March 25, more than one hundred women had signed up as members of one or another of eleven committees.[23] These ladies again came from the Anglo-American and German American communities. Though an advisory committee was made up of some of their businessmen husbands, Mrs. Stevens and her volunteers were virtually responsible for the entire organization and staging of the parade. As the procession would grow over the next few years, organizational preparation would grow with it, and the ladies would take on all of it with capable hands. The one main exception was crowd control; here they deferred to a committee of gentlemen, including Bryan Callaghan and Oscar Bergstrom, who would be responsible for securing the needed number of police. Already a grand charity ball was being planned at the same time for a somewhat earlier date. Since the sponsors and stagers of this ball were the community's military wives, several of whom were also working on the parade, the arrangements for both took a considerable amount of coordination. The parade organizers, many of whom served on several civic organizations and boards simultaneously, were used to multitasking and would pull both events off with finesse.

Nevertheless, much work needed to be done. Within the month's time, the invitations committee not only tapped important locals to march or ride but also sent messages to friends in surrounding towns, urging ladies to decorate carriages and participate. All carriages, horses, and cycles were to be decorated by their owners or users, this year with artificial as well as real flowers. A float committee worked to adorn larger vehicles and secure riders. The committee dealing with streets and stores not only arranged for extra street cleaning and vehicle clearance along the route but also encouraged stores along these streets and plazas to decorate their places of business. A large committee oversaw the planning of the battle proper in Alamo Plaza, plus the erection of a small viewing stand for special invited guests. To validate the significance of the parade even more, they invited Capt. William McMaster, a genuine San Jacinto veteran, to be present on that stand.[24]

The same contingents of decorated carriages, equestrians, and cyclists were planned, but additions to the parade already distinguished it from its French and Mexican predecessors. Aside from the Twenty-third Infantry Band, the Belknap Rifles—fresh from winning a drill competition in Indianapolis—would march in their white uniforms, their rifles hung with flower wreaths. The fire depart-

San Antonio's best-known Anglo-American drill team, the Belknap Rifles.
Courtesy Daughters of the Republic of Texas Library

ment was also be included, with all available engines decorated with floral finery. Six commercial floats also would participate. Whether or not to include commercial floats would remain a bone of contention through the 1890s. In the case of 1892, one of the firms, Wolfson's Department Store, was probably allowed because Mrs. Wolfson was a committee member and her husband's firm made a contribution to the parade. Another, Harnisch and Baer, was a popular ice-cream and confectionary spot with the ladies.

Mrs. Stevens and her committees had reason to be proud that year. The battle went without a hitch, spectators remaining spectators. Over five hundred carriages of every size participated, ranging from donkey carts, buggies, one-horse traps, and phaetons, to larger carriages and canopied surreys. There were also at least two large festooned coaches, called tallyhos. Evergreens, laurel, and moss abounded, but the real distinction was in the flowers, either real or very realistic imitations. These included roses of red, white, pink, and yellow (a yellow variety called Maréchal Neil was particularly favored); primroses of pink and yellow; and poppies. Occupants of the carriages wore dresses or boutonnieres matching the

A flower-decorated steamer truck in parade action.
Courtesy San Antonio Conservation Society

colors of their decorations. Some of the carriage entries had themes, making them small floats. A tallyho featured not only a virtual robe of blooms but children who each represented a different flower. One of the fashionable themes of this period was Japan and things Japanese (this was, after all, the era of *The Mikado*, performed in the city in 1889).[25] Thus a phaeton was decorated as a "Japanese chariot," crowned with a large Japanese parasol, fans, flowers, and laurel, its female occupants dressed in kimonos. Keeping to the same theme was a male cyclist, "gotten up in the character of a Japanese in full costume . . . [so that] his most intimate friends failed to recognize him. His wheel was decorated in the Japanese fashion with exquisite taste and was surmounted by a Japanese parasol, and when in motion he looked like a Japanese nobleman riding to his summer residence mounted on a wheel."[26]

The only mishap of the day came at the parade's start. The order to march was given prematurely, and the Belknaps and the fire department had to rush to catch up, not fully joining in until the procession neared Alamo Plaza.[27]

From 1892, the Battle of Flowers parade assumed the basic shape it would retain through the rest of the decade. From this point on, it would simply get bigger and more elaborate, the ranks swelled not only by more decorated vehicles but by added contingents of marchers, many of them the mainstays of other civic parades in the municipality.

In the following year under president Mrs. J. H. French, wife of the former mayor, commercial floats were banned, but by this point, the parade had become long enough to be divided into three sections. And the ladies went out of their way each year to extend an invitation to anyone and everyone in the city who wanted to decorate a vehicle, horse, or donkey, however modestly.[28] This is important because it explains why this parade was so successful while the Volksfests died. True, the planners of the Battle of Flowers were the wives of relatively well-off men, but the parade itself had basically a grassroots philosophy that all decorations were homemade and home-contributed, so no large sums needed to be raised for costly floats. The carriages, bicycles, and horses could be extravagantly decorated, but they could also march with minimal, inexpensive adornment: the "evergreens," for example, could be local "Texas cedar," free for the gathering.

The first of the three divisions in 1893 included 132 bicycles. The second featured the ex-firemen's band and the entire now-professional fire department (except for a skeleton crew to cover emergencies) under chief L. B. Peck, "rigged out in such profuse gaudiness as has never before been seen in this city."[29] Many of the latter vehicles featured the children of the participating firemen. The third division was led by the Twenty-third Infantry Band and contained a large group of the uniformed Knights of Pythias, who were having a convention in the city at the time. It also included the equestrians, who rode extravagantly caparisoned horses, and "a number of cowboys with a few greens."[30] The enormous number of decorated horse-drawn vehicles ranged from the "beautiful to the absurd to the shabby," suggesting that a wide social spectrum did actually participate.[31] At one end of the scale, the Turnverein contributed a flower-decked float with the members' children; at the other end was an "urchin in his rig, drawn by two angora goats."[32] The parade itself was over a mile long, necessitating an expanded route, which now spanned all three plazas.

The identification of the parade with the Battle of San Jacinto was becoming stronger. All four surviving veterans of the battle who lived in the area were invited;

Gen. H. P. Bee and Nat Mitchell rode in the parade; Captain McMasters and Sam McCullough witnessed it from their special stand in Alamo Plaza. There was also one added patriotic feature: the facade of the "Alamo Chapel" was decorated. This facade was originally to have been decorated in 1891, but the rain out had forced cancellation. In 1893, a special committee decorated it with flowers, wreaths, and mottoes. Besides the garlands of flowers and moss, the word "Bonham," on the right side, was surmounted by the motto: "March 6, 1836. Travis: those who will die for Texas cross this line, march!" On the left side was the word "Evans," above it the inscription: "Bowie: Lift my cot and carry me across this line!" The center had the motto: "Heroes and patriots from near and far, / Behold with joy the flag of the star," with the name "Crockett" and the Texas Flag emblazoned above.[33]

As the nineteenth century progressed, the battle of the Alamo had achieved mythic proportions. All visitor journalists from the 1850s onward had recounted versions of the story. Virtually all of them singled out Travis, Crockett, Bowie, and often Bonham as the battle's great leaders.[34] Sidney Lanier, visiting San Antonio in 1872 in hopes of curing his tuberculosis, recounted the legend of Travis drawing the line and Bowie having his bed carried across it.[35] In the next decade, a painting was made of the same incident by the Galveston artist Louis Eyth.[36] Whether the story of Travis and the line was truth or myth didn't matter by 1893; it had become part of the accepted canon (and we have already seen an allegorical representation of the canonical heroes in the 1892 German American Volksfest parade—see the illustration in chap. 6). The only less-famous hero the ladies included was Robert Evans, who achieved his niche in the pantheon by trying to blow up the Alamo's powder room, dying before he could do so.

Part of the mystique of the Alamo's fall was that nearly everyone involved perished. The motto "Thermopylae had her messenger of death; the Alamo had none" was attached to the legend by the 1840s. Though the Chapel was at first left derelict after 1836, it was restored and added on to by German builders John Fries and Michael and David Russi, hired by the U.S. Army in 1849 when it became a quartermaster's depot.[37] It was this fancifully restored facade that became a tourist attraction for intrepid visitors as early as the 1850s.[38] There was, however, little in the way of a movement to preserve it until the 1890s. Indeed, the "Chapel" had been dwarfed by the huge, ugly, crenellated emporium built over the remains of its adjacent barracks by Honoré Grenet in 1878. This was still standing (though somewhat toned down), owned by the firm of Hugo and Schmeltzer, in 1893.

But the Alamo, and particularly the "Alamo Chapel," had become a living

The decorated Alamo facade, replete with festoons and patriotic mottoes relating to the Alamo heroes. *Courtesy San Antonio Conservation Society*

icon, especially dear to the city's growing Anglo-American population (even though most of them had not been in Texas in 1836). In many ways, it became a symbol of manifest destiny, a place of martyrdom whose very tragedy heralded the coming of first the Republic of Texas, then the United States, replete with all the trappings of the nineteenth-century ideal of progress. Enhancing the attraction of the Alamo for Battle of Flowers participants was the redemption of its martyrs through the Texian victory at the Battle of San Jacinto—thus symbolizing triumph over tragedy.

By 1893, a movement was already afoot both to glorify the memory of the Alamo and the San Jacinto battle and to save the "Alamo Chapel." Four years earlier, in 1889, a women's patriotic group called De Zavala's Daughters had been formed in San Antonio. Its president and principal organizer was Adina de Zavala, a schoolteacher and the granddaughter of Tejano patriot Lorenzo de Zavala.[39] In 1893, this group was invited to join the Daughters of the Republic of Texas. The Daughters were likewise a patriotic group, made up of women who could trace their ancestry to Anglo-American inhabitants of the Republic of Texas or earlier. Adina de Zavala bore the name of one of the Republic's Tejano founders, but both her mother and grandmother were Irish Americans.[40] The De Zavala chapter of the Daughters of the Republic took a strong and early interest in the preservation of the city's other missions, as well as the Alamo. It is not surprising that some of its members were also part of the committee that oversaw the decoration of the Alamo's facade for the Battle of Flowers; they would continue to be instrumental in identifying the Battle of Flowers with Texas patriotism well into the next century.

In 1893, there were no problems with either the flower battle or the parade. Everyone started on time. The battle, which lasted about forty minutes, was staged to music by the Twenty-third Infantry Band, which occupied the bandstand in the middle of the plaza.

In each successive year, more and more citizens became involved in both the planning of and participation in the Battle of Flowers. In 1894, Mrs. John A. Frazer (wife of the vice president of the San Antonio National Bank) oversaw twelve different committees, including one to invite the inclusion of the German American organizations and *vereine* in the growing procession. Mrs. Frazer had an excellent pedigree for the job. Her father was William Girard Tobin, a prominent citizen of the city in the middle of the century, and her brother (also named William) was a fire chief as well as one of the founders of the Belknap Rifles. Her maternal grandfather, John W. Smith, had been at the Alamo during the siege. He survived because he had left several days before the final onslaught in an attempt to seek reinforcements from Seguin.[41]

The Alamo decorations had been preserved from the year before and were used again. The parade was still on a shoestring budget, so an ingenious arrangement was made to include more floats by recycling personnel and costumes from an earlier theatrical charity performance. This was a dance recital featuring local talent, staged at the Opera House at the end of March, entitled *Kermess*. Many of the same ladies who made up Battle of Flowers committees were involved in its production. *Kermess* consisted of a series of dances representing popular theatrical fashions of the day.[42] The general theme was the ever-popular "all nations." The program began with a dance by ladies and gentlemen representing Bretons: they were revealed in a pretty tableau when the curtain rose and performed a dance in wooden shoes. Following this were seven more scenes. First there were children dressed as Japanese (the *San Antonio Express* called them "the little Japs" and noted that their dance was, of all things, a polka).[43] Then came an eighteenth-century minuet, followed by men and women dressed as Neapolitan fisher-folk who danced a tarantella. The United States was represented by performers in lawn-tennis costumes, replete with rackets. A brave William Tobin did a solo as a Venetian gondolier and later sang an accompaniment for the next group, of gypsy dancers. The show ended with a tambourine dance.

Kermess was staged three times—to standing-room-only audiences; the last performance took place on March 29. The organizing sponsors had invested in imported costumes (whose availability may have determined the subjects of the dances). The Bretons' costumes came from Chicago, the eighteenth-century minuet garments from New Orleans.[44] Wisely, the Battle of Flowers planners realized that both performers and costumes could be recycled on flower-decorated floats.

The parade itself was again composed of two divisions, the first led by the ex-firemen's band (though this year minus the fire department itself); the Belknap Rifles in their dress uniforms; twenty-four local members of the Knights of Pythias in uniform; and students, likewise in uniform, from the West Texas Military Institute. The bicycles were also included here, and this year more women cyclists participated. Again some bicycles were elaborately decorated, including one disguised as a small ship, one as the liberty bell, and two cyclists dressed as clowns.[45]

The second division featured seventy-five horsemen and -women; the president and officers of the association in a decorated tallyho; and a number of delegates from the Benevolent and Protective Order of Elks, who rode in carriages. Another carriage contained several San Jacinto survivors. There was also a decorated delegation of carriages from the Daughters of the Republic of Texas and an ever-growing profusion of privately decorated vehicles. Interspersed with the carriages were the floats extending the theme of *Kermess*. These included "the little japs," the Neapolitan fishers, and the gypsies, each group in its own vehicle.

Everyone else was on a float of "all nations," escorted by a group of (Anglo-American) horsemen dressed as "Indians." There were also public-school floats, decorated and populated by schoolchildren.

The Elks' carriages included their mottoes "Charity, Justice, Brother Love and Fidelity" and "BPOE" spelled out in paper roses, as well as their trademark elk horns. Most of the other carriages were once again decorated with paper and real flowers, with their occupants dressed in matching ensembles. Also included were several broadly satirical floats of the "poor but in it" type bringing up the rear.

This parade again went off without a hitch. This is not surprising considering that a contingent of forty policemen kept order. These men were more than welcome, since everyone ignored the ropes put up in Alamo Plaza to separate battlers from spectators. A few small boys in the crowd did throw fallen flowers back on the combatants, but this was the extent of spectator participation To add to the festiveness of the occasion, many stores and other businesses along the route decorated their windows and facades with bunting, wreaths, and artificial flowers.

It was inevitable that other events would begin to attach themselves to this parade, as they were attached to the parades for the other festivals. In 1894, these were to come in the form of private affairs. The Maverick Building was closed to the general public for parade viewing, with entry permitted to invited guests only. The Casino Club threw a calico ball for its members the evening after the parade. More public was the charity ball thrown by the Liquor Dealers Association at Mission Gardens, open to anyone for the price of a ticket.[46]

ENTER THE GENTLEMEN—TEMPORARILY, 1895

In January, 1895, an event occurred that would strongly affect that year's Battle of Flowers celebration and would later permanently alter its dynamics. This was the founding of the San Antonio Businessmen's Club. This precursor to the Chamber of Commerce was formed to pursue investments, lower railroad rates, and tout San Antonio in the national spotlight.[47] By the end of the month, there were over four hundred members, many of them the spouses of the most active women planning the flower battles. James L. Slayden, husband of flower-battle executive-committee member Ellen Slayden, was elected the club's president.

Among the prime activities of the Businessmen's Club was to attract tourism and conventions to the city. One of their first successes was luring the Traveler's Protective Association (T.P.A.) to San Antonio for a convention to be held in

June. This was the main professional affiliation of traveling salesmen, or "drummers," of which there was a very large number at this time in the United States. The businessmen, looking for ways to entertain the largest convention in the city to date, instantly thought of the Battle of Flowers, which by this time was becoming a considerable tourist attraction in itself.

At their very first organizational meeting on March 25, the ladies were tendered a communication from the Businessmen's Club requesting that they either postpone or repeat their parade in June that year for the edification of the visiting drummers. The businessmen dangled a tempting carrot: the donation of five hundred dollars from the club to help them stage the procession. The Battle of Flowers parade had so far been operating on a shoestring each year. Though five hundred dollars seems a paltry sum in comparison to the thousands spent on the Volksfests, for the ladies it would mean the difference between just about making ends meet and staging a far more impressive show. The businessmen also offered them the use (at no extra cost) of the four bands they proposed to engage for the convention, including the "military band" of Carl Beck.[48]

The women, again under the leadership of Mrs. Frazer, hesitated: June would be a hotter month, and there would be fewer fresh flowers available. But spurred on by the five hundred dollars and an offer by the businessmen to help them raise more if needed, the ladies capitulated, and the parade was postponed until June 4. They did insist, however, that this postponement be a unique event; in 1896 and all following years, it was to return to its traditional date of April 21. "When the date was settled upon," reported the *San Antonio Light,* "the enthusiasm of the ladies seemingly increased, and they departed for their homes determined to give the T.P.A. boys an entertainment that they would never forget."[49]

Within the week, the feminine volunteers (now numbering over two hundred) rolled up their sleeves and got to work. The participation of the fire department and a military contingent was swiftly locked in, and a committee visited merchants to ask for donations of prizes for the most tastefully decorated carriage, bicycle, horse, fire engine, and float. Since the merchants were mostly husbands of the committee members, they agreed. A new idea was to marshal the little boys who had thrown flowers back at the carriages over the past few battles to gather the fallen blooms and return them to the combatants.[50] A month later, in early May, the ladies decided to advertise their fete nationwide and sent out invitations to all state offices in the United States and Mexico.

Because of the nature of the event, the parade in June had a somewhat different order and some added elements. There were three divisions. The first was heralded by the marshals Hermann Karber (former volunteer fire chief and perennial marshal from 1893 through 1897) and Fortunato Villareal. Mounted police, Carl Beck's Band, and the Belknap Rifles followed. Then came the decorated carriages, decorated children's carts and donkeys, and floats by the Art League and several others. The second division was atypical of the Battle of Flowers. Aside from a large contingent of military, including a band, Fifth and Seventh U.S. Cavalry members, and Light Battery E, it featured a T.P.A. band and six decorated T.P.A. floats, plus a gaggle of "cowboys" and "Indians" escorting a stagecoach.

The third and last division included the cyclists, the fire department, Solis' Mexican Band, and several commercial floats. Fewer decorated carriages participated than usual, but the procession was still lengthy due to the various additions. The T.P.A. floats struck a discordant note when contrasted to the rest: "[they were] conspicuous mainly for their lack of beauty. But while their pulchritude was of small degree, they . . . attracted the attention of the visitors from the North and East . . . because they were recollections of aboriginal days and are rapidly becoming extinct."[51] These floats were actually old transport wagons from the prerailroad days, mostly undecorated except for a few props. They more or less depicted the various historical stages of transport for traveling salesmen. The T.P.A. floats fared poorly when contrasted with the floral carriages and floats that reflected the now-traditional spirit of the Battle of Flowers. Perhaps the most impressive was contributed by the fraternal organization the Order of Chosen Friends. It boasted seven young ladies, each in a "gorgeous Grecian costume" of one of the colors of the rainbow. The float's front was adorned with a rainbow arch, and the back "was illustrated with the seven links of the order in the shape of a bending bow, surrounding the clasped hands of Friendship and bearing the initials of the motto of the order: Friendship, Aid and Protection."[52]

There was also one additional allegorical float, depicting Greek muses, contributed by the Art League. It was as elaborate as the Chosen Friends' float, with a Greek temple and altar and a table with two sculptures and a sculpted bust. The Muse of Art sat on a throne, while two other Muses (of Music and Literature) sat nearby on the ground; along the sides of the altar was a bevy of seated votaries.[53] Viewers would have been familiar with this sort of allegory from earlier Volksfest floats, notably "Commerce, Science and Art" of 1883 and "Industry, Art, Science and Learning" of 1890.

The *San Antonio Light* estimated a turnout of fifty thousand people, as the city's population was considerably swelled by visitors.[54] The businessmen were delighted with the procession. Although the ladies had pulled off another success, they were less happy. The weather was hot (which explains the relatively small number of carriages), no particular patriotic event was commemorated, the T.P.A. participants and their ugly floats were out of character with the parade as the women envisioned it, and they disapproved also of the commercial floats' presence.

THE BATTLE OF FLOWERS UNDER MRS. ELIZABETH OGDEN, 1896–99

The June experience led to a certain amount of confusion during initial plans for the parade in 1896. Mrs. Frazer had had enough after the businessmen's meddling of the year before. She resigned in early March, and for a short period there seemed to be no one to take her place. Finally, it was agreed that Mrs. Elizabeth Cox Ogden would assume the post.[55] Her willingness to take the position speaks much of this lady, because in 1896 she was seventy years old. But her lineage and energy were impeccable. The future Mrs. Ogden's parents had emigrated to Texas from Kentucky during the period of the Mexican Republic, and her father had served in Sam Houston's army.[56] At the age of ten, she was living with her family in Washington on the Brazos when Alamo survivor Mrs. Dickinson appeared there with her daughter and recounted the events of Santa Anna's siege. This meant that Elizabeth Cox was an Alamo contemporary, if not a survivor, and had heard the battle story firsthand. She married Duncan Campbell Ogden of New York, also of military inclination, who had come to Texas in 1838 and served with the army of the Republic of Texas. Ogden died in 1859, and Elizabeth never remarried. She raised two children, a son and a daughter. Her daughter, Cora, who married stockman Nathan T. Wilson, would also be active in planning various flower battles. Mrs. Ogden had long been involved in local charity work and for the next four years would prove to be a very capable leader, despite her years.

The ladies did accept one male advisor in 1896. Anna Goodman Hertzberg, who had been elected treasurer, would be one of the most active planners of this and future Battle of Flowers parades, but she was given invaluable aid by a local minister, Dr. G. Q. A. Rose. He acted as an informal financial advisor to the planners and headed a small fund-soliciting committee of businessmen. He would, however, never intrude on other parade matters, as the businessmen had done the year before. Otherwise, male volunteers were firmly relegated to the roles of marshals, police protection, and the participation of the fire department.[57]

The committees continued to swell in number. The carriage committee alone had over ninety volunteers. There was some altercation with fire chief William Tobin about the extent of decoration of the fire engines—apparently in 1895 they had been so buried under blooms that they nearly lost their identities. But this and other such problems were all eventually resolved.

A new element planned for this year was the erection of four floral "triumphal arches" in Alamo Plaza. They were to be placed on Crockett Street. One would extend to the park in the plaza, one would stretch over East Houston Street and Avenue D, and two would span the plaza itself.[58] The finance committee and Dr. Rose estimated that about one thousand dollars would need to be raised to cover the parade and the ambitious arches. Triumphal arches had made a sort of comeback in the nineteenth century, several of the most famous being permanent, such as the Arc de Triomphe in Paris and Washington Square Arch in New York. But there was a long tradition since Roman times of temporary triumphal arches spanning parade routes.

As it turned out, only one arch was actually constructed; it was placed across Avenue D (where the parade mustered) at the entrance to Alamo Plaza. The structure was entitled the San Jacinto Arch and was designed by the up-and-coming architect Atlee B. Ayers. Ayers's plan dictated a huge structure—forty feet wide (with twenty-eight feet of marching space between its two vertical buttresses), thirty feet high, and four feet broad—to be constructed of wood and painted white. The design called for "domestic columns" of roses and a frieze with garlands of more roses on top. The top and pedestal of the arch were envisioned to be covered with palms and the bases adorned with potted ferns, with cannons and flags situated above and around this greenery. The whole thing was to be outlined in multicolored incandescent lights.[59] Even this plan turned out to be far more ambitious than what was actually built. In its final version, the arch was twenty feet high, covered with white bunting, and decorated with streamers of leaves entwined with rope. Patriotic inscriptions on the two sides of the frieze read "Remember the Alamo" and "Remember Goliad," evoking the two disastrous massacres preceding the victory at San Jacinto.[60] All the planned flowers, urns, columns, and other ornaments had fallen by the wayside, mostly due to a seventy-five-dollar budget. But the plan was also abandoned because streetcars ran under the arch and the streetcar company would not stop service so that the arch could be more elaborately decorated.[61]

Event-wise, a modest festival quietly continued to grow around the parade. A band concert was planned in Alamo Plaza to entertain the crowds after the battle. A private charity ball was also sponsored by the San Antonio Library and Women's Exchange, an organization to which many of the Battle of Flowers ladies belonged. It would be a cotton ball held in Beethoven Hall. Various embellishments, including entertainment and the election of a king and queen, were to be part of it. Much was made of this first queen, Miss Ida Archer of Austin, in later accounts of Battle of Flowers fetes written in the royalty-obsessed twentieth century. It must be remembered, however, that Miss Archer was a private society queen at a private society ball; she did not take part in the public spectacle of the procession. The distinction of the first presence of a queen in a San Antonio parade belongs to the Juneteenth procession put on later that year.[62]

On parade day, the crowds were so dense that there was barely room for the marchers to pass. By this time, the route had become standardized, quite similar to the path established in 1893. The parade now had four divisions but was basically similar in makeup to the earlier, pre-1895 parades. Bicycles were now in the first division. The second division was military, consisting of a mounted cavalry band and four companies of infantry, one company of cavalry, and a contingent of artillery. The third division had the Belknaps, the officers of the association, a carriage with San Jacinto veterans, and the cavalcade. The numerous decorated carriages made up the fourth division. At the parade's end came the more modestly decorated carts—some drawn by goats—an amplified collection of "cowboys" and "Indians," and the decorated fire engines. The latter were less elaborately adorned than they had been the previous year, to the gratification of fire chief Tobin.

There were several floats in the third division, two sponsored by schools, others by individuals. One was the now-ubiquitous "All Nations," sponsored by real estate mogul Jay E. Adams. The high school's float had a classical theme, while West Texas Military Academy contributed "Baseball and Football." The Daughters of the Republic of Texas rode on their own patriotically decorated float. Floats were still a minor part of the parade, and they conformed to no overall theme. Their number still depended on which freight and lumber companies would contribute flatbed wagons for the occasion. Some of the floats' ornamentation and costumes was governed by expediency: the baseball and football players wore their uniforms and carried their gear. The high school entry featured six girls in classical robes, three in yellow and three in purple, to match the other decorations surrounding them. Classical garb and props were always a symbol of artistic high culture at this time, not only in San Antonio but throughout the United States. The high school float was no exception. It was sort of an amalgam of the Chosen Friends and Art League entries of the year before. The floats were generally decorated by the sponsoring group, and as many flowers, real and fake, were piled on as possible.[63]

In short, the 1896 Battle of Flowers returned to its 1894 identity. Unfortunately, one tragic occurrence marred the event. The ladies had made arrangements (through influential former congressman Thomas M. Paschal) to have a twenty-one-gun salute fired in honor of the day. The salute began at Fort Sam Houston at 3:30, but when Corp. George E. Parkhurst prepared to fire the twelfth of these, it exploded prematurely, killing him and injuring two attending privates when the shock wave threw them to the ground.[64] It was the only fatality directly associated with any of San Antonio's festivals during this period. It also postponed thoughts of having such a salute again for some years.[65]

Given the inclination of the ladies of the Battle of Flowers committees toward charitable acts, it would be imagined that they would have immediately done something to aid the deceased corporal's wife and children. However, the subject was not brought up until February 20 of the next year, and then it was not raised by any of the ladies, but by L. Clarke Irvine, secretary of the Businessmen's Club. Irvine reminded the ladies that Parkhurst's widow and orphaned children were now nearly destitute and that something should be done to raise some funds for them—perhaps through a charity ball after the parade.[66] The ladies at first resisted, declaring that San Jacinto Day was for the celebration of San Jacinto fighters only. Finally, they agreed to dedicate the proceeds of that year's Daughters of the Republic–sponsored cotton ball to the family. But this came only after the reading of a pathetic letter about the Parkhurst survivors written by the wife of Fort Sam Houston's doctor and much debate.[67]

In 1897, Mrs. Ogden was into the second year of her four-year presidential stint, and Mrs. Hertzberg was elected first vice president. Not at all a San Jacinto–era descendent, Anna Hertzberg originally hailed from New York. She was the wife of jeweler Eleazar Hertzberg and added a note of high culture and urban sophistication to the festival. She was a professionally trained, talented musician. In 1901, she would found the Tuesday Musical Club, which exists to this day. She was also the first woman elected to office in Texas, serving on the San Antonio educational board.[68]

Dr. Rose declined to serve as business advisor any longer, and the job fell to L. Clarke Irvine, the secretary of the Businessmen's Club. He would prove valuable in securing a committee of businessmen to raise the modest sum needed to hold the festival that year. Since the arch idea was discarded, it was estimated that only about five hundred dollars would be needed. The flower battle was continuing to attract tourists to the city. The gentlemen saw the wisdom of raising the money, securing special railroad rates—and then stepping back to let the ladies reign.[69] The men did make one additional suggestion: to invite bands from outlying towns to come to the city for a band contest. Just about every small town of the period had one, and after the contest, all participating bands would march in the Battle of Flowers parade. That would kill three birds with one stone: the bands could be obtained for the cost of reduced railroad rates, they would provide additional length to the parade, and they could also give performances for citizens in the plazas the night before the parade. There would thus be popular entertainment available as well as the private ball. The ladies liked the idea and adopted it.[70]

The band contest caught on quickly. Prizes were donated by local stores for the best bands; they included helmets, uniforms, and "one $10 violin."[71] Other, more valuable instruments were later added. Not to be outdone, Joske Brothers' Department Store offered the prize of a cut-glass vase to be awarded to the most beautifully decorated bicycle in the parade itself. The vase was exhibited in one of the store's windows for several weeks before the procession, both as an incentive for cyclists to decorate and as good publicity for Joske's.

In the end, bands from the Texas towns of Yoakum, Hallettsville, York Creek, La Grange, and Austin came, accompanied by enthusiastic booster contingents of local citizens. The band contest was scheduled for the morning and early afternoon of April 21; the parade would then be held at its customary 5 P.M. time. For the climax of the band contest, all the bands massed together at the end of the competition to play two selections, "America" and the "Coon Schottische" "Ma Angelique." All of them then joined the Fifth U.S. Cavalry Band and Carl Beck's Band for what must have been a very noisy parade.

The parade itself was made up of its usual decorated contingents. Joining the Belknap Rifles and the military marchers was the recently founded and gaudily dressed San Antonio Zouaves militia company, as well as some militia companies from other South Texas towns.[72] Several school floats participated, and a few advertising floats did as well.

The Daughters of the Republic became an increasingly integrated element in the parade, due to their Alamo affiliation. By this time they presented floats with members almost yearly (at least one decorated personally by Adina de Zavala). In 1897 they sponsored the cotton ball. They also assumed most of the responsibility for decorating the Alamo—in 1897, it featured a large Texas star of electric lights, besides patriotic portraits, festoons, and flowers.

The San Antonio Zouaves, drilling in their distinctive "oriental" uniforms, 1890s. *Courtesy Witte Museum, San Antonio, Texas*

To complete the continued success of the parade as an urban event, both stores and private houses off the route were decorated. This had already become a custom in Mexican American neighborhoods in honor of Diez y Seis celebrations. Streets were cleaned the morning of the parade; it can be inferred that the profusion of horses, donkeys, and goats in the procession must have left them quite in need of another sweeping afterward. However, very few spectators would have noticed the pavement. The *San Antonio Express* headlined the parade as "A Riot of Flags and Flowers . . . Most Brilliant and Successful Floral Carnival Held Yet. It Was a Medley of Beauty. A Dream of Fair Women and an Inspiration to Patriotism."[73]

By 1898, the Battle of Flowers parade had grown from an almost impromptu event to a famous, carefully planned one. Not only was the battle becoming a San Antonio civic institution, but its fame had spread sufficiently around Texas to prompt imitations. In the summer of 1897, the city of Waco had staged their own flower parade, which they entitled "Carnival of Beauty," and planned another for 1898.[74] Waco had added its own twist: along with a parade it had staged a beauty

Mrs. Hermann Kampmann's decorated carriage, which contributed to the description of the parade as "A Riot of Flags and Flowers," 1897.
Courtesy San Antonio Conservation Society

contest and, in so doing, attracted more out-of-town visitors than San Antonio had for its own procession and battle.

The San Antonio's Businessmen's Club, which had restrained itself from meddling in the ladies' plans (except when invited) since 1895, sat up and took notice. At the very first planning discussions in February, 1898, the businessmen, noting the success of the previous band contest and the threat of rivalry from Waco, made a proposal to extend the Battle of Flowers into a proper two-day festival, or carnival, with additional events.[75] They began lobbying the idea as soon as formal organizational sessions convened in early March. At first, Mrs. Ogden, Mrs. Hertzberg, and the ladies at large were inclined to view the idea favorably.

Decorated carriages near the Alamo in the Battle of Flowers parade, 1898.
Courtesy U.T. Institute of Texan Cultures, Laura Long

The new Businessmen's Club secretary, Milton Everett, continued to speak of it in meetings throughout March.[76] Since the meetings were held at their clubroom, the businessmen thought that they could invade any or all of them and eventually have their way. Everett and his cohorts began pushing harder, suggesting that gubernatorial candidates from all over Texas be invited to San Antonio to join the festival. They augmented their plan to include stump speeches held on April 21 and relegated the parade and band concert to April 22.[77]

That was overkill. Taking advantage of the absence of Mr. Everett on March 25, the ladies decided to return to their usual scheme of having the parade and battle on April 21. As a consolation, they sent the men off to organize the band contest, which, as in the previous year, would be held on parade day. The Daughters of the Republic again decided to stage a cotton ball the night of the parade.

But in the end, an event *was* scheduled for the next day, April 22. The women of the San Antonio Library and Women's Exchange, who had sponsored the first cotton ball, had let the Daughters of the Republic do it the following year. The latter would continue the custom in 1898. Not to be outdone, the library women decided to hold a "paper carnival" and ball on April 22. Female attendees were obliged to wear costumes of tissue paper, while their escorts had to swathe themselves in tissue-paper accessories. The library women had actually been talking of holding such a fete for several months, and the night after the flower battle seemed to offer the proper opportunity.[78]

The parade that year was composed of the usual contingents. Once again the Knights of Pythias, who were in San Antonio for another convention, were added, along with a couple of commercial wagons that managed to wangle their way in. This year, there were to be so many carriages that they would have their own division, with lighter carts and phaetons separated out into another section. The parade was long enough now to have seven divisions, each with its own marshal. The marshals were to be strictly in uniform: "black clothes with black ties and black crushed hats, Hessian boots, white trousers, and stove pipe and derby hats will be strictly tabooed."[79] Among the division marshals was Juan T. Cardenas, who had finally attained social cachet within the Anglo-American world (though Antonio P. Rivas had already served as a marshal two years earlier, in 1896).[80] Although from the very first parade the ladies had insisted that anyone with a decorated vehicle could participate, it seems that less affluent people had become more hesitant than ever to do so by the end of the decade. Consequently, Justice Enoch Griff-Jones (1898's grand marshal) made an exhortation for "all classes of citizens to follow the procession in carriages or any vehicle."[81]

Both marchers and viewers preparing to watch or participate in the parade had reason to be particularly patriotic. For several months, exacerbated by the explosion of the U.S.S. *Maine* in Havana harbor in February, a conflict with Spain had been brewing. Speculation was growing about the participation of federal troops from Fort Sam Houston and the Belknaps and Zouaves if a conflict erupted. By April 21, anticipation of an incipient war had reached a fever pitch. At around 2 P.M., or just about when the band contest was winding up, all the steam whistles and bells in the city gave a deafening blast to announce that war had indeed begun.[82]

The excited crowd vented their patriotic emotions on the parade, with its large contingent of military and militia. A small impromptu float decorated and sponsored by a Miss Finnegan represented a boat, "handsomely draped in the national colors, and at each corner was a little boy with a shield on which was emblazoned 'On to Cuba.'"[83] A legend later grew up that both the Belknaps and the Zouaves dashed to the post office on Alamo Plaza to enlist in midparade, but this was not the case. They were too busy assisting the police in keeping order among both marchers and spectators and made their commitments afterward.[84]

The Excelsior Guards were not involved in either the parade or the enlistment, though African Americans, as we shall see, would provide the Spanish-American War with heroes. In general, there is little evidence that the African American community at large participated in any significant numbers in the flower battle (in spite of the enigmatic reference by the *Express* in 1891), though theoretically they could have done so. They certainly did not attend any of the associated balls. They held their own celebration to honor San Jacinto Day on the evening of April 21 at Convention Hall. That same evening, the Excelsiors drilled in Alamo Plaza.[85]

The Spanish-American War was short, as wars go—it was over by December, 1898. The following year, a patriotically inspired parade such as the Battle of Flowers had something extra to celebrate—although the ladies still did not want to obscure the original observation of the San Jacinto victory. They started planning their parade in February but from the beginning had to engage in something of a power struggle with the city's omnipresent businessmen. Dangling financial aid once more as an incentive, secretary C. N. Kight of the Businessmen's Club attended the flower battle committee's very first meeting of the year on February 16. Once more he made a pitch to extend the festival for two days and suggested that it was time for the men to intervene in an active way.[86]

The ladies had just approved a charter for the Battle of Flowers organization and were obviously wary of interference from the businessmen. The women organizers had created a successful formula, and the very long 1898 parade had been staged at a cost of seven hundred dollars. Most of the contributions had been in small, individual amounts, some as little as fifty cents. The businessmen were now proposing an ambitious fund-raising enterprise to finance their idea of a two-day festival, which they wanted to name "Spring Carnival." They had appointed jeweler and club member Ben Hammond to act as organizer and liaison to the ladies. Substantial changes were proposed, not so much in the flower parade and battle itself but in its route, which they wanted to extend to encompass more city streets. They also wanted to place a reviewing stand in Main Plaza for Governor Joseph D. Sayers, whom they proposed to invite. Each carriage would stop and be reviewed by him in the course of the procession. For the evening of April 21, they suggested a performance by Carl Beck's Band in Alamo Plaza and also holding the cotton ball again (which returned in 1899 to the auspices of the San Antonio Library and Women's Exchange). On the second day, the men would stage their own patriotic parade with their own groups (including commercial entries). This second procession would end in Alamo Plaza not with a battle but with a tableau of a "living flag," formed by schoolchildren dressed in appropriate colors on a special stand.[87]

It should have been obvious by this time that the ladies, neither weak nor malleable creatures, would not allow the men to call the shots. Mrs. Ogden, Mrs. Hertzberg, Mrs. Wilson, Mrs. W. P. Baugh, and the other organizers insisted on an autonomous flower parade. With charm and steely resolve, they relegated the men to their side of the fence and graciously gave them a second day for their festivities. The women then proceeded to plan their procession as they had done in former years, still inviting anyone who would decorate a vehicle to participate.

Following what was now a tradition, bicycles, carriages, donkeys, equestrians, and the fire department would all be there. But even as traditional components and identity were guarded, the parade continued to grow. In composition, it was becoming more and more like other festival processions of the time in San Antonio. This can be seen in the final announced parade order. As a tribute to the Spanish-American War, local veterans of the Red Cross Hospital Corps, both male and female, marched, along with the Sixth Infantry Band, with the regimental officers and regulars of its Third Battalion. The Belknap Rifles and the Zouaves were included, fresh from mustering out of the army.[88] Boys from the West Texas Military Academy and the more recently established Peacock Military Academy participated; the latter also furnished their own float and their own pony, donkey, and bicycle brigades. One hundred orphans from Saint John's Orphanage carried American flags, the United Commercial Travelers (another "drummers" group, which was having a convention in the city) walked with "flower grips" in hand, and assorted fraternal organizations complemented the other contingents. Official carriages containing the Battle of Flowers officers and the surviving San Jacinto veterans were to be expected. Added to these were carriages with city and county officials (including Mayor E. Marshall Hicks) and a carriage holding Confederate veterans. There were three other bands besides Carl Beck's and the Sixth Infantry's, including the Hallettsville Silver Cornet Band, but no band contest was held.[89]

In spite of all this added volume, the parade was still loved and applauded for its traditionally adorned vehicles and animals, the best of which received donated prizes. The *San Antonio Express,* as usual, hyperbolically hailed it as "A

Chapa and Dreiss's "Battleship Texas" float, Battle of Flowers parade, 1899. The building above the wagon is not part of the float. The personnel includes Mr. and Mrs. F. A. Chapa, Mr. and Mrs. L. Dreiss, Mrs. Erma Elmendorf, Mrs. Regina Beckmann, Mrs. Emelia Baetz, Mr. Samuel E. Blaze, and Mr. Antonio Flores Rivas, Jr. *Courtesy San Antonio Conservation Society*

Dream of Beauty."[90] One commercially sponsored float was featured, but it was of a patriotic and nonadvertising nature. This was the "Battleship Texas," sponsored by the firm of Chapa and Dreiss. Members of both families and employees of the business stood on board. This float was very much in the spirit of the Battle of Flowers tradition. It was homemade: waves were painted around its skirt, and the ship itself was adorned with greens and bristling with several small cannons and one large one, out of which was shot a white dove as the float passed the post office.[91]

Even a cold front arriving precipitously, with a drop in temperature and clouds of dust, did not dim the enthusiasm of the spectators or the participants.

Now that the streets were paved, adverse weather was just an annoyance, no longer an insurmountable problem.

THE MEN'S VERSION: THE 1899 "PATRIOTIC PARADE"

While the ladies went about their preparations, the Businessmen's Club was occupied with its own plans. Governor Sayers had accepted their invitation to visit the festival, and the gentlemen planned a formal reception for him at noon on April 21.

The men's "patriotic parade" on April 22 was organized into three divisions. The first was completely military in nature. The Red Cross and the Sixth Infantry marched again, the latter enriched by three additional companies, making a total of twelve hundred men (the Red Cross women were thus rendered inconspicuous). Also present were 125 members of Light Battery K. But the real hit of this division was the Tenth Cavalry, with its band. The Tenth Cavalry, composed of African American men, had become famous as "the black demons of San Juan Hill, rescuers of the Rough Riders" in the late war.[92] If the parade couldn't have the beloved Rough Riders, whom Theodore Roosevelt had personally trained in San Antonio, they could have the Riders' saviors.[93] This marked the first and only time that an African American contingent appeared in a nineteenth-century Anglo-American parade in the city as an invited entity, aside from Reconstruction and Knights of Labor–dominated processions.

The second division had more repeats from the parade of the day before. It included the fire department (in undecorated vehicles), Carl Beck's Band, the Hallettsville Band, city and county officials in carriages, and the traveling salesmen and fraternal organizations previously seen.

The businessmen considered the third division to be their own best feature. It consisted of various "Karnival Krew Klubs."[94] These were social organizations of gentlemen from both San Antonio and outlying towns who had taken responsibility for providing special allegorical floats, which were accompanied by their marching members. These associations were loosely based on the carnival organizations of New Orleans's Mardi Gras, in that they sponsored processional events and marched as well; however, the link existed more in name than in fact.

Four related allegorical floats were sponsored by the Krews under the title "Our New Citizens." These celebrated America's conquests from Spain (though with some liberties). Each showed a battleship, and each featured young people representing the appropriate countries. The *Oregon* came first, replete with engineers, stokers, and an allegory of "Hawaii," with an African American girl holding a Hawaiian flag. Second was the *Olympia,* "Dewey's Flagship." It carried another African American child representing the Philippines, bearing Aguinando's battle flag. The third, according to the *San Antonio Express,* was "an exact counterpart of the 'Texas,' the battleship which figures so prominently in the Battle of Santiago." The 'Texas' represented 'Cuba,' with a Mexican girl who supported a large Cuban flag. This battleship, like the others, was a dull lead color, as she appeared during the war." Last came the *Gloucester,* representing Puerto Rico, on which a Mexican child waved the Stars and Stripes.[95]

The liberties taken were rather broad. Obviously, Hawaii was not a spoil of the Spanish-American War but had been appropriated as a U.S. territory in 1898. The *Gloucester,* Morgan's converted yacht, was never a proper battleship, as were the others. The "exotic" nature of these conquests was represented to the public by children from non-European ethnic groups. Thus, "Hawaii" and the "Philippines" were both African American girls, while "Puerto Rico" and "Cuba" were played by Mexican Americans. All four of these entries were ambitious by San Antonio standards, if somewhat inaccurate. The only problem with these floats was that all but the unassuming "Gloucester" broke axles on the uneven paving or streetcar tracks before the parade started, thus never appearing in the procession; the mesquite block pavement, which had seemed like such an innovation a decade earlier, was proving a problem.

The Krew members who were to march as escorts to these floats were dressed to represent "Uncle Sam and All Nation's Band," a humorous comment on the "all nations" theme. Their number included the likes of Uncle Sam, Cuban Bugler, Jewish Horn, German Horn, French Horn, Chinese Cymbals, Italian Organ Grinder, and Irish, English, and "Negro" Cornets. About their costumes, one can only guess.

Such cultural paragons were preceded by the "Karnes City Hayseed Orkester" and followed by a bevy of commercial floats. All were of the type seen in earlier Volksfest parades, advertising products. The only special patriotic contribution came from Wolfson's—their float represented Havana's Morro Castle fortress, with a Cuban soldier on guard.

The parade route followed a slightly different path from the previous day's parade, beginning at Travis Park rather than near Alamo Plaza, though it did finish up at that plaza after circling the others. There marchers were greeted by six hundred children on the specially constructed grandstand dressed in red, white, or blue, placed to compose the American flag (forty-seven of them carried white stars). Under the direction of Professor Laurence D. Daggett (piano tuner and music teacher), the combined group sang the "Star-Spangled Banner." They also sang other patriotic songs, including the anthem of the Spanish-American War, "Hot Time in the Old Town Tonight."[96] Though the businessmen made much of this event, this was not the first time a "living flag" display had been seen in the city. The year before, a float with children in colors making up the Mexican flag had graced the Diez y Seis procession.[97]

The Businessmen's Club was very happy with their spectacle. Ben Hammond considered his parade "more popularly interesting than the flower fete itself."[98] But that was the insider's view. As the *San Antonio Light* put it the day after the fete, "If the military and living flag features had been cut out, there would have been very little to attract in the parade, aside from the advertising floats and trades displays."[99] The unique spirit that animated the Battle of Flowers was certainly missing, but the men thought that they had done a great job.

THE BATTLE OF FLOWERS: A REPRESENTATIVE SAN ANTONIO PARADE?

No festival in the city of San Antonio would ever be like the flower battle. The sheer beauty and elegance of its decorated vehicles and animals were unique, as was its "floral battle." The spectacle was very much family fare, both in its participants and in its viewing public. It was common to see whole families in the parade in a decorated carriage or simply a carriage filled with children. The later accusations of elitism in this first decade were only partially true (though in the next century elitism would become the norm). The ladies really did want as many people included as possible, citing the parade's homemade decorations as an example that anyone with a cart, a goat, or a donkey and "a few greens" was welcome. The patriotic and fraternal additions were augmentations that brought the components of this parade into San Antonio's traditional mold, but they were not its justification for existence.

There was also an additional appeal to the senses—pleasant smells. Contemporaries who witnessed the battle remarked that "from the scattered flowers on the Plaza of the Alamo a subtle perfume arose which seemed to permeate the city with a magical influence."[100] It was a nice change from manure and other contemporary street smells, to be sure.

Again, the *San Antonio Express* invoked the Mardi Gras and Veiled Prophet parades in comparison. However, such a comparison was even less relevant in the case of the Battle of Flowers than it was in the case of the Volksfests. The grassroots spirit of decoration, the family orientation of the parade, and the featuring of ladies as both stars and planners were different in essence from the spectacles of New Orleans and Saint Louis. Only the parade's success as a genuine yearly tradition that attracted an increasing number of out-of-town spectators as well as locals made the Battle of Flowers comparable to the other two processional spectacles.

The advent of the Battle of Flowers occurred in the same decade as the "Anglification" of San Antonio's downtown streets and plazas (as well as its government) was definitively accomplished. A lady in a pastel dress would certainly not have been advised to ride in a delicate phaeton decorated with flowers on the cluttered, unpaved, saloon-filled Main or Military Plazas of the 1870s!

It should be noted that nobody would even have thought of the battle or the parade if Nice had not originated its Carnival flower fete in 1876. As it was, the Battle of Flowers was not the only American festival inspired by the one in France. On January 1, 1890, members of the Valley Hunt Club in Pasadena, California, staged their first Tournament of Roses. This festival too featured a profusion of flower-decorated carriages, and it marked the beginning of a tradition that would eventually lead to a nationally televised annual spectacle.

But although the initial inspiration was the same—as was, perhaps, the superficial appearance of the two parades in their first year—the Battle of Flowers and the Tournament of Roses developed very differently. The urban centers that birthed them were quite distinct, as were the deeper reasons for their founding, even though both attracted numerous tourists. The Tournament of Roses was the idea of a man named Professor Charles F. Holder, who had moved to southern California from New York after the blizzard of 1888 and was amazed to see roses blooming in Pasadena in January. He approached the Valley Hunt Club with the idea of a festival to celebrate California's climate—and to encourage both urban growth and tourism. The club members (particularly Dr. Francis F. Rowland, who had seen the Nice festival) were very enthusiastic about the plan, and the festival was born.[101]

California's festival never staged a flower battle, and its organizers were men, even though the Hunt Club's wives and children rode in decorated carriages and on lavishly decorated horses. There was also no patriotic event underlying the Tournament of Roses; it was purely local civic promotion.

There were other differences. The California parade was immediately associated with sports contests. At first these were footraces. The races were later succeeded by a full-fledged tournament with jousting knights. Eventually, the jousts were replaced by a college football game, which remains to this day the king of New Year's bowl contests. Participating ladies were at first and ever after living decorations in their carriages. They also graced the elaborate floats conceived within a unifying pageant theme that soon became the parade's most prominent feature. Ladies continued to ride with the cavalcade, but a controversy arose about the propriety of their riding astride in split skirts (they were not allowed to do this until 1893). By 1896, surrounding communities were sending floats. From the beginning, as in Nice, the parade entrants made a ruling of fresh flowers only ("roses in January" remained the basic premise). Perhaps the main thing that the two processions had in common was the age-old theme of the coming of spring (which occurred, it seems, four months earlier in Pasadena than in San Antonio).

The development of the two parades and their festivals continued to diverge in the next century. The Tournament of Roses would feature Hollywood stars as the centerpiece of many floats as the movie industry began to thrive in southern California. Huge sums would be spent on fresh flowers to decorate these displays. Commercial floats became commonplace. And the one-two punch of parade and football game would become an institution.

The Battle of Flowers would continue its patriotic association and, if anything, would make it stronger. Although the actual flower battle would not survive very long into the next century, the parade would become the centerpiece of a weeklong city celebration that continues to grow to this day. The flower parade began to have an overall theme and more elaborate floats owing to the increasing popularity of the pageant movement after the turn of the twentieth century, but many floats continued to be designed and decorated by their sponsors. Even though today most of the flowers are artificial, they are still a prominent feature of the parade and decorate antique carriages and automobiles. The floats are still generally noncommercial, those sponsored by businesses expected to conform to a theme and not to overtly hawk their wares. Most importantly, the parade in the twenty-first century is still entirely organized and run by women.

At the end of the nineteenth century, none of this future growth was clear. As a matter of fact, in 1900, Mrs. Ogden announced that she would no longer serve as president (she would die in 1903). No one else wanted to assume the responsibility—except for the members of the Businessmen's Club. This was the opportunity they had been waiting for. Since the ladies would not be staging anything in this April of 1900, they would do so, but the results would be very different.

CHAPTER 8
SPRING CARNIVAL, 1900
"IN CHARGE OF THE BUSINESSMEN'S CLUB"

> We have planned a Street Fair and Plaza Carnival as a new and highly attractive diversion and have spared neither pains or time to insure all attractions and programmes being of a high order, and making the state, especially south and west Texas, familiar with these facts. The evidences are positive that our city will be thronged with people during the carnival covering dates April 16th to 21st inclusive.
> —William H. Aubrey, *San Antonio Light,* April 2, 1900

Euphoric from their perceived success in the patriotic parade on the day following the 1899 Battle of Flowers, the Businessmen's Club decided to expand their role in 1900. By February, they had agreed to use the name Spring Carnival, which they had already tried (and failed) to impose on an expanded festival in 1898.[1] The carnival would cover a six-day period, from April 16 through April 21, with the Battle of Flowers parade as its climax. The ladies would still be responsible for their parade and perhaps a ball to follow, and the businessmen for everything else.[2]

On March 3, Mrs. Ogden handed in her formal resignation as president of the Battle of Flowers executive committee. When two meetings called to reorganize failed to reach a quorum, doubt grew as to whether there would be a flower parade at all. In the end, no one would take charge of the parade, not even the Daughters of the Republic (who might be expected to jump into the breach), so the Battle of Flowers would not be held in 1900.[3]

No longer constrained by feminine decorum, the businessmen rushed ahead with elaborate plans for the weeklong festival. The president of the association, attorney William H. Aubrey, also headed the Spring Carnival executive committee. Aubrey was assisted by several of the other Businessmen's Club directors and officers. Among them were real estate dealer Jay E. Adams (a transplanted New Yorker); Frank Arnold, manager of the Lone Star Brewery; insurance man Thomas L. Conroy; architect Alfred Giles; and C. N. Kight, founder of the club and its secretary. All of them had worked on the previous year's patriotic parade, and all had served on the committee to welcome Governor Sayers before the procession. Jay E. Adams's interest in the seasonal parade was already established, for he had personally sponsored an "All Nations" float in the 1896 Battle of Flowers parade.

These gentlemen were powerful figures in San Antonio's Anglo-American community, and the event would be a totally Anglo-American show. They envisioned a festival that was part San Antonio International Fair, part honky-tonk carnival, part extended convention, and part Mardi Gras pageant and social event.

If there couldn't be a Battle of Flowers, it would be replaced by six parades—one held each day to include different organizations to take advantage of the numerous conventions that had scheduled their meetings in San Antonio that week. The Daughters of the Republic, the Confederate Veterans, and the Grand Army of the Republic were among these groups; they were expected to give the carnival some of the patriotic tone otherwise missing without the flower battle. The businessmen undoubtedly considered other groups scheduled to meet at that time: the conventioneers of the Knights Templar, the Nobles of the Mystic Shrine, and the Women's Relief Group might be called on to participate, but the State Undertakers and Embalmers Association and the National Association of Sanitary Engineers would be less likely prospects, since their organizations had little to do with patriotism.

It was this spirit of eclectic assortment that would characterize the entire Spring Carnival. The basic idea was not only to make the festival last a whole week but to draw all of downtown into it and then attract as many citizens and out-of-towners as possible. The organizers therefore adopted elements from many festival sources. From their own trade fair, they appropriated the idea of a walkway lined with trade booths. For the Spring Carnival, this walkway would be recreated downtown by closing Commerce Street to traffic from Alamo Street to Main Plaza (except for the cross-streets) and setting up the booths there. The booths themselves would be offered to any business that cared to rent them for the week at a modest fee.[4] A festive air would be imparted to the street by spanning it with eight garlanded and illuminated arches, one at each intersection, so that people could enjoy the wares in the evening as well as the day. Aesthetic unification would be achieved by adopting official "carnival colors," dark red, yellow, and blue, and encouraging everyone to decorate stores, booths, and anything else with bunting in those hues, provided by the club.

The businessmen also decided to designate the north end of Main Plaza and the west end of Alamo Plaza as *lugares festivos* (festive places) by building temporary enclosures and filling them with attractions for which admission would be charged.

These were all basically commercial midway acts, hired by Thomas Conroy from the Pan American Carnival Company. The shows in Main Plaza were strictly for men, perhaps because of its past reputation and because it was close to the bordello district now firmly ensconced a few blocks to the west. These included a "wargraph with moving war pictures, Sapho the artist's model, an illusion styled 'Darkness and Dawn'; Happy Holmes' dancing girls in the turtle dance, Sen Sen and Hulahula, labeled 'too warm for the ice box'; Hi Ki, the Filipino wild man; Will Stout, the fat boy and Jennie the double lady."[5] The attractions in Alamo Plaza were more family oriented; they included the "educated horse, Esau, the snake eater, the ossified man, Morris' new show, electrical fountain, incubator with live infants and the electrical theatre."[6]

Perhaps the only feature that the businessmen borrowed from the city's Mexican American heritage (except for the words *lugar festivo* and *alegria*) was one of its least savory legacies. Cockfights, long an underground activity locally, would be publicly staged over the entire week. They would take place at the usually clandestine pit called the Western Star, at the corner of Laredo and West Commerce Streets.[7]

The most glittering feature of the carnival was borrowed from New Orleans's Mardi Gras. The Spring Carnival would feature a public display of royalty, a king who would reign over the festivities for the entire week. He would make his appearance on the first day, ride in a public procession through the city streets, and be crowned in an elaborate ceremony later that evening in Beethoven Hall.

Mention has been made several times in previous chapters of the lack of "royalty" in any of the city's festivals. The exceptions were the historical or mythical figures featured in Volksfest themed floats or in private balls associated with the Battle of Flowers toward the end of the nineteenth century. A precursor of what would become a preoccupation in the twentieth century can be seen in the "queens" featured in Juneteenth parades from 1896 onward. What the Businessmen's Club was proposing for Spring Carnival was, however, something far more elaborate.

San Antonio's carnival king would bear the name King Alegria (King Happiness). In many ways he was based on King Rex of Mardi Gras, who arrived by steamer to lead his own parade.[8] Since the San Antonio River was too narrow to allow a maritime entrance, the planners invented the story that King Alegria would be coming from Mexico by train. This was a bit of a stretch, as he would actually be boarding his railroad car about twenty miles south of San Antonio. The International and Great Northern Railroad, which was also offering special rates to visitors, contributed three railroad cars and an engine for the event.[9] Like that of King Rex, the identity of King Alegria was not kept a secret, as was the identity of Saint Louis's Veiled Prophet, though it was supposedly not revealed until April 16. Thomas Conroy of the Businessmen's Club was chosen for the role. All the cliches of nineteenth-century mock titles for mock royalty were attached to this king. He was "King of Carnival" but was also styled "Prince of Molokai," and his lord high chamberlain (C. N. Kight) carried the title "Ukiah Coto, High Klamath to His Majesty."[10]

What differentiated King Alegria from King Rex was the fact that he arrived accompanied by his queen, who also rode with him in the public procession that followed. At Mardi Gras, women consorts were absent from public display: all female roles in the parades were played by men. Honored ladies reigned exclusively (as they did at the Veiled Prophet celebration in Saint Louis) at the balls that followed. But in San Antonio, women had been participating in parades and on floats since the city's festival parades began. Given the display of feminine elegance and charm in the Battle of Flowers, it would be unthinkable to exclude them here. The lady chosen for the queen's part in Spring Carnival was Lola Kokernot, daughter of a prominent stockman, who had been part of the debutante circuit in the city for the past two years.[11] She would have an entourage of "ladies in waiting" selected from young women of the city's social elite, replete with gentlemen escorts.

Far more pomp was to be attached to the king and queen's arrival and progress than merely their reception at the International and Great Northern depot at 10 A.M on April 16. The planners had originally thought to have a flatcar with an artillery piece on it that would fire a round at intervals as the train approached San Antonio. This proved impractical, and a ten-gun salute (the customary military one for visiting foreign rulers) was scheduled to be fired by Light Battery K of Fort Sam Houston as "their majesties" descended from the train at the depot.

Waiting for them would be a series of open carriages draped (as was the train) in carnival colors. There were also dignitaries: Mayor Hicks and Governor Sayers, a military escort led by General McKibbin of Fort Sam Houston, and (as always) the Belknap Rifles and Carl Beck's Band. The procession would wind from the depot along downtown streets, circling Main and Military Plazas, and would finish in Alamo Plaza, where the mayor would give a short welcoming speech and deliver the keys of the city ("an elaborate affair, handsomely decorated in carnival colors") to their majesties.[12] This would take place on the balcony of the San Antonio Club, above the Opera House.

Later that same evening the Grand Carnival Ball would be held in Beethoven Hall. The businessmen put the ball into the hands of their wives. Many of them had served on Battle of Flowers committees and were experienced at planning fancy fetes.[13] Atlee B. Ayers, the architect responsible for the triumphal arch for the Battle of Flowers, was commissioned to design the double throne for the king and queen.

The royal parade was the first of the six that the Businessmen's Club planned for Spring Carnival week. For April 17, they announced an orphans' and schoolchildren's parade to Beethoven Hall. There the children would view a play called *Nan the Mascotte*. On April 18, there would be a morning parade of about seven hundred visiting and local members of the fraternal order of Knights Templar. The following day would have two processions, one of fraternal orders in the morning and a trades-display parade (with commercial floats and advertising wagons) in the afternoon. That same evening, the planners scheduled a military ball. April 20 would bring the Confederate veterans and the Grand Army of the Republic; in the evening, there would be a masked ball with the king and queen presiding. Finally, April 21 would feature a patriotic parade at 5 P.M. organized by Texas veterans and the Daughters of the Republic, which would substitute for the Battle of Flowers. This final parade would culminate, as had the patriotic parade the year before, with the "living flag" in Alamo Plaza, again organized and staged by Professor Daggett. Each day of the carnival would feature band concerts in Alamo or Main Plaza—or sometimes in both. And of course, the beautifully lit Commerce Street and the *lugares festivos* would give visitors and citizens alike something to occupy themselves with between these activities. Conspicuously missing were the orations, athletic contests, and other community-sponsored recreational pastimes that characterized the city's ethnic and patriotic festivals of the era; for Spring Carnival, it seems, there was no room for amateurs.

The businessmen, ever-conscious of tourism as their Volksfest predecessors had been, had organized a veritable visitor's bureau, which would attempt to match out-of-town attendees with available hotel and boardinghouse space. Bureau kiosks were to be placed at the various train depots. From these, the travelers would be directed to the most convenient streetcars to reach their lodgings.[14]

It all sounded marvelous. A full week of parades, dances, concerts, and other activities—and the lining of the businessmen's pockets via booth and store sales and a cut of the receipts of the *lugares festivos*—not to mention a great deal of publicity for San Antonio as the most important metropolis in Texas at that time. But, much like Edgar Schramm and his committee staging the 1891 Volksfest, the planners suffered from an attack of hubris. The reality was that some things worked out well, and others didn't.

The *Light* and the *Express,* posters, and a great deal of talk and publicity had been touting the carnival for months. But on its first day, April 16, everything was not quite ready. The sideshow acts for the *lugares festivos* had not yet arrived, nor were all the Commerce Street booths finished; those that were finished were promptly plastered with advertisements and bills rather than carnival colors. It would take another day before these defacements could be removed and all the booths be in full operation. There had already been a problem with the installation of the arches. Each was designed to have a hanging emblem at its center: stars, crescent moons, globes, shields. Each was to be draped in evergreens and moss, and each featured between three and five hundred incandescent bulbs on arch and emblem. On the night of April 15, the hanging globe on the arch at Commerce and Navarro Streets caught fire; the arch and over thirty bulbs were destroyed. Fortunately, it could be reconstructed before opening night.[15] By the second evening, when all the lights were on and all the bunting-draped booths were open, Commerce Street was truly transformed. Visitors could stroll along under the lights; look at and purchase wares from the booths; and buy such goodies as popcorn, Mexican dishes, ice cream, orange- and lemonade, and "California chewing candy."

The king and queen arrived on schedule, to be greeted by the mayor, Governor Sayers, and General McKibbin. Unfortunately, the need for artillery at the post for other activities reduced the ten-gun salute to two guns. Otherwise, the arrival, procession, and speeches of welcome went without a hitch.

The ball that evening had the social reporters in ecstasy. Trust the ladies to manage a good show. Beethoven Hall was swathed in evergreens and carnival bunting and gleamed with a large quantity of electric lights, many of them, particularly around the stage, giving a peacock effect of green and blue. The king and queen's architect-designed throne was surmounted by a red canopy adorned with lights, a red cloth behind them. Admission to the ball was by ticket, and the guest list appears to have been exclusive (this would not be the case for the masked and military balls to be held later). The general public could, however, purchase tickets to look on for a modest fee, which would restrict them to the hall's balcony.[16]

When the ball-goers arrived, the stage of Beethoven Hall was concealed by

Commerce Street with illuminated arches. These are actually from a later incarnation of Spring Carnival in the early twentieth century. The 1900 arches were quite a bit more elaborate. *Courtesy U.T. Institute of Texan Cultures*

King Alegria, his queen, and their court, Beethoven Hall, April 16, 1900. Queen Lola Kokernot appears to be rather bored; King Thomas Conroy looks more *incómodo* than *alegre*. *Courtesy U.T. Institute of Texan Cultures, Ann Russell*

its curtain. At a given signal, it parted to reveal the enthroned king and queen, flanked by twenty-eight pairs of ladies and their escorts. The ladies were dressed in white, though not identical, gowns. The king and queen wore sumptuous raiment worthy of the finest Volksfest actors.[17]

The activity on Commerce Street and the events of the first day proved to be Spring Carnival's high point. The special railroad rates did not go into effect until April 17, so the first night most of the people on the streets and viewing the ball were local. Even though everything was not yet operational, the carnival received a good response. San Antonians loved the lights, the bunting and festoons, and what goods were available. When the out-of-towners did come, they too enjoyed Commerce Street and the grotesque novelties of the *lugares festivos*, available for a modest admission fee.[18]

But by the second day, things were not quite so smooth, particularly in the parade department.[19] The superintendent of public schools refused to declare a school holiday on April 17, so only the orphans (Catholics, in blue uniforms, and Protestants—but no African Americans) marched in a very small parade and got to see the entertainment. Governor Sayers, who was supposed to participate in additional ceremonies that day, had to return to Austin, so these ceremonies were canceled. On the other hand, business boomed on Commerce Street and in the *lugares* and only stopped when the lights were turned off at midnight.

On April 18, it rained. The Knights Templars valiantly paraded, but there weren't many people watching them, and a scheduled light artillery drill at Fort Sam Houston was cancelled because of the inclement weather. The rain also faded the carnival bunting and other booth adornments, making the street decorations of the second half of the week less flamboyant than in the first half. Things were somewhat better on April 19, when the weather cleared, but the grand morning parade of the numerous fraternal organizations of the city failed to materialize. In the end, only the Woodmen of the World, the fire department, and Carl Beck's Band appeared. The biggest crowd of the week did attend the afternoon trades parade, but the large contingent of trade-union members invited to march did not show up, as their bosses declined to give them the day off. There were a few union floats, showing members at their trades, but several were dogged by accidents. The cooks' and waiters' float broke an axle before the parade and did not participate; the Sunset Railroad float lost a wheel halfway through; and the boiler on the blacksmiths' float blew up, though no one was injured and it managed to finish the parade. The military ball that night boasted an encore of the king and queen's tableau.

The most successful parade in terms of representation was the Confederate veterans and Grand Army of the Republic procession on April 20. Most of the members in town for the convention marched. In addition, the San Antonio Zouaves under their captain, Eugene Hernandez, performed a thrilling drill in Alamo Plaza. The king and queen made one last appearance at the masked ball in the evening. By this point, the *lugares festivos* had run out of paying customers, so they opened their displays for free.

Perhaps most disappointing of all was the parade that occurred on what should have been the Battle of Flowers day. The veterans opted out of the procession, as did the Daughters of the Republic. The Daughters were content to present retired General Carlos Bee, who delivered an oration after the parade in Alamo Plaza and was given a bouquet. The procession ended up being mostly recycled trades-display floats, hurriedly reassembled for the occasion, and a small contingent of decorated bicycles and donkeys. The only redeeming feature was the repeat of the "living flag."

The biggest crowds of the carnival had come in for the parade of April 21 and were bitterly disappointed. They expected flowers and pageantry and got adver-

The fallen arch with light-studded globe at Commerce and Navarro Streets, after the vicious early-morning storm, May 4, 1900. *Courtesy U.T. Institute of Texan Cultures,* San Antonio Light *Collection*

tisements instead. Other Texas cities, which had looked on enviously at San Antonio's yearly parade and "battle," were glad to take it over. Thus, San Antonio's loss was Fort Worth's gain in 1900. They staged a flower battle that year with great success.

In the end, people got tired of the carnival. It was too much of a good thing and too much of the *same* thing. Local viewers became bored with so many parades, and none of these processions had the visual elegance of the Battle of Flowers. How many times could one see a sideshow or shop at the Commerce Street booths? If the businessmen had planned a three-day festival, like the Volksfest and Diez y Seis organizers did, perhaps the glow would not have worn off. Perhaps, too, without the taste of the Battle of Flowers women, the spectacles were similar to the point of monotony. And the easy interchange among San Antonio's various ethnic and cultural factions was conspicuously missing.[20] Was this deliberate discrimination, or were the businessmen so insensitive that they let the philosophy of manifest destiny get the best of them? By the end of the festival, order began to break down as well. It seems that the police had also become tired of the crowds and the incessant street noise: there were incidents of stabbing and a number of pickpockets at work.

The only things that were generally agreed to have been an unqualified success were the Commerce Street arches. An editorial in the *San Antonio Express* urged the city to keep them up for a while—perhaps leaving them up permanently and illuminating them every time there was a convention, another festival, or some similar event.[21] They did remain up, but only for a little over two weeks. On May 7, 1900, an unusually severe storm struck the city at 4:00 A.M., knocked down the capstone of the Alamo Fire Insurance Building, and completely demolished the San Antonio Loan and Trust Company, then under construction at the corner of Commerce and Navarro Streets. When the building fell, so did the arch over the intersection. For safety's sake, the other arches were removed shortly afterward. However, the idea of an illuminated arch was successful enough that more of them—and more elaborate lighting of not only the streets but also public buildings—would become de rigueur for the city's subsequent festivals.

The weeklong concept of Spring Carnival may not have been a total success in 1900, but it became the seed from which the far more varied Fiesta San Jacinto grew in subsequent years. Mercifully, the Battle of Flowers would return in the new century as the festival's centerpiece, though the role of its female organizers was temporarily strictly limited by overall businessman control. This by-now-traditional event would not only provide the element of good taste, conspicuously missing from the 1900 carnival, but would also return a patriotic focus to the event, and the ladies would recover full sovereignty over their contribution. Unfortunately, however, the prevailing Anglo-American tone of Spring Carnival would dominate the entire festival for decades to come.

EPILOGUE
SAN ANTONIO
ON PARADE

Through the later nineteenth century, the parades and festivals of San Antonio treated here were certainly in the American spirit of their times; the shape, history, and cultural demographics of this particular city gave them their own unique, regional character. Much of this was due to the particular makeup of immigrants who chose to settle in the city. Immigration was still welcomed in the United States in the decades after the Civil War. The skills of both workers and farmers were still very much needed, and confidence in immigrants' adaptability to U.S. culture was high.[1] In South Texas, part of the ethnic mix was present long before the state joined the Union. There had been a cultural interchange between Mexican and Anglo-American settlers since the days of Mexican republican rule. The proximity to Mexico, even after Texas became part of the United States, would always be a vital element in San Antonio's life and culture—far more so than Europe, which was so much further away.[2] The arrival of German immigrants by the end of the 1840s added a new ingredient, which was welcomed in this sparsely populated region. The other European groups that arrived were considerably smaller, as were the free post–Civil War African Americans. All, however, enriched the local culture in greater or lesser degrees.

San Antonio in the second half of the nineteenth century was no idealistic Emerald City, where everyone lived in blissful harmony. The frontier mentality was not long distant, and military and "cowboy" culture had a pronounced tradition of rowdiness. This was certainly reflected during the 1870s and 1880s in the public life around Main and Military Plazas and subsequently further west, toward San Pedro Creek, as these plazas became more genteel. Missing was organized conflict along ethnic lines, such as the gangs that operated in New York City and other American cities during this era. Part of the reason for this was that there was no big influx of any single immigrant group in San Antonio during the post–Civil War period, other than the Anglo-Americans. Though Anglo-American prejudices would eventually lead to greater social inequalities in the twentieth century, they were not yet so overt in the nineteenth (except in the case of African Americans). It was only with the large flood of immigrants and refugees due to the upheavals in Mexico after 1910 that the dynamics would change. At that point the city's resident Anglo-Americans would feel threatened enough to more rigidly enforce their sense of cultural superiority.[3]

In contrast, nineteenth-century San Antonians of varying ethnic origins were not particularly interested in imposing their mother culture on nongroup citizens. German Americans openly promoted their own cultural institutions, whether *vereine* or choirs, but did not proselytize beyond their immediate community— and indeed, even the diverse *vereine* represented distinct subgroups within their own social fabric. Mexican Americans blithely preserved their own customs in a similar way. Crossovers between ethnic groups were not uncommon, particularly among Catholic residents. African Americans, excluded by other groups, created their own culture and values, at this point and in this particular city firmly rooted in the Anglo-American traditions that had been forced on them decades or even centuries before. Though they certainly suffered discrimination, the overt hostility that resulted in lynchings in other Texas towns was conspicuously absent in San Antonio.

In late nineteenth-century San Antonio, people of various ethnic origins thus managed to live side by side with relatively little conflict. Manifest destiny was looming on the horizon but had not as yet completely triumphed. There was still enough space for all, though some had better choices of where and how to live than others. In any case, whatever tensions or inequalities that did exist on a day-to-day level were put aside on festival days, when the particular group sponsoring the celebration had control of the downtown streets of the parade route and of the festival venue afterward. The sponsors displayed their pride in their ethnicity and their own social institutions in the parades they staged. At the park venues, besides celebrating among themselves, they served as hosts to the rest of the community and allowed outsiders to see, hear, and taste what they had preserved from their "old-country" way of life. But underneath every festival was a basically American organization, reflecting the sponsors' pride as citizens of their adopted land.

There were also early and continuing crossovers among various individuals within festival host groups. Thus we find that Tejano-descended Antonio P. Rivas, a pillar of the Mexican American community, also was a member of the mostly German volunteer Fire Company 1 and participated in the German American Volksfests. Fortunato Villareal had an even wider involvement. He was a member of the Turnverein Hook and Ladder Company and the Casino Club and therefore a Volksfest luminary (he even played Beowulf in the parade-pageant of 1891). Like Rivas, he was involved in the Mexican Social Club, becoming its president in 1899, and supervised fireworks for the Diez y Seis celebration of 1892. But he was also grand marshal for the 1892 Columbus Day parade, marshal in various Battle of Flowers parades, and active in planning Spring Carnival in 1900.

Villareal was an extremely eclectic case, apparently moving easily through everyone's social circles. Many, however, spanned Mexican American and Anglo-American social spectra via intermarriage. This permitted them membership in social clubs of both groups and therefore legitimate participation in both groups' festivals, whether as orators, marchers, or marshals. Edward Froboese Jr., whose German-born father had married a Tejana, is a good example. He belonged to both the Mexican Social and Casino Clubs and participated over the years in Diez y Seis, Columbus Day, and the Battle of Flowers. In addition, he was one of the "Indians" who attacked the "immigrant wagon" during the 1892 Volksfest parade.

Another way of spanning several of the groups was through politics. Here, Bryan Callaghan Jr. provides the best-known example (though he also qualified through two generations of intermarriage). As mayor of many terms, Callaghan was careful to court everyone and to ride in everyone's processions (except Juneteenth). But he also played active committee roles across the board, serving as organizer of receptions for several festivals and on the Committee on [Police] Protection for the Battle of Flowers. Juan T. Cardenas, though less "official" as far as political office holding went, managed a similar diversity of participation, including serving a turn as a marshal in the Battle of Flowers parade. Oscar Bergstrom, of German parentage, was a lawyer and politician and was much sought after as an English-language orator for the Fourth of July and Columbus Day. At various other times, he marched as a marshal for the Sociedad Mutualista Mexicana in the Diez y Seis parades of 1883 and 1884, was an assistant marshal for the 1883 Volksfest procession, and served on the Committee on Plazas for the Battle of Flowers in 1892.

Finally, some groups transcended nationality altogether and appeared in any parade that needed to fill space. Good examples were Carl Beck's "Military" Band and the Belknap Rifles, who seem to have had appropriate uniforms for any occasion

German Americans and Anglo-Americans perhaps had the most in common, though the German Americans spent a lot of energy in trying to preserve the best of their home culture within the American framework. But, though the

Fortunato Villareal, Hugo and Schmeltzer salesman, Turnverein Hook and Ladder Company member, Mexican American Social Club member, and festival bon vivant. *Courtesy Daughters of the Republic of Texas Library*

vereine were as German American as the *mutualistas* were Mexican American, the "German" Casino Club and the "Anglo" San Antonio Club boasted many of the same members from among the city's professional and business elites.

Only the African Americans remained apart, as they did all over America. Their presence in Fourth of July parades during Reconstruction was considered an affront by Anglo-Americans of Confederate ancestry. The same was felt, but to a lesser extent, about the African American workers' presence in the Knights of Labor–dominated Diez y Seis parade of 1886. Fire Company 3 did march in various Fourth of July parades well into the 1880s, but it did not appear every year. When African Americans did grace floats, such as in the 1883 and 1892 Volksfests and in the 1898 patriotic parade's battleship floats, they portrayed either demeaning stereotypes (such as representatives of "Cotton Culture" in 1883) or exotic allegories. The only exception to this attitude was the appearance of the Tenth Cavalry in the 1898 patriotic parade, their presence legitimized by their rescue of the Rough Riders.

The parade route used by all groups remained nearly the same throughout the whole period, including, for the most part, all three downtown plazas. Subtle variations depended on the aims of individual groups—such as the short route of the 1882 Volksfest from Alamo Plaza to Wolfram's Central Gardens; or the desire for Diez y Seis paraders to keep marching all the way to San Pedro Springs Park, even after the introduction of streetcars, because the procession was a part of the lead-in to the *grito* ceremony. In general, however, as the century wore on, the route of all holiday processions was similar. The most noticeable change was in the starting point of each group's parade as ethnic groups coalesced more into individual neighborhoods. Thus, by the late 1890s, Diez y Seis marchers tended to muster west of San Pedro Creek, at Milam Square; Juneteenth gathered its participants at East Commerce and Chestnut Streets; and Battle of Flowers participants prepared themselves just north of Alamo Plaza on Avenue D.

The host group was always honored for its festival. Following a general trend in the nineteenth century, speeches in several languages were not only tolerated but applauded; it was a reaffirmation of both culture of origin and the transition of individuals to English-speaking Americans. Though most of the festivals boasted food booths, orations, dances, and fireworks, the ethnic distinctions within these activities were relished by hosts and visitors alike. But here too was a certain amount of "melting pot" crossover, particularly of the culinary sort. Good examples are Madame Candelaria's Mexican food stand among the sausages and beer at one of the Volksfests and the diversity of food offerings on Commerce

Street during Spring Carnival.[4] Similar crossovers were sometimes also found in festival music: Batista's Mexican Military Band cheerfully played an entire program of John Philip Sousa's music following the Battle of Flowers parade in 1896.[5]

Just about every group adopted some symbols of Texas heritage that would seem inappropriate to later generations. Cowboys (real or impersonated) and "Indians" (always impersonated) rode in all festival parades with the exception of Juneteenth, and it is quite possible that some authentic African American cowboys participated in the latter. The Alamo became enough of an icon that not only was it patriotically decorated for the Battle of Flowers but Alamo heroes and Santa Anna's surrender to Sam Houston graced floats in two separate Volksfest parades. The scene of the battle of the Alamo also turned up in a Columbus Day fireworks display.

The festivals were predominantly wholesome and family oriented, whether held in the morning, afternoon, or evening. Though Anglo-Americans prejudicially expected disorder to occur among African Americans and lower-class Mexican Americans, this apparently was never the case at any Juneteenth or Diez y Seis celebrations of the nineteenth century. The Anglo-American newspapers constantly commented (with apparent surprise) on the decorum at these festivals. Indeed, the main example of disorder in this period was in the floral battle of the first Battle of Flowers parade—exactly where it was least anticipated.

For the parade watchers, and for those outside of the host group who attended the park festivities, the experience was universal. Anyone could be on the downtown streets to watch a parade (contemporary photographs reveal African American observers at white parades and vice versa). Anyone could come to the parks. The similarity of organization across the board of both parade and festival provided a comfortable note, even if the external trappings were regarded as exotic. During the 1860s and up to 1877, San Antonio was still an isolated place. Anybody's festival was an anticipated event within limited urban social options, and most of the city's population would turn out, along with contingents from neighboring towns who cared to brave the roads.

On occasion some external pressure could be brought to bear on an individual festival to temporarily change its face: the presence of the Knights of Labor and that organization's agenda in their parade during the 1886 Diez y Seis festival comes to mind, as does the T.P.A. convention of 1895, which changed the date of that year's Battle of Flowers parade. But these were one-shot events, and they did not permanently affect the pattern of festivities in San Antonio during this period.

As the city grew and became better connected to the outside world via the railroads, the festival crowds got bigger. Part of this was due to the increase in population (though less of the city's total population might actually witness a parade). But part was due as well to San Antonio's self-awareness as a tourist destination. With the railroads came special promotional rates to and from other cities to draw in the crowds. Festival organizers often sent out announcements and posters to neighboring towns (and, in the case of the Battle of Flowers, to every state's government) to encourage more visitors.

Experiencing a parade in 1866 was very different from doing so in 1898. Right after the Civil War, the city's narrow streets and one- to two-story buildings were on a very human scale. There were no obstructions from electric or streetcar overhead wires. The parades themselves were not very long and, except for uniforms and band music, not overwhelmingly spectacular. What floats there were had a distinctly homemade air. Spectators and marchers existed in close proximity to each other, except, perhaps, in the plazas. Everyone was pretty much at the same eye level; even second-story or rooftop spectators were not that far away. And the smallness of the population made it quite possible for the spectators to personally know most of the marchers.

By the end of the century, with the advent of taller buildings, paved streets, and many-barred utility poles, perceptions would have been quite different. Watchers packed all available floors, so some would have had truly bird's-eye views. Often the streets were so densely packed that those in the rear could see very little, if anything at all. The parades were of much greater length, often with multiple divisions, each containing a band. There were more floats, of a somewhat more sophisticated nature. Marchers wore a diversity of uniforms and insignia. The greater number of spectators and participants from outside the city (particularly visiting conventioneers) made personal acquaintance between marchers and viewers less likely. All in all, though the streets were still narrow, the parades would have presented a grander but more remote spectacle by the end of the century.

With this urban and population growth, the question arises as to whether San Antonio's parades and festivals themselves became increasingly sophisticated as the century wore on, as did the ever more spectacular processions that marked the Mardi Gras and Veiled Prophet celebrations in New Orleans and Saint Louis. After all, both the Volksfest and Battle of Flowers organizers constantly made reference to these large and famous festivals as benchmarks to which they aspired.

The answer is both yes and no. Certainly, as San Antonio grew, so did its festivals. This is seen not only superficially, in the length of its parades, but in the planning and execution of both the parades and their attached festivals. With the exception of the German American Volksfests, most of the earliest parades of each group, from the Fourth of July to the Battle of Flowers, were thrown together with a sort of "we can put on a show" mentality. Most were organized on relatively short notice by a fairly small group of people, whether a newly formed *mutualista* society or a group of middle-class friends. The more they grew in subsequent years, the more advance planning and bureaucratic committees were necessitated.

Some of the local variations within the general festival model depended on the social and cultural customs of the sponsoring group. Therefore, the Battle of Flowers grew partially from the custom of Anglo-American upper-middle-class women riding through the city in the late afternoons. The Volksfests drew their propensity for pageant floats from the German Americans' own literary traditions and their general love of knowledge.

Some festivals had rather sporadic beginnings, false starts, and strange metamorphoses. The Fourth of July, in its many guises, is a good example of this. Some also survived and even thrived in spite of schism and rivalry, such as Diez y Seis and Juneteenth. Others, like Columbus Day and the Volksfests, flowered but did not outlast the century. Nineteenth-century Columbus Day parades were eventually discontinued because San Antonio's Italian American population proved too small to sustain them. The Volksfests died because the German American population was gradually losing its identity in the greater Anglo-American melting pot and because their pageants were too ambitious for their time and place. Additionally, the German Americans' insistence on charging admission fees led to a certain amount of resentment among the population at large.

All in all, the most successful festivals and parades started small and grew within their means. Perhaps the best example is the Battle of Flowers, which throughout the 1890s was staged on a shoestring budget (never over seven hundred dollars). The fete only got into trouble (temporarily) when an exterior group of businessmen tried to redefine its character, first by the postponement of 1895 and later by Spring Carnival, when the flower battle did not occur at all. The Battle of Flowers would survive because it would resume after 1900 with its scope largely intact and would only gradually grow and change in character as the city did.

The other two festivals that survived into the twentieth century, Diez y Seis and Juneteenth, did so partially because, like the Battle of Flowers, they were identified with patriotic events. The impetus for the former two—real commemorations of liberty—was probably more legitimate than the impetus for the latter, which was after all the excuse for a festival rather than its cause. But San

Jacinto Day received its legitimization with the definitive canonization of the Alamo by the increasingly dominant Anglo-American elite after 1900.

The unifying American character of all the parades was helped along by a few groups who participated in all of them. Military units from the local army post marched at one time or another in every group's parade. The various fire companies, whether volunteer or professional, participated, either decorated or undecorated depending on the occasion. Politicians were ever ready to advertise themselves, both in the parades and as orators. And what would a parade be without at least one band?

As fraternal organizations proliferated during the late nineteenth century, more and more of them joined the processions. These included the mutual aid societies and labor groups as well as fraternities such as the Odd Fellows (both black and white), the Woodmen of the World, the Knights of Pythias, and the Sons of Hermann. Ladies' auxiliaries, such as the Daughters of Ruth, and coed ones, like the Sociedad Benito Juarez de Señoras y Señoritas and the Society of the Knights and Ladies of Honor, provided some of the earliest female marchers. Indeed, San Antonio's featuring of women in various parades far exceeded their participation in Mardi Gras or in the all-male Veiled Prophet processions. The ladies played allegorical roles on carriages and floats as early as the 1860s, assumed all the women's roles on the Volksfest pageant floats, and (of course) dominated the Battle of Flowers. Conspicuously missing were suffragettes or other early feminists in any of the processions. San Antonio's women, in whatever capacity, kept their festive participation within accepted social conventions of their place and time.

Over time, the parades were certainly longer and had an ever increasing range of participants. But whether they grew more visually sophisticated is another matter. With the exception of the Volksfests, most of the allegorical entries in the processions remained pretty much the same during the entire last third of the nineteenth century. "Columbia," "Mexico," "Germania"or the "Goddess of Liberty," and women representing the various states of the union repeatedly graced many different festival parades. Equally popular were members of both sexes as "all nations," whether comic or ornamental.[6] Floats with patriotic themes, whether Columbus's ship or the U.S. Navy's, were frequently included. So were floats of a modest nature with a nominal theme, such as baseball and football teams riding on flatbeds, children in a bathtub, or little girls dressed as flowers on flower-decorated tallyhos.

More serious and ambitious historical pageant-type floats found their apex in the Volksfest processions and in the less elaborate 1886 Junta Patriótica parade celebrating Mexican Independence. But such floats were also to be found in single entries that resonated enough to be recycled in succeeding years, such as Juneteenth's antebellum slave cabin and Columbus's ship in the Columbus Day festival. In general, though, these types of representations were the exception rather than the rule. It appears that excess sophistication in float themes did not appeal to San Antonians at this time. The costly 1891 German American pageant, with its elaborate ancient and literary mythology, was remembered and remarked upon for its glamour rather than its content. Indeed, it appears that unsubtle, glittery, and easily identifiable symbols had the greatest success, whether displayed by brightly dressed bands; uniformed volunteer firemen; military or militia companies in their dress uniforms; decorated fire engines and bicycles; or insignias worn or carried by *mutualistas, vereine* or fraternal orders. By the last years of the century, while the Veiled Prophet, Mardi Gras, and Tournament of Roses parades grew ever more expensive, overdecorated and overproduced, San Antonio's viewers enthusiastically cheered the likes of Chapa and Dreiss's clearly homemade "Battleship Texas."

It is also interesting to note that commercial entries in most San Antonio parades of the era were relatively inconspicuous. Trades floats did participate in some of the Volksfest processions, particularly the early day and torchlight parades, but the Battle of Flowers ladies fought a constant battle against the Businessmen's Club's desire to include them in the flower procession. Indeed, the trades-display element was pretty much played down until the 1900 Spring Carnival, which was, in just about every way, planned with commerce in mind. In general, however, none of the other late nineteenth-century festivals we have discussed was, in its spectacles or events, overtly driven by commerce. The primary goals were community values, both ethnic and American cultural pride, grass-roots participation, and entertainment for the host community and the greater population. This was true even though organizers had the secondary goal of luring out-of-towners to gather for the occasion and shop in the city's emporia, enrich the pockets of its hoteliers and boardinghouse proprietors, and buy food and drink at the festival booths. By this time, San Antonio was already developing into an attractive tourist center and gearing up its economy to cater to out-of-town visitors.

The park festivals, whether at San Pedro Springs, Riverside Park, or a large beer garden, remained remarkably constant throughout the later nineteenth century. Orations continued to be the introductory cornerstone of each event. Ethnic food only increased in variety and elaboration. Dances, sports, and fireworks, in varying proportions, made up the other events of the day. Generally, the initial one-day events grew to two or three days as the century wore on.

Even the Battle of Flowers, planned as a single-afternoon event, eventually became the impetus for a concomitant festival, Spring Carnival; this occurred particularly after 1900, when the flower parades resumed. But Spring Carnival was markedly different from the earlier festivals in the city. It was commercial, planned by a different (though related) group than the ones that organized its parades, and initially had no patriotic or ethnic festival at all attached to it. In these respects, it had more in common with the Veiled Prophet celebration than other San Antonio festivals. It would not be until 1913 that San Jacinto Day (the ostensible reason for the Battle of Flowers in the first place) would be associated with the entire carnival, when it was officially renamed "Fiesta San Jacinto."[7] This joint coalition of businessmen and Battle of Flowers ladies would see the Spring Carnival transform itself into Fiesta during the twentieth century. And Fiesta would come to dominate the festival year in San Antonio, much as Anglo-American values dominated the festival itself, despite its Hispanic name. As it reached predominance, it would assume characteristics also coming into fashion elsewhere in the United States, such as theme-based parades, pageants, and the adulation of festival "royalty." All of this would be a departure from the essentially democratic tradition of ethnic and patriotic festivals that had reigned in San Antonio for over a third of a century before 1900. T. R. Fehrenbach has characterized nineteenth-century San Antonio's makeup as "a society with many concentric but very separate circles, in which private concerns were more important than public"[8] But nineteenth-century San Antonio's diverse society *was* reflected in the public sphere through its celebrations. In this aspect, the society was not manifested as independent, closed circles at all but rather as a fascinating tapestry, of very uneven weave—some subsidiary patterns intersecting, some twined together and even sharing threads, and others autonomous; some parts of bright colors and others more subdued; some sections woven finely and tightly and others less disciplined and freer; but all making up one clearly articulated festive fabric, identifying this particular municipality in its place and time.

NOTES

INTRODUCTION
1. Peter D. Salins, *Assimilation, American Style,* 44–45.

PROLOGUE
1. Although teams of horses or oxen could be commandeered by the volunteer fire chiefs to pull the fire apparatus in time of emergency, they were basically hand drawn until 1881, when the first horse-powered apparatus was purchased.

2. *San Antonio Express,* July 3, 1870, 3.

3. Ibid. At this time, "lunch" referred to a buffet-style meal, which was not necessarily restricted to midday; bars offered "free lunches" all night.

4. *San Antonio Express,* July 5, 1898, 5.

5. See Daniel Glassberg, *American Historical Pageantry: The Uses of Tradition in the Early Twentieth Century,* 9–28.

CHAPTER I
1. One of the "downs" can be garnered from an article that appeared in the *National Gazette and Literary Register* (Philadelphia), June 18, 1822: "At San Antonio where has once been a wealthy and populace [*sic*] city, nothing but wretchedness is visible. That place is garrisoned by about 75 soldiers, who were nearly destitute of ammunition. The people of that place have once been in a state of ease and affluence, but, in consequence of the soldiers of the Spanish and Republican armies having been quartered in, and pillaging them, for several years, together with their own indolence, they are now reduced to the most abject state of poverty" (n.p.).

2. Frederick Law Olmsted, *A Journey through Texas, or A Saddle-Trip on the Southwestern Frontier: With a Statistical Appendix,* 150. The church was actually restored in 1840 after flood damage in 1819 and a major fire in 1828, but it had not been kept up. See Daniel Fox, Dan Scurlock, and John W. Clard Jr., *Archeological Excavations at San Fernando Cathedral, San Antonio, Texas: A Preliminary Report,* 7.

3. Richard Everett, "Things in and about San Antonio," *Frank Leslie's Illustrated Newspaper,* Jan. 15, 1859, n.p.

4. Olmsted, *A Journey through Texas,* 163.

5. Olmsted, *A Journey through Texas,* 154, mentions that Mexican Americans were expelled from Austin in 1853 and Seguin in 1853. There was a movement among certain Anglo-Americans to also expel them from San Antonio, but they were outnumbered by the Germans, who declared that such policy was "not the right and republican way."

6. Included under the umbrella of "Anglo-Americans" are small numbers of French, Irish, and other settlers of European origin, excluding the Germans.

7. The citizens of San Antonio actually voted against secession, even though the secessionists manipulated some of the ballots and got cart drivers from New Mexico to vote three times. However, Bexar County and the state of Texas both voted in favor of seceding. See Billy Joe Sayers, "'That Horrific Tragedy': The Initial Impact of Secession and the Beginning of the Civil War upon San Antonio and South Central Texas" (master's thesis, The University of Texas at San Antonio, 1982), 63.

8. See the account by Edward King, "Glimpses of Texas—I: A Visit to San Antonio," *Scribner's Monthly: An Illustrated Magazine,* Jan., 1874, 306–308.

9. King, "Glimpses of Texas," 310.

10. See Vinton Lee James, *Frontier and Pioneer Recollections of Early Days in San Antonio and West Texas,* 134.

11. Harriet Spoffard, visiting the city in 1877, described the streets as "exceedingly narrow, and by no means clean . . . [T]he sidewalks are narrower yet, and worn in ruts by the tread of many feet." See Harriet Spoffard, "San Antonio de Bexar," *Harper's New Monthly Magazine,* Nov., 1877, 836.

12. Small portable bathhouses had actually existed from the 1850s for the more modest German and Anglo-American residents—see Olmsted, *A Journey through Texas,* 157.

13. In 1892, for example, a cholera outbreak that started in Europe and spread to both New York and Mexico was apprehensively followed by San Antonians day by day. Fortunately, it never reached the city. See *San Antonio Express,* Sept. 16, 1892, 6; and Sept. 18, 1892, 3.

14. *San Antonio Express,* Apr. 16, 1891, 8. See also the advertisement for Bradford's Female Regulator, as well as Dr. McGork's Invigorator for men, guaranteed to restore "Lost Manhood" (*San Antonio Express,* Oct.16, 1892, 6).

15. Sidney Lanier, who visited San Antonio in 1872 for his health, noted the number of consumptives walking the city's streets, including himself. See Lanier's memoir, "San Antonio de Bexar," 90.

16. People also lived close to downtown because of the continuing fear of Comanche raids, even though the last had occurred two miles from the city in 1870. See William Corner, *San Antonio de Bexar: A Guide and History,* 129. As late as 1879, when Gustav Frasch built his stone residence on Avenue C, some distance up the new, unpaved road, friends were fearful of the potential of Indian attacks. See Cecilia Steinfeldt, *San Antonio Was: Seen through a Magic Lantern: Views from the Slide Collection of Albert Steves, Sr.,* 168.

17. King, "Glimpses of Texas," 327; Pearson Newcomb, *The Alamo City,* 79.

18. James, *Frontier and Pioneer Recollections,* 136–42, lists prominent businesses along Commerce Street.

19. James Rock and W. L. Smith, *Southern and Western Texas Guide for 1878,* 173, carefully list the number of practitioners of each of 172 professions in San Antonio but merely comment on the "usual number" of saloons.

20. Spoffard, "San Antonio de Bexar," 847, also remarks on the lack of such ameni-

ties as theater and opera; cites the role of the church in respectable ladies' social lives; and observes their education, most of them speaking Spanish and German besides English. The Ursuline convent school was the preferred place of education for Catholic ladies, and "several of the matrons have an acquaintance with the dead languages [Latin and Greek] which would allow them to fit their own boys for college."

21. Ibid.

22. To give just two examples from the first half of the nineteenth century, Bryan Callaghan Sr. married Concepción Ramon, while Lorenzo de Zavala's second wife, Emily West, was from New York.

23. Frank Richard Prassel, "Leisure Time Activities in San Antonio, 1877–1917" (master's thesis, Trinity University, 1961), 38.

24. Cornelia Crook, *San Pedro Springs Park: Texas' Oldest Recreation Area*, 43–44.

25. Crook, *San Pedro Springs Park*, 49–55.

26. *San Antonio Express*, July 4, 1876, 4.

27. Spoffard, "San Antonio de Bexar," 838, reports on the clutter of the streets: "Narrow as they are, they are incumbered [*sic*] in every way and made still narrower." They included carts full of stone, canvas-covered prairie schooners and their oxen on both streets and plazas, donkeys with large or small loads, entire Mexican families moving across town on encumbered wagons, army trains of covered mule-drawn wagons, strolling consumptives coughing away, Charros in full costume, equestrian ladies, and street venders.

28. *General Directory of the City of San Antonio, 1879–80*, 53–54.

29. *San Antonio Herald*, June 23, 1878, 4; *General Directory of the City of San Antonio, 1879–80*, 57–58. Between its opening in 1878 and May, 1879, it carried 105,000 passengers.

30. Lewis Fisher, *Crown Jewel of Texas: The Story of San Antonio's River*, 13. The San Antonio Water Works was incorporated by Jean Baptiste Lacoste in 1877. It was subsequently purchased by George Brackenridge, who added the second station in 1884.

31. Corner, *San Antonio de Bexar*, 55.

32. Andrew Morrison, *The City of San Antonio*, 6.

33. Fisher, *Crown Jewel of Texas*, 17.

34. The term *macadam* derives from crushed macadamia shells, originally used in the process. In San Antonio, however, stone replaced the shells.

35. According to Joseph Galleghy, *From Alamo Plaza to Jack Harris's Saloon: O. Henry and the Southwest He Knew*, 49, the first mesquite block paving was laid at 828 Avenue D, north of Alamo Plaza, by Walter Scott on May 17, 1882.

36. San Antonio was not the only Texas city with wooden paving. Galveston had it too—and earlier, when the Strand received it in the 1870s, other streets being paved later. See David G. McComb, *Galveston: A History*, 104. During the devastating hurricane of 1900, all of it popped out of its bed and floated away.

37. Steinfeldt, *San Antonio Was*, 106.

38. Stephen Gould, *The Alamo City Guide*, 3; Morrison, *City of San Antonio*, 4.

39. For studies of both the up and down sides of Callaghan's career, see Mary Beatty Edelen, "Bryan Callaghan II: His Earlier Political Career, 1885–1899" (master's thesis,

Trinity University, 1971); and David R. Johnson, John A. Booth, and Richard J. Harris, *The Politics of San Antonio: Community, Progress and Power,* 9–14.

40. *General Directory of the City of San Antonio, 1879–80,* 58.

41. Steinfeldt, *San Antonio Was,* 124. The sumptuous Menger Hotel appealed more to tourists and wealthy visitors, while the Vance House (the former military building), later called the Mahnke Hotel after its later owner, and the Maverick Hotel, also originally a military structure, were preferred by businessmen and traveling salesmen (ibid., 118–23).

42. The most detailed account of these killings appears in Elton R. Cude, *The Wild and Free Dukedom of Bexar,* 91–124.

43. Frances Kallison, "100 Years of Jewry in Texas" (master's thesis, Trinity University, 1977), 21, 69.

44. King, "Glimpses of Texas," 321.

45. Gould, *Alamo City Guide,* 138.

46. Barbara Rabke, "Theater in San Antonio, 1886–1891" (master's thesis, Trinity University, 1964), 11. The operas included *The Bohemian Girl, The Chimes of Normandy, La Traviata, Faust, Carnival of Venice,* and *Il Trovatore.*

47. Rabke, "Theater in San Antonio," 19–29.

48. By 1890, there were eight public elementary schools for whites, three for "coloreds," and a Central High School for whites only (Corner, *San Antonio de Bexar,* 32). Riverside High School was established for African American students in 1891; see Kenneth Mason, "Paternal Continuity: Afro-Americans and Race Relations in San Antonio, Texas, 1867–1937" (Ph.D. diss., University of Texas at Austin, 1994), 211.

49. *San Antonio Light,* Oct. 22, 1885, 1.

50. Earlier, such decorations were mostly restricted to the plazas. See the circa-1870 image of parade marshals and a band in Military Plaza.

51. See, for example, the description of street decorations for the 1882 Volksfest in the *San Antonio Express,* June 3, 1882, 4.

52. See Alwyn Barr, "Occupation and Geographic Mobility in San Antonio, 1870–1900," *Social Science Quarterly* 51 (Sept., 1970): 396–403.

53. Charles Thomas Logan, "Quaint San Antonio," *Frank Leslie's Popular Monthly,* July, 1898, 90.

54. Morrison, *City of San Antonio,* 9. The infamous "Bat Cave" was just one of the old buildings torn down to make way for its construction.

55. Corner, *San Antonio de Bexar,* 24–25.

56. Corner, *San Antonio de Bexar,* 39, cites Giles as also having earlier designed the county jail and the county courthouse, on Soledad Street.

57. The Alamo was not properly a chapel. It served as the mission's church (though it was never completely finished before the mission itself was dissolved). In nineteenth-century newspapers and other texts, however, it was referred to as the "Alamo Chapel," and that is what I shall call it for the remainder of this book.

58. Corner, *San Antonio de Bexar,* 39. This was designed by M. E. Bell of Chicago, with modifications by W. A. Freret of Chicago and J. Reily Gordon of San Antonio.

59. Charles Ramsdell, *San Antonio: A Pictorial and Historical Guide*, 111, mentions seeing a *jacal* in the area of La Villita as late as the 1940s.
60. Morrison, *City of San Antonio*, 11.
61. Corner, *San Antonio de Bexar*, 6.
62. Prassel, "Leisure Time Activities in San Antonio," 32, 37.
63. Numerous studies have been written about the mythification of the Alamo, among them Susan Prendergast Schroeder and Tom W. Gläser, *Alamo Images: Changing Perceptions of a Texas Experience*; Edward Tabor Linenthal, *Sacred Ground: Americans and Their Battlefields*; and Holly Beachly Brear, *Inherit the Alamo: Myth and Ritual at an American Shrine*. The full-blown myth was recounted in the 1850s both by Olmsted, *A Journey through Texas*, 55; and Richard Everett, "Things in and about San Antonio."
64. See the *San Antonio Express*, Apr. 22, 1894, 1; Apr. 22, 1896, 2.

CHAPTER 2

1. Mary P. Ryan, *Women in Public: Between Banners and Ballots, 1825–1880*, 22.
2. Ibid.
3. Glassberg, *American Historical Pageantry*, 9.
4. Fred Mosebach, "Fourth of July Antedates All Patriotic Celebrations in San Antonio," *San Antonio Express*, June 28, 1936, 10C, errs when calling it the oldest patriotic celebration in San Antonio; there are even earlier records of the celebration of Diez y Seis (see chap. 5).
5. Newcomb, *The Alamo City*, 23–24.
6. *San Antonio Herald*, July 3, 1859, 2.
7. Quoted in Ellen Bartlett Ballou, "Scudder's Journey to Texas in 1859," 9. Scudder does remark that the Texas Independence Day parade of the same year was somewhat more elaborate, being augmented by Mexican War veterans and "a large assemblage of young Texans" (10), but says nothing about the Fourth of July.
8. Washington's Birthday was even more sporadically celebrated than the Fourth of July. A clause included in the volunteer fire companies' statutes mandated that the companies celebrate it, but aside from a parade now and then, the rest of the city generally ignored it as an excuse for a public festival. See note 14, this chapter.
9. Steinfeldt, *San Antonio Was*, 177–78.
10. The Alamo Rifles barely survived the Civil War, but they survived long enough to march in the Fourth of July parades of 1875, 1876, and 1877. See *San Antonio Express*, July 6, 1875, 3; July 6, 1876, 4; July 4, 1877, 4.
11. The fire apparatuses of the 1850s in San Antonio were hand-drawn, though the volunteer fire chief was authorized by the city to commandeer teams of horses or oxen to get to fires if the situation was serious. The horses described by Scudder were thus not trained to pull the hand pumpers of the day. See Hector Cardenas, *San Antonio Fire Department History*, 24.
12. Cardenas, *San Antonio Fire Department History*, 23–25. The few exceptions in the 1870s to the Germanic membership were A. P. Rivas, who was a member of Fire Company 1; H. B. Adams and H. B. Andrews in Fire Company 2; C. Gillespie, William

Carr, and Ed Sommers of Sunset Hose Company 1; George Morgan of the Second Ward Hose Company; and Thomas Abbot, George Caen, Jose Cassiano, and Thomas and Charles Mullaly, members of Mission Hose Company 4. See *Roll of Members of the San Antonio Fire Department.*

13. Cardenas, *San Antonio Fire Department History,* 25–26. Mason, "Paternal Continuity," 162, erroneously gives the founding date for these fire companies as 1877.

14. *Statutes of the San Antonio Volunteer Fire Companies,* statute 2. Though the first surviving statutes date from 1875, the continuing presence of the volunteer fire companies from 1859 onward suggests that mandatory participation on Washington's Birthday and the Fourth of July were written into their rules from their inception.

15. There seems to have been some misunderstanding or dispute that prevented the Turnverein from joining the others in the correct location. See the *San Antonio Daily Ledger and Texan,* July 5, 1860, 2.

16. Ibid.

17. *San Antonio Daily Ledger and Texan,* July 3, 1861, 2.

18. Slaves were allowed time off from labor during certain holidays. See William H. Wiggins Jr., *O Freedom! Afro-American Emancipation Celebrations,* 25.

19. See the *San Antonio Herald,* July 4, 1866, 3.

20. Harold Shapiro, "The Labor Movement in San Antonio, Texas, 1865–1915," *Southwestern Social Science Quarterly* 36 (Sept., 1955): 160. This was a close-knit society, dedicated to noneconomic activity, and little is known of its activities.

21. Mason, "Paternal Continuity," 96.

22. Ryan, *Women in Public,* 33; Glassberg, *American Historical Pageantry,* 18.

23. James, *Frontier and Pioneer Recollections,* 142.

24. Mosebach, "Fourth of July Antedates," 10C.

25. In 1870, the African American community held a Fourth of July picnic at Guenther's Mill (*San Antonio Express,* July 4, 1870, 3).

26. Arnoldo de León, *The Tejano Community, 1836–1900,* 30.

27. Glassberg, *American Historical Pageantry,* 18, cites a similar appearance of the Goddess of Liberty and girls representing the original thirteen colonies in a centennial Fourth of July parade in Des Moines, Iowa, in 1876.

28. *San Antonio Herald,* July 3, 1869, 3.

29. *San Antonio Express,* July 4, 1870, 3.

30. Turnverein papers, Witte Museum.

31. I am oversimplifying San Antonio's complicated political situation in the 1870s. For an excellent, coherent analysis, see David R. Johnson, "Frugal and Sparing: Interest Groups, Politics and City Building in San Antonio, 1870–85," 33–57.

32. *San Antonio Express,* June 18, 1871, 3.

33. Turnverein papers, Witte Museum.

34. *San Antonio Express,* July 4, 1874, 3. There is no mention of a parade in 1873, but there are missing issues of San Antonio newspapers, and the *Express,* at this time, did not publish on Mondays.

35. Glassberg, *American Historical Pageantry*, 10–11, 18.
36. *San Antonio Express*, July 6, 1876, 4.
37. As Ryan, *Women in Public*, 43, puts it, "At this time men usually provided the participation, ladies provided decoration." The presence of these ladies may also have been a late Reconstructionist manifestation. Mason, "Paternal Continuity," 230, points out that AME churches were closely identified with Reconstruction.
38. For personal information on Joseph E. Dwyer, see below.
39. *San Antonio Express*, July 4, 1876, 4.
40. *San Antonio Express*, July 1, 1884, 4.
41. *San Antonio Light*, July 4, 1884, 1.
42. *San Antonio Light*, July 5, 1884, 1. Crawford had active links to the Mexican American community. In Diez y Seis parades of the period, he would serve as a marshal for the Sociedad Mutualista in 1884 and for the Sociedad Benevolencia in 1885. He was also a member of the Mexican Social Club.
43. Ryan, *Women in Public*, 48.
44. *San Antonio Light*, Sept. 12, 1881, 1.
45. Glassberg, *American Historical Pageantry*, 9–11.
46. *San Antonio Express*, July 5, 1896, 2.
47. Callaghan was the chairman of the reception committee and a member of the large executive committee. For a complete roster of members of all the committees, see the *San Antonio Light*, June 19, 1898, 3.
48. There was a brief period in which there was a question of whether all of the diverse elements invited could be managed within one parade. This was resolved quickly, but the decision to split the postparade festivities among two venues took a bit more time. See the *San Antonio Express*, June 21, 1898, 5.
49. Ibid.
50. See chapter 1.
51. *San Antonio Express*, Apr. 23, 1899, 6.
52. See Glassberg, *American Historical Pageantry*, 18.
53. *San Antonio Express*, Apr. 5, 1899, 4.
54. *San Antonio Express*, Apr. 23, 1899, 6.
55. *San Antonio Express*, Apr. 5, 1900, 7.
56. *San Antonio Light*, July 5, 1900, 5. Unfortunately, though three hundred pounds of beef were bought and barbecued, a near-riot of rowdy boys made access to the meat impossible for many.

CHAPTER 3

1. One exception to this late freeing of slaves in Texas was the case of Gen. Sam Houston, who freed his slaves as soon as he heard about Lincoln's intention to issue the Emancipation Proclamation (in September, 1862) and then paid his former bondsmen to help harvest his crops. See Patricia Smith Prather and Jane Clement, *From Slave to Statesman, Servant to Sam Houston*, 70–71.

2. William H. Wiggins Jr., "Juneteenth: A Red Spot Day on the Texas Calendar," 237.

3. Scholars also trace these secular festivities back the slave celebrations of Pinkster and Election Day. See Wiggins, *O Freedom!*, 28–36.

4. The situation was somewhat more flexible under Spanish and Mexican rule, when it was possible for free Africans to marry into the prevailing cultural and racial mix that came to be known as *mestizaje*. See Mason, "Paternal Continuity," 9–12. Mason's masterful dissertation remains the premier study on African Americans in San Antonio in the late nineteenth and early twentieth centuries and will be much quoted in this chapter.

5. Barr, "Occupation and Geographic Mobility," 400–401.

6. Mason, "Paternal Continuity," 73.

7. The number of free blacks in San Antonio before the war was tiny. Horace Scudder, visiting the lone as yet undenominational "colored church" in the city in 1859, estimated its congregation at "about twenty blacks and one or two whites." See Ballou, "Scudder's Journey to Texas," 10.

8. Sayers, "'That Horrific Tragedy,'" 71.

9. For a history and provisions of this charter, see Johnson, "Frugal and Sparing," 39–40.

10. Mason, "Paternal Continuity," 129.

11. Ibid., 151.

12. Jacqui Malone, *Steppin' on the Blues: The Visible Rhythms of African American Dance*, 54–55.

13. The Presbyterian church on Commerce Street allowed slaves to worship alongside their masters before the Civil War, but though they were allowed to attend the church after the war, they were segregated, their children put into a separate Sunday school, and the church eventually burned down under mysterious circumstances. See Mason, "Paternal Continuity," 281.

14. This church survives to this day as Saint Paul's United Methodist Church.

15. Mason, "Paternal Continuity," 292.

16. Saint Paul's church was at the center of Juneteenth organizing activities. Meetings were held there, and many of its members served as program and other committee chairs for the event over the years (Oscar Gooden, telephone interview by the author, July 6, 2000).

17. Mason, "Paternal Continuity," 315.

18. Ibid.

19. I am indebted to Vera Williams Young for this information (interview by the author, July 4, 2000, San Antonio, Texas). Boyd was later promoted to box clerk at the post office.

20. I am indebted to Oscar Gooden, historian of Saint Paul's United Methodist Church, for this information (telephone interview).

21. *San Antonio Herald*, June 12, 1866, 3.

22. In 1867, there was an African American camp meeting held outside of the city, but there is no mention of any "Juneteenth" activities in connection to what was basically a religious revival. See *San Antonio Herald*, June 19, 1867, 3.

23. *San Antonio Express*, June 19, 1881, 4, states that the event was celebrated "as heretofore by the colored people of the city."

24. *San Antonio Express*, June 20, 1879, 4. I have not been able to find any information on the Order of the Golden Links. The *Express* does not specify which one of the AME churches supplied the Sabbath school children.

25. The Loyal Union League also marched in some Fourth of July celebrations of the Reconstruction era. See chapter 2.

26. Mason, "Paternal Continuity," 137–40. It should be noted, however, that Walker's rather patronizing obituary in the *San Antonio Express* (Feb. 21, 1901, 6) states that he was a Democrat and was "rewarded by his frequently being named on the list of delegates to Democratic conventions." A biography of Walker is yet to be done.

27. *San Antonio Express*, June 17, 1881, 4. This celebration was held on June 18 rather than June 19. There is no report of who was in the parade or of the route, though there is the remark that the procession began in Military Plaza, so it may have taken the same route as the 1879 one. The earliest accounts of these festivals in the *Express* are rather lax.

28. *San Antonio Express*, June 17, 1881, 4; June 19, 1881, 4.

29. *San Antonio Express*, June 20, 1882, 4; *San Antonio Light*, June 19, 1882, 4. Though the festival was Juneteenth, it was traditional to read the Emancipation Proclamation and not Granger's later Galveston statement.

30. *San Antonio Express*, June 20, 1883, 1; *San Antonio Light*, June 20, 1883, 1. The *Express* also published a complete roster of the members of the festival's organizing committee, many of whom were drawn from the small black entrepreneurial community, including barbers and blacksmiths. At least one member of the committee, James Martin Jr., a coachman, would be active through the rest of the century in these festivals.

31. For the dates of the San Antonio Rifles and Belknap Rifle charters, see *General Directory of the City of San Antonio, 1883–84*, 54. For the date for the charter of the Excelsior Guards, see *General Directory of the City of San Antonio, 1887–88*, 51. It is clear from the *Express*'s publication of the Juneteenth order of march for 1883 that the Excelsior Guards already existed by that year, under their commander, Capt. John van Duze. The Belknaps and the Rifles met at their own armories, both on Houston Street, to drill. The Excelsiors drilled every Thursday at Chestnut and Crockett Streets.

32. Mason, "Paternal Continuity," 266; *San Antonio Express*, Sept. 17, 1893, 7.

33. *San Antonio Express*, Sept. 17, 1893, 7.

34. William H. Wiggins Jr., "'They Closed the Town Up, Man!' Reflections on the Civic and Political Dimensions of Juneteenth," 290.

35. *San Antonio Express*, June 20, 1888, 5; June 20, 1890, 5; June 20, 1896, 5; June 20, 1898, 5; *San Antonio Light*, June 20, 1892, 4; Gooden, telephone interview.

36. The Sunset Band, which marched in 1883, seems to have been short-lived. It appeared only in that one Juneteenth parade, then vanished. Whether it was African American is not clear, but probably likely.

37. The Granger Guards appeared only in the 1884 parade. The Eighth Cavalry Band caused a delay in the parade. It was originally scheduled to depart Milam Square

at 9 A.M., but the band did not show up until 11 A.M. See the *San Antonio Light,* June 19, 1884, 1.

38. *San Antonio Express,* June 20, 1884, 3. Zachariah (or Zack) Irvin, whose name was also spelled "Irwin," "Irven," and "Irving" by the newspapers at various times, would be grand marshal again in 1886. The fourth marshal was Joseph Hughes, possibly a cook.

39. *San Antonio Express,* June 20, 1884, 3.

40. A digest of Newcomb's speech is in the *San Antonio Express,* June 20, 1883, 1.

41. *San Antonio Express,* June 20, 1884, 3.

42. Katrina Hazzard-Gordon, *Jookin': The Rise of Social Dance Formations in African-American Culture,* 78.

43. Henson, who served terms as minister of Methodist congregations in other cities before and after his time in San Antonio, had already preached at Saint Paul's in 1881. Besides being a church activist, he was also grand chancellor of the colored Knights of Pythias. He died while conducting a prayer meeting in his last post in Waco in 1905. I am indebted to Oscar Gooden for this information (telephone interview).

44. Mason, "Paternal Continuity," 338.

45. Information supplied by Oscar Gooden (telephone interview).

46. Shapiro, "The Labor Movement," 161–62.

47. The two companies were dissolved when they dared asked for monetary compensation, a perquisite that had been enjoyed by their white counterparts since the 1850s. See Cardenas, *San Antonio Fire Department History,* 25. Zack Irvin would continue to be active in Juneteenth celebrations, serving on the finance committee in 1890 and on the organizing committees of the San Pedro Springs festivals of 1892 and 1893.

48. *San Antonio Express,* June 20, 1890, 5; June 21, 1892, 4.

49. Mason, "Paternal Continuity," 34. By the 1930s, the black percentage had declined to 7.7 percent, or just about what it was in 1865.

50. The *Light* estimated that two thousand people attended the 1883 event and only about thirteen hundred the celebration of 1899.

51. *San Antonio Light,* June 19, 1890, 8.

52. Hazzard-Gordon, *Jookin',* 72, points out that in the African American community (as in the rest of nineteenth-century society), upper-strata voluntary organizations and social clubs generally dominated social dance events.

53. Charles H. Brooks, *The Official History and Manual of the Grand United Order of Odd Fellows in America,* 159, 171.

54. See, for example, the *San Antonio Express,* June 20, 1892, 4.

55. The Black Union Veterans were African American members of the Grand Army of the Republic, which was composed of men who had fought for the Union during the Civil War.

56. *San Antonio Express,* June 21, 1892, 5.

57. *San Antonio Light,* June 20, 1895, 4.

58. Quoted in the *San Antonio Light,* May 16, 1893, 3. None of the nineteenth-century African American newspapers survive, except for this excerpt.

59. *San Antonio Express,* June 20, 1894, 5.

60. They may also have been donations rather than lent items: 1893 was the last year a German American Volksfest was held in San Antonio. Perhaps the Volksfest association realized by the summer of 1894 that these wagons would no longer be needed.

61. *San Antonio Express,* June 20, 1896, 5.

62. Hazzard-Gordon, *Jookin',* 71, cites an Emancipation Day celebration in Washington D.C., in 1882 that featured several queens. In general, female royalty in other festivals did not parade at this time. Queens of Mardi Gras and the Veiled Prophet celebration in Saint Louis appeared at balls, but not on the streets in the parades preceding them.

63. There was a "queen" of the cotton ball held in conjunction with the Battle of Flowers celebration of April, 1896, but that was at a private affair, not a parade, as we shall see. Even in New Orleans, there were no official "queens" until the 1800s, and—as at the Veiled Prophet celebration in Saint Louis, which crowned its first "Queen of Love and Beauty" in 1894—the practice was restricted to private balls. See Thomas M. Spencer, *The St. Louis Veiled Prophet Celebration: Power on Parade, 1877–1995,* 57.

64. *San Antonio Express,* June 20, 1898, 5.

65. I am indebted to Vera Williams Young for the text of this program.

66. *San Antonio Express,* June 19, 1899, 7.

67. Malone, *Steppin' on the Blues,* 71. This dance formed the backbone of one of the earliest black musicals, *Clorindy—The Origin of the Cakewalk,* which premiered in New York in 1897, with a cast of twenty-six singers and dancers.

68. *San Antonio Express,* June 19, 1900, 4.

69. Ibid.

CHAPTER 4

1. The original text of Father Hidalgo's speech is as follows: "Mis amigos y compatriotas; no existe ya para nosotros ni el rey ni los tributos. Esta gabela vergonzosa, que sólo conviene a los esclavos, la hemos sobrellevado hace tres siglos como signo de la tiranía y servidumbre; terrible mancha que sabremos lavar con nuestros esfuerzos. Llegó el momento de nuestra emancipación; ha sonado la hora de nuestra libertad; y se conoceís su gran valor, me ayudereís a defenderla de la garra ambiciousa de los tiranos. Pocas horas me faltan para que me veáis marchar a la cabeza de los hombres que se precian de ser libres. Os invito a complir con este deber. De suerte que sin patria ni libertad estaremos siempre a mucha distancia de la verdadera felicidad. Preciso ha sido dar el paso que ya sabeís, y comenzar por algo ha sido necesario. La causa es santa y Dios la protegerá. . . . Viva, pues, la Virgen de Guadalupe! Viva la América, por lo cual vamos a combatir!" Quoted in Pedro García, *Con el cura Hidalgo en la guerra de independencia,* 44. The translation is mine.

2. De León, *Tejano Community,* 7.

3. A fascinating account of this deportation can be found in Hieronymus Münzer, *Viaje por España y Portugal, 1494–1495,* 17–18: "I saw in a certain house persons of both sexes placed on sale. They were [Guanches] of Tenerife, that is one of the Canary is-

lands in the Atlantic ocean, that rebelled against the king of Spain, and were conquered by him, who put up the entire population for sale. There was a merchant of Valencia who brought 87 of them in a ship, of which 14 died of seasickness and the change in climate. The others were put up for sale. They are dark men, but not black like the barbarians. Their women were well formed, of strong and rather long limbs; but they are bestial in their customs, because up until now they have not lived under any law, but were idolaters." Münzer, a German jeweler, made a yearlong journey through Spain and wrote a memoir about it. The translation is mine.

4. The hardships of the hardscrabble life in the Canary Islands apparently made it easy for the islanders to be induced to colonize, for they had already been sent to colonize other outposts in New Spain. See Jesus F. de la Teja, "Land and Society in Eighteenth Century San Antonio de Bejar, a Community on New Spain's Northern Frontier" (Ph.D. diss., University of Texas at Austin, 1988), 67.

5. Gerald E. Poyo, "The Canary Islands Immigrants of San Antonio: From Ethnic Exclusivity to Community in Eighteenth Century Bexar," 46–47. I will use "Tejano" to refer to those members of the Hispanic community who were in San Antonio before 1836 or to their descendants and "Hispanic" for those who arrived later.

6. Jesus F. de la Teja and John Wheat, "Béxar: Profile of a Tejano Community, 1820–1832," 17–18.

7. See for example, the account of the club's monthly ball in the *San Antonio Express*, Jan. 3, 1892, 8.

8. The various terms "Tejano," "Hispanic," and "Mexican American" have had different meanings at different times. Here, the term "Tejano" refers to those whose families in San Antonio predate the Civil War, while the more general term "Mexican American" encompasses everyone, including newer arrivals both from Mexico and from other towns in South Texas.

9. See chapter 1.

10. For good analyses of the Tejano role in later nineteenth-century politics, see de León, *Tejano Community*, 23–49; and Kenneth Stewart and Arnaldo de León, *Not Room Enough: Mexicans, Anglos and Socio-economic Change in Texas, 1850–1900*, 42–58.

11. See Edelen, "Bryan Callaghan II," esp. 13–87.

12. De León, *Tejano Community*, 7.

13. Hinojosa and Poyo, *Tejano Origins in Eighteenth-Century San Antonio*, 15–16. Note that the *junta patriótica* was also responsible for organizing religious festivals, such as Corpus Christi, Christmas, Holy Thursday and Good Friday, and the Feast of San Felipe de Jesús. See de León, *Tejano Community*, 7.

14. De León, *Tejano Community*, 7.

15. *San Antonio Herald*, Sept. 18, 1868, 3. The writer for the *Herald* was unsure about which war the Mexicans dated their independence from and had to research it; the *Herald* published a short account in the same article. There is no mention of where the Club Mexicano-Texano went to celebrate or of how they celebrated.

16. Angel Navarro also married Concepción Ramon, the widow of Bryan Callaghan Sr., and so was the future mayor's stepfather.

17. Charles Merrit Barnes, *Combats and Conquests of Immortal Heroes: Sung in Song, Told in Story*, 231.

18. *San Antonio Herald*, Apr. 17, 1855, 2; *General Directory of the City of San Antonio, 1879–80*, 93; *1881–82*, 73; *1883–84*, 73.

19. *San Antonio Herald*, Sept.16, 1869, 3. Also see chapter 2.

20. Alejo Perez also carried the cachet that his mother was an Alamo survivor.

21. Barnes, *Combats and Conquests*, 231. The present-day Rivas Street is located to the north and west of the original one, running from approximately Twenty-ninth Street east nearly to Interstate 10.

22. The 1900 census lists Rivas as living at the ancestral residence at 527 West Houston Street (originally Rivas Street), along with his son, daughter and son-in-law, and a live-in servant.

23. *San Antonio Express*, Sept. 16, 1877, 4.

24. *San Antonio Express* Sept. 17, 1878, 4.

25. Ibid.

26. There was an earlier society called Los Yndesoluleles, but its members appear to have been confined to the upper class. They included José Cassiano and Manuel Pereida. See *General Directory of the City of San Antonio, 1878–79*, 79.

27. Jose Amaro Hernandez, *Mutual Aid for Survival: The Case of the Mexican-American*, 10.

28. They were published as *Ley Fundamental de la Sociedad Benevolencia Mexicana para auxilios mutuos. Fundada en la Ciudad the San Antonio, Condado de Bexar, Estado de Texas, el 1 de Mayo, 1875, reformado en 1885 y regenerado en 1889*.

29. *Ley Fundamental*, 7–23, 27. The dress and decorum stipulations are in article 78.

30. Julie Leininger Pycior, "La Raza Organizes: Mexican American Life in San Antonio, 1915–1930, as Reflected in Mutualistas Activities" (Ph.D. diss., Notre Dame, 1979), 9.

31. See the *San Antonio Express*, Sept. 16, 1879, 3; Sept. 17, 1880, 4; Sept. 14, 1881, 4; Sept. 15, 1881, 4; Sept. 16, 1881, 4; Sept. 17, 1882, 1.

32. San Antonio wasn't the only city to have politically oriented mutual aid societies; see, for example, the discussion of the Sociedad Unión of Laredo, also dominated by Democrats, in Roberto I. Calderón, "Unión, Paz y Trabajo," 70–71.

33. *San Antonio Express*, Aug. 9, 1883, 4.

34. Frederick C. Chabot, *With the Makers of San Antonio*, 259, mentions Juan T. Cardenas's parents, but not Juan. The birth dates that Chabot gives for Juan's parents (1796 for his father, 1801 for his mother) are those also given in Juan's obituary in the *San Antonio Express*, Sept. 1, 1903, 10. Does Chabot's lack of mention of Juan Cardenas himself indicate that he thought he was less than socially acceptable? In addition, Cardenas seems to have prevaricated about his origins somewhat. In the 1870 census, he stated that both his parents were born in Mexico, but in the census of 1880, he stated that they were both born in Texas.

35. See his obituaries in the *San Antonio Express*, Sept. 1, 1903, 10; and in the *San Antonio Light*, Sept. 1, 1903, 3.

36. *San Antonio Herald*, Aug. 8, 1868, 2.

37. This, however, was not an elected office—Cardenas was filling out an unexpired term.

38. After the massive influx of Anglo-Americans and the concomitant decline in the Hispanic population, there was not a critical mass of the latter to force election of any of their community. See de León, *Tejano Community*, 33–45.

39. *San Antonio Express*, Sept. 1, 1903, 10.

40. The Eighth Cavalry Band also played for the 1883 Volksfest and for the Fourth of July in 1884.

41. The Mutualista uniform was nearly identical to that of the Benevolencias the previous year, except that the latter wore black gloves and wore their insignias on the opposite breasts.

42. *San Antonio Express*, Sept. 16, 1883, 4; *San Antonio Light*, Sept. 17, 1883, 1.

43. See Juan T. Cardenas's obituary, *San Antonio Express*, Sept. 1, 1903, 10.

44. *San Antonio Express*, Sept.16, 1884, 4; *San Antonio Light*, Sept. 17, 1884, 1.

45. The text of Breckenridge's speech was published in full in the *San Antonio Light*, Sept. 17, 1884, 1.

46. *San Antonio Light*, Sept. 16, 1884, 1.

47. *San Antonio Light*, Sept. 7, 1885, 3; Sept. 9, 1885, 3.

48. *San Antonio Express*, Sept. 17, 1885, 2.

49. *San Antonio Light*, Sept. 15, 1881, 1.

50. *San Antonio Light*, Sept. 17, 1885, 3. The play however, was considered by the *Light* as "mediocre to an American theater-goer."

51. Turner Hook and Ladder Company 1 was invited by the Mutualistas to march, but it is unclear whether they actually participated, as no complete parade roster was published by either the *Light* or the *Express* that year. See Turnverein papers, Witte Museum.

52. In exchange, the Sociedad Mutualista would march in the Columbus Day parade the following month.

53. *San Antonio Light*, Sept. 16, 1885, 5.

54. See chapter 1.

55. Herminio Rios and Lupe Castillo, "Towards a True Chicano Bibliography: Mexican-American Newspapers, 1848–1842," *El Grito: A Journal of Contemporary Mexican-American Thought* 2 (summer, 1970): 17–24. De León, *Tejano Community*, 197–99, lists several weekly and biweekly papers published during the period. Which was published by Warren is not indicated in either source.

56. *San Antonio Light*, Sept. 17, 1885, 3.

57. Shapiro, "The Labor Movement," 161–62.

58. *San Antonio Express*, Sept. 16, 1886, 8.

59. *San Antonio Light*, Sept. 16, 1886, 4; *San Antonio Express*, Sept.16, 1886, 8. It is worth noting that the *Express* also misspelled "triste" as "tristi." All descriptions that follow come from these two articles.

60. *San Antonio Express*, Sept. 16, 1886, 6.

61. Tableaux became so popular that handbooks were published during this period with descriptions, illustrations, and instructions. See, for example, Tony Denier, *Parlor Tableaux, or Animated Pictures for the Use of Families, Schools and Public Exhibitions;* and J. A. Hill, *Hill's Book of Tableaux.*

62. Shapiro, "The Labor Movement," 162.

63. Hernandez, *Mutual Aid for Survival,* 65.

64. La Unión's statutes, a copy of which survive in the Special Collections of Our Lady of the Lake University in San Antonio, are very similar to those of the Sociedad Benevolencia.

65. *San Antonio Express,* Sept. 16, 1893, 8.

66. *San Antonio Light,* Sept. 16, 1891, 4; *San Antonio Express,* Sept. 16, 1891, 8. The theme of "Mexico" and the "United States" joining hands on a float was a favorite one for municipal festivals all along the U.S.-Mexican border.

67. *San Antonio Light,* Sept. 16, 1891, 8.

68. *San Antonio Express,* Sept. 16, 1887, 5.

69. The most prominent of these included the Hispanic Gran Círculo de Obreros and the Anglo-American/German Independent Workingmen's Club. See, for example, the *San Antonio Express,* Sept. 15, 1896, 5.

70. *San Antonio Express,* Sept. 17, 1892, 6.

71. These were also branches of sisterhoods from other parts of South Texas, Corpus Christi and Brownsville, respectively. See Hernandez, *Mutual Aid for Survival,* 65.

72. For these festivals see the *San Antonio Express,* Sept. 16, 1894, 3; Sept. 16, 1896, 5; Sept. 16, 1898, 5; the *San Antonio Light,* Sept. 16, 1896, 7; Sept. 17, 1896, 8; Sept. 15, 1898, 6; Sept. 16, 1898, 8. Ed and his cowboys had previously appeared in the Fourth of July parade the same year.

73. The Zouaves were formed in 1896. See Barnes, *Combats and Conquests,* 147–52. Charles Merritt Barnes was a Zouave.

74. *San Antonio Express,* Sept. 17, 1895, 8.

75. *San Antonio Express,* Sept. 5, 1896, 8.

76. The *Express* spells the word "casqueronis." It would be a few decades before these turned up as a feature in Hispanic celebrations in San Antonio. By the late twentieth century they had been appropriated by the Anglo-American community for their "Fiesta week."

77. See William H. Beezley, "The Porfirian Smart Set Anticipates Thorstein Veblen in Guadalajara," 175–76.

78. Beezley, "The Porfirian Smart Set," 180.

79. *San Antonio Express,* Sept. 17, 1892, 1; Sept. 15, 1895, 1. Such flower festivals were also held on other occasions; see the *San Antonio Express,* Apr. 13, 1891, 4.

80. See McComb, *Galveston: A History,* 121–47.

81. There would be a similar cancellation of San Antonio's Diez y Seis parade a century later, as a result of the bombing of the World Trade Center and the Pentagon on September 11, 2001.

CHAPTER 5

1. Alberto Pecorini, "The Italian in America, 1891–1914," 175–76.
2. The Italian Americans of Philadelphia had a float of Columbus in the bicentennial celebration parade of the arrival of William Penn in 1876. See Glassberg, *American Historical Pageantry*, 23.
3. And this represents quite an increase over the six Italians counted in San Antonio in the 1860 census! See Valentine Belfiglio, *The Italian Experience in Texas*, 46.
4. See *General Directory of the City of San Antonio, 1879–80*, 69; *1885–86*, 43; and *1887–88*, 39. Also see Institute of Texan Cultures, *The Italian Texans*, 11, and the file on Antonio Bruni, Institute of Texan Cultures.
5. For example, see de León, *Tejano Community*, 31.
6. Other founders who signed the Società's charter included Agostino Rubino, Francesco Rubiolo, José Cassiano, Luigi Moglia, and Paolo Columbo. See Belfiglio, *The Italian Experience in Texas*, 72.
7. See the *San Antonio Light*, Aug. 31, 1892, 4, commenting on scheduling conflicts between the Columbus Day festivities in 1892 and the 1892 Volksfest: "The Italians had not made a success in celebrating the Fall of Rome and had changed about to celebrate the discovery of America."
8. *San Antonio Express*, Sept. 19, 1885, 3.
9. I am indebted for this information to Reg Little, of Alamo Fireworks (telephone interview with the author, Aug. 21, 2000).
10. *San Antonio Light*, Oct. 12, 1887, 4.
11. *San Antonio Express*, Oct. 13, 1887, 5.
12. *San Antonio Light*, Oct. 12, 1889, 4.
13. For accounts of the years 1889 through 1891, see the *San Antonio Express*, Oct. 13, 1889, 3; Oct. 14, 1890, 2, Oct. 23, 1891, 8; and Oct. 13, 1891, 4. Also see the *San Antonio Light*, Oct. 13, 1890, 1; Oct. 10, 1891, 4; and Oct. 13, 1891, 4.
14. *San Antonio Express*, Oct. 22, 1891, 6.
15. *San Antonio Express*, Oct. 22, 1891, 6; Oct. 21, 1891, 6.
16. Belfiglio, *The Italian Experience in Texas*, 72. This society was founded by Alberto Solero and fifteen other Italian Americans.
17. The Italian Americans may have also lent their "Columbus" float to the German American parade. See chapter 6.
18. The Christopher Columbus Society, which still exists, sponsors "Italian Spaghetti and Meatball Dinners" to this day. Did they serve up such fare at the Springs?
19. *San Antonio Express*, Oct. 20, 1892, 2; *San Antonio Light*, Oct. 22, 1892, 2.
20. *San Antonio Express*, Sept. 23, 1892, 6.
21. Donated to the city by the Christopher Columbus Society in 1957, the bronze image of Columbus is placed in the small park fronting the Christopher Columbus Society Hall and San Francesco di Paola Church, at the intersection of West Martin and Columbus Streets.
22. *San Antonio Express*, Oct. 22, 1893, 3.
23. There was a Giovanni Giovanetti active during this period in Florence, but he

was a sculptor. There was also a painter and painting teacher working in Lucca by the name of Raffaele Giovannetti, who was known as both a history painter and a portraitist. This Giovannetti was patronized by Lucca's nobility and was already a professor in his home city by 1822—he would therefore have been *very* old to travel to America for a medal in 1895. See E. Bénézet, *Dictionnaire critique et documentaire des peintres, sculpteurs, dessinateurs et graveurs*, 5:21.

24. *San Antonio Express*, Oct. 22, 1893, 3.
25. *San Antonio Light*, Oct. 19, 1894, 5.
26. *San Antonio Light*, Sept. 16, 1895, 4; Oct. 19, 1895, 5.

CHAPTER 6

1. Walter Struve, *Germans and Texans: Commerce, Migrations and Culture in the Days of the Lone Star Republic*, 46–47.
2. Terry G. Jordan, *German Seed in Texas Soil: Immigrant Farmers in Nineteenth-Century Texas*, 33.
3. Glen E. Lich, "Goethe on the Guadalupe," 54–62.
4. Larry Lane Bybee, "The Germans in San Antonio (1844–1920): A Study in Cultural Persistence" (master's thesis, The University of Texas at San Antonio, 1980), 14–15.
5. Chabot, *With the Makers of San Antonio*, 270–74, 386–87.
6. But even the less-educated German immigrants formed farmers' and workers' *vereine*, which, among other goals, had the objective of cultural improvement. See Rudolph Leopold Biesele, *The History of German Settlements in Texas, 1831–1861*, 220.
7. Biesele, *The History of German Settlements in Texas*, 223.
8. See Mack Walker, "The Old Homeland and the New," 72–81.
9. Among them was Vinton Lee James; see Steinfeldt, *San Antonio Was*, 144–50; and James, *Frontier and Pioneer Recollections*, 98.
10. August Siemering, founder of the *Freie Press*, was also a founder of the *San Antonio Express*.
11. James Patrick McGuire, *Iwonski in Texas: Painter and Citizen*, 41.
12. Ben Thompson and "King" Fisher went to see a performance of the drama *Lady Audley's Secret* at Turner Hall the night they died in the shoot-out at the Vaudeville Theater. See Cude, *The Wild and Free Dukedom of Bexar*, 113; and chapter 1.
13. Louis B. Englke, "The Old Schuetzen Verein Was a Way of Life," *San Antonio Express*, Dec. 3, 1950, 9, points out that the Scheutzenverein had its regular shooting competitions on Sundays, when good Protestants and Catholics were in church. The major competition, the "King's Shoot," was held on Pentecost Sunday.
14. For example, Horace Clark, Charles Campbell, and W. H. McAllister sang with the Beethoven Männerchor in the 1890s.
15. It used to be thought that this was a massacre by Confederates of unarmed German Union sympathizers. See Stanley S. M. McGowan, "Battle or Massacre? . . . Nueces, 8/10/1862," *Southwestern Historical Quarterly* 104 (July, 2000): 64–86.
16. Adolf Douai had already been expelled from New Braunfels in 1852. His views were too extreme even for that all–German American town. But it was his constant and

strident antislavery position that would earn him the wrath of more apolitical German Americans in San Antonio. There had been a convocation of the Texas State Convention of Germans in 1854, at which an antislavery position was taken, but this was still a minority stand. See Jordan, *German Seed in Texas Soil*, 182.

17. The paper continued after Douai's expulsion, renamed in 1856 the *Texas Staats-Zeitung* under Gustav Schleicher, until the destructive riot of 1861.

18. August Santleben, *A Texas Pioneer: Early Staging and Overland Freighting Days on the Frontiers of Texas and Mexico*, 318.

19. Steinfeldt, *San Antonio Was*, 138.

20. Ibid., 116–18, mentions several of the German saloons and their proprietors, including John Bosshardt's Eureka Saloon (1877), Ernst Dosch's Deer Horn Saloon (after 1870), and William Reuter's elegant Parlor Bar.

21. See also chapter 1.

22. Bybee, "The Germans in San Antonio," 62–63.

23. James V. Reese, "The Early History of Labor Organizations in Texas, 1838–1876," *Southwestern Historical Quarterly* 72 (July, 1968): 6, 14.

24. See chapter 1.

25. *San Antonio Express*, Sept. 16, 1869, 3. See also James Patrick McGuire, *Iwonski in Texas*, 29–30.

26. *San Antonio Express*, Sept. 1, 1869, 3

27. George L. Mosse, *The Nationalization of the Masses: Political Symbolism and Mass Movements in Germany from the Napoleonic Wars through the Third Reich*, 88.

28. San Antonio's German American choirs hosted a three-day *sängerfest* in 1870, which also featured a parade and picnic at San Pedro Springs Park (prematurely terminated by a violent hailstorm). Like the Humboldt anniversary, this was not an annual affair, since the venues for *sängerfests* rotated among various Texas German American communities. For the 1870 event, see the *San Antonio Express*, Sept. 10, 1870, 2; Sept. 10, 1870, 3; and Sept. 11, 1870, 3. Also see the *San Antonio Herald*, Sept. 12, 1870, 3.

29. Mosse, *The Nationalization of the Masses*, 58–62.

30. Ibid., 84–85.

31. Ibid., 62–63, 90–93.

32. For example, Biesele, *The History of German Settlements in Texas*, 223 and note 69, cites a Volksfest that was held after the first *sängerfest* in New Braunfels in 1853.

33. Obituary for Max Lindner, *San Antonio Express*, Feb. 26, 1901, 10; Feb. 27, 1901, 10. Lindner was thirty-one when he came to San Antonio. In San Antonio, he had a colorful career not only as a pharmacist but as the publisher of a satirical weekly called the *Lantern*, which made him many political enemies. He served as chief deputy tax assessor under Louis Huth and later abandoned the pharmacy business to work for the Mutual Electric Company. He died at the age of fifty-two, his physical health destroyed by his repeated bouts with malaria and his mental state decimated by a nervous breakdown that occurred in January, 1901.

34. Dr. Lindner is not mentioned in published accounts of the initial Volksfest meet-

ings, but he is credited with the idea in an article in the *San Antonio Express,* May 12, 1882, 4. Unfortunately, no minutes survive from Volksfest meetings prior to 1890.

35. *San Antonio Express,* Jan. 17, 1882, 4.

36. The community had already charged a fee for the picnic at the 1870 *sängerfest*—fifty cents per adult male. *San Antonio Express,* Sept. 11, 1870, 3.

37. *San Antonio Express,* Jan. 18, 1882, 4.

38. This is an observation made by Theresa Gold in a letter to the author (Dec. 12, 2001). It is backed up with individual membership listings in city directories of the 1870s and 1880s. One of the notable exceptions was Ed Froboese Sr., who was a charter member of the Scheutzenverein and also a member of the Turnverein.

39. *San Antonio Express,* Apr. 11, 1882, 4.

40. Ibid.

41. Were costumes from this parade perhaps the ones bought by Lindner?

42. *San Antonio Express,* June 2, 1882, 4.

43. *San Antonio Express,* June 3, 1882, 4. Adolph Wagner would also be on one of the historical floats the next day, as an Indian chief on the float depicting the "Landing of Lasalle."

44. For an excellent analysis of the origins and traditions of Mardi Gras, see Samuel Kinser, *Carnival American Style: Mardi Gras at New Orleans and Mobile.*

45. Spencer, *The Saint Louis Veiled Prophet Celebration,* 3–16. Spencer gives a history and complete analysis of this festival, and my discussion of the Veiled Prophet parade is based on his study.

46. Glassberg, *American Historical Pageantry,* 1–5.

47. See the detailed descriptions in the *San Antonio Express,* June 3, 1882, 1.

48. Ibid.

49. The *San Antonio Express* (ibid.) gives an elaborate description of this float: "Log cabins, well made with cedar poles occupied the rear of the car, and the settlers were arranged in the foreground in different occupations, some cooking, a blacksmith, shoemaker, guards, cowboys, Indians, etc."

50. Ibid.

51. Ibid. One of the set-pieces was set off early inadvertently by Dr. Lindner.

52. *San Antonio Express,* June 4, 1882, 4.

53. Mosse, *The Nationalization of the Masses,* 90–94. There was even a National Festival Society formed in Germany in 1897.

54. *San Antonio Express,* Jan. 8, 1883, 4; Jan. 15, 1883, 4; and *San Antonio Light,* June 21, 1883, 1.

55. Runge was experienced in this post; he had already served several terms as recording secretary for the Turnverein.

56. *San Antonio Light,* July 9, 1883, 1.

57. Professor Katzenberger also composed a march for the occasion of the Volksfest and dedicated it to the planning committee.

58. *San Antonio Light,* Aug. 2, 1883, 1. Most of these were provided by the city's electric company, but some came from private sources. The *San Antonio Light,* Oct. 4, 1883,

1, reported that "Mr. W. W. Walling had, at great inconvenience to himself, donated his electric light for use in the Volksfest."

59. The *San Antonio Express*, Oct. 5, 1883, 2, commented that "the ten electric lights cast a lurid sheen over the grounds [of Central Gardens]."

60. *San Antonio Light*, Sept. 20, 1883, 1.

61. *San Antonio Light*, Oct. 5, 1883, 1.

62. Ibid. The arch was designed and executed by Mr. A. F. Beckmann, architect.

63. A float depicting "Cotton Culture," sponsored by the city's British Association, broke a wheel before the parade started and was never seen.

64. *San Antonio Express*, Oct. 4, 1883, 4.

65. The allegorical ladies were Amelia Schreiner (Commerce, with an anchor), Emma Degan (Art, with the wand of Hermes), and Miss Hausman (Science, with a sword). All wore "Grecian" robes (ibid.).

66. *San Antonio Express*, Oct. 7, 1883, 1. The sextet did get to perform later at Central Gardens.

67. *San Antonio Express*, Oct. 6, 1883, 4.

68. *San Antonio Light*, Oct. 6, 1883, 1.

69. *San Antonio Express*, Oct. 7, 1883, 1.

70. Ibid.

71. *San Antonio Light*, Oct. 6, 1883, 3.

72. *San Antonio Light*, Oct. 8, 1883, 1.

73. *San Antonio Light*, Oct. 5, 1883, 1; Oct. 26, 1883, 1.

74. *San Antonio Light*, Oct. 26, 1883, 1.

75. *San Antonio Light*, Mar. 17, 1884, 4; Mar. 20, 1884, 1; Mar. 27, 1884, 1.

76. *San Antonio Express*, June 19, 1884, 8.

77. *San Antonio Express*, Aug. 21, 1884, 1; Aug. 25, 1884, 1; Sept. 3, 1884, 2.

78. There may also have been economic reasons: at one of the last meetings, on September 21, George Kalteyer, noting the lack of enthusiasm for the project, commented that "times were dull" and speculated that everyone might be in a better financial state the following year (*San Antonio Light*, Sept. 21, 1884, 1).

79. *San Antonio Express*, July 28, 1883, 3.

80. See the belated invitation to the Turner Hook and Ladder Company from the Volksfest Association, dated Oct. 9, 1885. They were evidently left out of the earlier invitation list. They did participate. The letter is in the Turnverein papers, Witte museum.

81. *San Antonio Express*, Oct. 23, 1885, 3.

82. *San Antonio Light*, Oct. 22, 1885, 3.

83. *San Antonio Express*, Oct. 23, 1885, 3.

84. Ibid.

85. *San Antonio Light*, Oct. 24, 1885, 1. The San Antonio Männerchor is otherwise unknown.

86. *San Antonio Light*, Oct. 22, 1884, 1.

87. *Protocoll Buch der Central Comites zur . . . des Deutschen Tages in San Antonio*,

Daughters of the Republic of Texas Library, German-English School Records 890, Aug. 24, 1890, 1.

88. *Protocoll Buch,* Sept. 10, 1890, 3. The Mission Hose Company was the eighth and last volunteer fire company in the city. It was organized in 1885. See Cardenas, *San Antonio Fire Department History,* 28.

89. *San Antonio Light,* Oct. 11, 1890, 1.

90. Ibid., 4.

91. *Protocoll Buch,* Sept. 15, 1890, 7.

92. The German Americans of San Antonio were not unique in mining such a source, for Mardi Gras floats themselves were recycled in the Philadelphia centennial parade in 1876. See Glassberg, *American Historical Pageantry,* 26.

93. *San Antonio Light,* Sept. 27, 1890, 5; Sept. 30, 1890, 3.

94. *Protocoll Buch,* Oct. 1, 1890, 14.

95. *San Antonio Express,* Oct. 11, 1890, 8.

96. A complete set of photographs of these floats is in the Library of the Institute of Texan Cultures. Steinfeldt, *San Antonio Was,* 202–12, was the first to publish a complete set of these floats; however, she erroneously dates them circa 1905 and does not identify their subject matter. T. R. Fehrenbach, *The San Antonio Story,* 162, published one ("Barbarossa") that is likewise not identified as to subject matter and is dated by him as 1893.

97. *San Antonio Light,* Sept. 30, 1890, 31; Oct. 11, 1890, 8; *San Antonio Express,* Oct. 12, 1890, 3.

98. Lich, "Goethe on the Guadalupe," 71.

99. Carl von Iwonski had hastily produced a history painting of the subject for the same celebration, which later hung in the Casino Club. It was not, however, used as a source for the float design. The painting is reproduced in James Patrick McGuire, *Iwonski in Texas,* 5. It was raffled off later in February and was won by Fridolin Wild, who then donated it to the Casino Association. See James Patrick McGuire, *Iwonski in Texas,* 30–31.

100. *San Antonio Light,* Oct. 13, 1890, 1.

101. *Protocoll Buch,* Oct. 15, 1890, 17. Follow-up meetings were held on December 20, 1890, and December 29, 1890.

102. *Protocoll Buch,* Jan. 3, 1891, 19.

103. *San Antonio Express,* Feb. 7, 1891, 3.

104. *San Antonio Light,* Feb. 20, 1891, 1.

105. He also brought some of these figures, already made, with him from New Orleans.

106. *San Antonio Light,* Feb. 20, 1891, 1; *Protocoll Buch,* May 14, 1891, 28; May 26, 1891, 28–29.

107. *San Antonio Express,* Oct. 1, 1891, 3.

108. Steinfeldt, *San Antonio Was,* 190–92.

109. For example, see those illustrated in Henri Schindler, *Mardi Gras, New Orleans,* 80–81, 88–89, of the Proteus parade of 1886 and the Rex parade of 1904. The lithographer of the *Light* supplement was Kockert and Walle.

110. See chapter 4.

111. The newspapers gave fairly extensive citations of float personnel. For example, Mrs. Lulu McAllister Griesenbeck impersonated "Columbia," and Miss Hulda Rommel played "Germania" (*San Antonio Light*, Oct. 10, 1891, 4), while the six young men who played the Rhine Maidens were Tom Tengg, August Peters Jr., Eddy Degener, George Wurzbach, Walter Jenull, and Master Bartholomaie.

112. *San Antonio Express*, Oct. 10, 1891, 6.

113. *San Antonio Light*, Oct. 12, 1891, 4

114. *San Antonio Express*, Oct. 10, 1891, 6.

115. *San Antonio Express*, Oct. 12, 1891, 5; *San Antonio Light*, Oct. 12, 1891, 2.

116. *Protocoll Buch*, Oct. 24, 1891, 42–43; Jan. 4, 1892, 45.

117. *Protocoll Buch*, Feb. 8, 1892, 45; Feb. 15, 1892, 47; Feb. 22, 1892, 48.

118. *Protocoll Buch*, July 7, 1892, 49.

119. *San Antonio Express*, May 16, 1893, 5.

120. See chapter 5.

121. *Protocoll Buch*, Aug. 20, 1892, 55.

122. *San Antonio Express*, Oct. 11, 1892, 5.

123. See chapter 5.

124. Reproduced in Pauline A. Pinckney, *Painting in Texas: The Nineteenth Century*, figure C-11. The same painting served as a source for the scene of Santa Anna's surrender in the earliest film about the Alamo, *The Immortal Alamo* (1911), directed by Gaston Méliès. See the still in Frank Thompson, *Alamo Movies*, 22.

125. Steinfeldt, *San Antonio Was*, 176–77.

126. *San Antonio Express*, Oct. 11, 1892, 5.

127. *San Antonio Light*, Oct. 29, 1892, 4. There were, however, Mexican food stands inside the garden, and more affluent Mexican Americans certainly attended all events.

128. Ibid.

129. *San Antonio Express*, May 16, 1893, 5.

130. *San Antonio Express*, June 13, 1893, 6.

131. Some of the protagonists in this pre-Disney period were called by alternate names. Thus, Cinderella was referred to by her German name, Ashenbrodel; Snow White was Snow Drop; and Red Riding Hood was Red Cap.

132. *Protocoll Buch*, June 23, 1893, 81; July 3, 1893, 82–83.

133. *San Antonio Express*, Oct. 7, 1893, 6.

134. Ibid.

CHAPTER 7

1. Helene van Phul, *History of the Battle of Flowers*, 1–2.

2. See chapter 4. At least one of these flower battles was described in the local press; it was perhaps for a Cinco de Mayo celebration in Mexico City in 1890. See the *San Antonio Express*, Apr. 28, 1890, 1.

3. In a recap of the festival published in the *San Antonio Express* the Sunday after the parade the anonymous author of the article "Society and the Flowers" (*San Antonio Ex-*

press, Apr. 26, 1901, 9) credits the initial impetus to Alexander, who proposed the idea on April 4.

4. C. James Haug, *Leisure and Urbanism in Nineteenth-Century Nice*, 49–51.

5. Mary Etta McGimsey, *A Parade with a Purpose*, 3, suggests a series of meetings being held, the first at the home of Col. H. B. Andrews and his wife during the early months of 1891.

6. *San Antonio Express*, Mar. 7, 1882, 4.

7. *San Antonio Express*, Apr. 17, 1891, 8. Ballard's suggestion may also be the source of the idea that he had something to do with the origin of the Battle of Flowers, which became part of the official mythology. See, for example, Barnes, *Combats and Conquests*, 121.

8. The Benjamin Harrison presidential papers (Library of Congress microfilm series 2, reel 76) include a telegram from the citizen's committee of San Antonio, dated April 7, inviting Harrison to visit the "largest city in the state."

9. *San Antonio Express*, Apr. 18, 1891, 4.

10. The Benjamin Harrison presidential papers include no invitation to the Battle of Flowers.

11. *San Antonio Express*, Apr. 14, 1891, 8.

12. *San Antonio Light*, Apr. 14, 1891, 4; *San Antonio Express*, Apr. 14, 1891, 8.

13. On the other hand, many of the San Antonio Club members were also members of the German American Casino Club, and some of the Catholics among them also belonged to the Mexican Social Club.

14. Prassel, "Leisure Time Activities in San Antonio," 100.

15. *San Antonio Express*, Apr. 17, 1891, 8.

16. *San Antonio Express*, Apr. 18, 1891, 8.

17. *San Antonio Light*, Apr. 20, 1891, 1, 8; *San Antonio Express*, Apr. 21, 1891, 4.

18. *San Antonio Express*, Apr. 24, 1891, 5.

19. The *San Antonio Express*, Apr. 26, 1891, 9, printed a long list of the more prominent entries on its society page. Since Mrs. Slayden was the paper's first society editor, this is not surprising.

20. The same Belknap members entered the same float in the German American parade in October, where it was not appreciated at all.

21. *San Antonio Express*, Apr. 26, 1891, 9.

22. *San Antonio Express*, Oct. 29, 1892, 3. This never quite came off anyway, because the oxen drawing the wagon were spooked by the firing of blanks by the "cowboys" and bolted from the line of march.

23. For a complete list, see the *San Antonio Express*, Mar. 25, 1892, 8.

24. They invited a second veteran, Nat Mitchell, but he did not show up. See the *San Antonio Express*, Apr. 22, 1892, 6.

25. Rabke, "Theater in San Antonio," 35.

26. *San Antonio Express*, Apr. 22, 1892, 6.

27. *San Antonio Light*, Apr. 22, 1892, 1.

28. See Mrs. Ellen Maury Slayden's remarks in the *San Antonio Express*, Apr. 1, 1893, 6.

29. *San Antonio Express*, Apr. 22, 1896, 6.

30. *San Antonio Light*, Apr. 22, 1891, 1.
31. Ibid.
32. Ibid.; *San Antonio Light*, Apr. 22, 1893, 8.
33. *San Antonio Express*, Apr. 22, 1896, 6.
34. See, for example, Richard Everett, "Things in and about San Antonio," n.p.; King, "Glimpses of Texas," 323; and Spoffard, "San Antonio de Bexar," 845–46.
35. Lanier, "San Antonio de Bexar," 84–87. Lanier attributes his source of the story of Travis drawing the line to the Zuber family, at whose house Moses Rose, supposedly the only man who did not "cross the line" and left, stopped after leaving the besieged fort. For the truth or myth of the story of Travis drawing the line, see Walter Lord, *A Time to Stand*, 201–204.
36. The painting had been made for a book project by James DeShields, entitled *Tall Men with Long Rifles*, though it was never used. See Pinckney, *Painting in Texas*, 188 and figure 107.
37. For a discussion of the genesis of the restored facade, see Frank Thompson, *The Alamo: A Cultural History*, 83–86.
38. See, for example, Richard Everett, "Things in and about San Antonio," n.p.
39. Gale Hamilton Shiffren, *Echoes from Women of the Alamo*, 112–13.
40. For a discussion of the Daughters of the Republic of Texas, see Brear, *Inherit the Alamo*, 84–95.
41. *San Antonio Light*, Apr. 21, 1894, 1.
42. The craze for national dances, both on the stage and in the ballroom, was a phenomenon that spanned the entire nineteenth century in both Europe and the United States. See Lisa C. Arkin and Marian Smith, "National Dance in the Romantic Ballet," 11–68.
43. *San Antonio Express*, Mar. 27, 1894, 3
44. *San Antonio Express*, Mar. 11, 1894, 9.
45. Descriptions of participants in this parade come from the *San Antonio Express*, Apr. 22, 1894, 1, 3; and the *San Antonio Light*, Apr. 21, 1894, 1. By now, the parade was front-page news in both papers.
46. *San Antonio Light*, Apr. 21, 1894, 1.
47. *San Antonio Express*, Jan. 8, 1895, 5; Jan. 14, 1895, 5; Jan. 15, 1895, 5.
48. *San Antonio Express*, Mar. 25, 1895, 5; *San Antonio Light*, Mar. 28, 1895, 4.
49. *San Antonio Light*, Mar. 28, 1895, 4.
50. *San Antonio Express*, Apr. 5, 1895, 5.
51. *San Antonio Express*, June 4, 1895, 8.
52. *San Antonio Express*, June 5, 1895, 8.
53. Ibid. The *Express* description concluded: "One of the beauties of the float was its simplicity, nothing being overdone[!]."
54. *San Antonio Light*, June 5, 1895, 4.
55. *San Antonio Express*, Apr. 19, 1896, 3.
56. For an elaborated biography of both Mr. and Mrs. Ogden, see Chabot, *With the Makers of San Antonio*, 339–43.

57. See, for example, the planning meeting reported by the *San Antonio Express*, Mar. 24, 1896, 3, at which Dr. Rose and fire chief John Tobin were the only males present.

58. *San Antonio Express*, Apr. 1, 1896, 3.

59. *San Antonio Light*, Apr. 2, 1896, 4.

60. *San Antonio Express*, Apr. 22, 1896, 2.

61. *San Antonio Light*, Apr. 21, 1896, 7.

62. *San Antonio Light*, Apr. 3, 1896, 4.

63. The floats were only briefly described, and no known photographs of them survive. See the *San Antonio Express*, Apr. 21, 1896, 2.

64. *San Antonio Express*, Apr. 21, 1896, 5.

65. Barnes, *Combats and Conquests*, 124, does not mention the accident and erroneously assumes that the salute became an annual event beginning in 1896.

66. *San Antonio Express*, Feb. 20, 1897, 5.

67. *San Antonio Express*, Feb. 28, 1897, 4; Apr. 11, 1897, 4.

68. Kallison, "100 Years of Jewry," 109.

69. *San Antonio Express*, Mar. 14, 1897, 5.

70. *San Antonio Express*, Mar. 21, 1896, 4. There is still a band contest associated with the Battle of Flowers, but now it is invitational and restricted to school bands. Participants still march in the parade.

71. *San Antonio Light*, Apr. 4, 1897, 1.

72. According to Charles Merritt Barnes, who was a member, the Zouaves were founded July 4, 1896. See Barnes, *Combats and Conquests*, 147.

73. *San Antonio Express*, Apr. 22, 1897, 1–2.

74. *San Antonio Express*, Feb. 11, 1898, 5.

75. *San Antonio Express*, Feb. 11, 1898, 5.

76. *San Antonio Express*, Mar. 1, 1898, 5; Mar. 4, 1898, 5; Mar. 10, 1898, 6.

77. *San Antonio Light*, Mar. 3, 1898, 7.

78. *San Antonio Express*, Mar. 28, 1898, 10 (the society page).

79. *San Antonio Express*, Apr. 20, 1898, 6.

80. *San Antonio Express*, Apr. 20, 1898, 6. On Rivas, see the *San Antonio Express*, Apr, 1, 1898, 6. There were twenty-five marshals in the 1898 Battle of Flowers parade, with a number drawn from San Antonio's varying ethnic communities, including Antonio Battaglia, Leopold Guerguin, Lucien Lacoste, Louis Heuermann, and Otto Wahrmund.

81. *San Antonio Express*, Apr. 20, 1898, 6.

82. *San Antonio Express*, Apr. 22, 1898, 5; *San Antonio Light*, Apr. 22, 1898, 3. The *Light* places the whistle blast about 1 P.M.

83. *San Antonio Express*, Apr. 22, 1898, 5.

84. *San Antonio Light*, Apr. 22, 1898, 3. Charles W. Barnes relates that the Zouaves were in line for the coming parade and happened to pause in front of the telegraph office when the war notification came out, deciding to volunteer then and there. This may be the seed of the parade enlistment story. See Barnes, *Combats and Conquests*, 147.

85. *San Antonio Light*, Apr. 22, 1898, 3.

86. *San Antonio Express*, Feb. 17, 1899, 3.

87. *San Antonio Express*, Mar. 17, 1899, 5; Mar. 3, 1899, 5; Mar. 24, 1899, 8; Mar. 31, 1899, 5; Apr. 7, 1899, 5; *San Antonio Light*, Mar. 3, 1899, 4; Mar. 17, 1899, 8; Mar. 24, 1899, 4, 8; Apr. 7, 1899, 5.

88. The San Antonio Zouaves had to march with dummy guns, since enough real rifles could not be secured in time (*San Antonio Light*, Apr. 21, 1899, 4).

89. *San Antonio Express*, Apr. 21, 1899, 7; *San Antonio Light*, Apr. 21, 1899, 4.

90. *San Antonio Express*, Apr. 22, 1899, 5.

91. *San Antonio Light*, Apr. 22, 1899, 5.

92. Ibid.

93. See chapter 2.

94. Though these clubs were sometimes abbreviated as "K.K.K.," they had nothing to do with the Ku Klux Klan.

95. *San Antonio Express*, Apr. 22, 1899, 6; *San Antonio Light*, Apr. 23, 1899, 8. In late nineteenth-century San Antonio, we have seen that several ethnic groups managed to live side by side with relatively little conflict.

96. *San Antonio Light*, Apr. 23, 1899, 8.

97. See chapter 4.

98. *San Antonio Express*, Apr. 22, 1899, 6.

99. *San Antonio Light*, Apr. 23, 1899, 8.

100. *San Antonio Express*, Apr. 22, 1897, 2.

101. For a very brief history of the early tournaments, see Joe Hendrickson, *The Tournament of Roses: A Pictorial History*, 4–9.

CHAPTER 8

1. See chapter 7.

2. *San Antonio Light*, Feb. 24, 1900, 4.

3. *San Antonio Express*, Mar. 4, 1900, 12.

4. This meant, of course, that the businessmen could persuade the merchants along Commerce Street to allow the booths in front of their stores. With the cooperation of Mayor Hicks, this was soon achieved. See the *San Antonio Express*, Feb. 24, 1899, 8; Mar. 17, 1900, 8.

5. *San Antonio Light*, Apr. 17, 1900, 5.

6. Ibid. Did this company also provide the traveling incubator babies?

7. *San Antonio Light*, Apr. 4, 1900, 4. The people who entered the fighting birds were, however, Anglo-Americans.

8. Henri Schindler, *Mardi Gras, New Orleans*, 66–69.

9. *San Antonio Express*, Mar. 31, 1900, 10.

10. *San Antonio Light*, Apr. 9, 1900, 5. That these titles derived from tribal Indian names, and the place from an island in the Hawaiian chain, didn't faze the planners in the least—indeed, "Molokai" was also spelled "Malaki" and "Molekin" in the newspapers.

11. *San Antonio Express*, Apr. 1, 1900, 12.

12. *San Antonio Light*, Mar. 18, 1900, 8.

13. It should be noted, however, that the principal organizers of the various Battle of Flowers processions, such as Mrs. Frazer, Mrs. Hertzberg, Mrs. N. T. Wilson and Mrs. G. G. Watts, to name just a few, were conspicuously absent from any planning committees for Spring Carnival.

14. *San Antonio Express*, Apr. 15, 1900, 7.

15. *San Antonio Light*, Apr. 16, 1900, 8.

16. *San Antonio Light*, Apr. 10, 1900, 10.

17. *San Antonio Express*, Apr. 17, 1900, 7.

18. The only people who were not enthralled were the owners and potential patrons of Wolfson's Department Store on Main Plaza, whose entrance was blocked by the *lugar festivo*.

19. Reports of the activities for the rest of the week can be found in the *San Antonio Express*, Apr. 17, 1900, 7; Apr. 18, 1900, 7; Apr. 19, 1900, 4; Apr. 20, 1900, 4; Apr. 21, 1900, 4; Apr. 22, 1900, 10, 12; *San Antonio Light*, Apr. 17, 1900, 5; Apr. 18, 1900, 8; Apr. 19, 1900, 4; Apr. 20, 1900, 4; Apr. 21, 1900, 4; Apr. 22, 1900, 1.

20. Only that perennial gentleman Fortunato Villareal was involved in the Spring Carnival—he was on several military ball committees.

21. *San Antonio Express*, Apr. 23, 1900, 4.

EPILOGUE

1. See the long article in the *San Antonio Herald*, June 24, 1871, 2, for the general tone of American attitudes toward immigration just after the Civil War.

2. The *Herald*, the *Express* and the *Light* all featured European news as well as news from Mexico, but the attention given to Mexico and Mexican affairs always occupied a substantial part of every edition.

3. Discriminatory attitudes of the time are perhaps best seen in the availability of nineteenth-century festival photographs. The Volksfests and Battle of Flowers parades are relatively well documented. Though photographs of Juneteenth festivals at the end of the century exist in some of the official brochures published to commemorate them (now in the collection of Vera Williams Young), there are no extant photographs of the African American volunteer fire companies or baseball teams. Most of the nineteenth-century photographs of the Mexican American community that survive were taken by Anglo-American photographers and show a stereotyped view of their "exoticness": food sellers and other vendors from Military Plaza, "picturesque" *jacales,* and the like. The one surviving photograph of Diez y Seis included in this book is from a stereograph that was part of a series on "quaint" Mexican American life, probably designed for tourists.

4. *San Antonio Light*, Oct. 3, 1885, 1; *San Antonio Express*, Apr. 17, 1900, 7.

5. *San Antonio Express*, Apr. 21, 1896, 5.

6. "All nations" as a festival or pageant theme at the time appears to have excluded most of the countries of Africa, South America, and Asia, except for China and Japan.

7. Jack McGuire, *A Century of Fiesta in San Antonio*, 44.

8. Fehrenbach, *The San Antonio Story*, 157.

BIBLIOGRAPHY

DOCUMENTS AND MANUSCRIPTS

Bybee, Larry Lane. "The Germans in San Antonio (1844–1920): A Study in Cultural Persistence." Master's thesis, The University of Texas at San Antonio, 1980.

Edelen, Mary B. "Bryan Callaghan II: His Early Political Career, 1885–1899." Master's thesis, Trinity University, 1971.

Kallison, Frances. "100 Years of Jewry in San Antonio." Master's thesis, Trinity University, 1977.

Landolt, Robert Garland. "The Mexican-American Workers of San Antonio, Texas." Ph.D. diss., University of Texas at Austin, 1965.

Mason, Kenneth. "Paternal Continuity: Afro-Americans and Race Relations in San Antonio, Texas, 1867–1937." Ph.D. diss., University of Texas at Austin, 1994.

Phul, Helene van. *History of the Battle of Flowers*. 1931. Manuscript in the collection of the Daughters of the Republic of Texas Library, San Antonio, Texas.

Prassel, Frank Richard. "Leisure Time Activities in San Antonio, 1877–1917." Master's thesis, Trinity University, 1961.

Protocoll Buch der Central Comites zur . . . des Deutschen Tages in San Antonio. Daughters of the Republic of Texas Library, German-English School Records 890.

Pycior, Julie Leininger. "La Raza Organizes: Mexican American Life in San Antonio, 1915–1930, as Reflected in Mutualistas Activities." Ph.D. diss., Notre Dame, 1979.

Rabke, Barbara. "Theater in San Antonio, 1886–1891." Master's thesis, Trinity University, 1964.

Remy, Caroline M. "A Study of the Transition of San Antonio from a Frontier to an Urban Community from 1875–1900." Master's thesis, Trinity University, 1960.

Rogers, Will C., III. "A History of the Military Plaza to 1938." Master's thesis, Trinity University, 1968.

Roll of Members of the San Antonio Fire Department. Turnverein Collection, Witte Museum, n.d.

Sayers, Billy Joe. "'That Horrific Tragedy': The Initial Impact of Secession and the Beginning of the Civil War upon San Antonio and South Central Texas." Master's thesis, The University of Texas at San Antonio, 1982.

Smith, Horace R. "History of Alamo Plaza from the Beginning to the Present." Master's thesis, Trinity University, 1966.

Ley Fundamental de la Sociedad Benevolencia Mexicana para auxilios mutuos. Fundada en la Ciudad de San Antonio, Condado de Bexar, Estado de Texas, el 1 de Mayo, 1875, refamado en 1885 y regenerado en 1889. 1889. University of Texas at Austin, Center for American History.

Statutes of the San Antonio Volunteer Fire Companies. Turnverein Collection, Witte Museum, 1875.

Strong, Bernice Rhoades. "Alamo Plaza: Cultural Crossroads of a City, 1724–1900." Master's thesis, University of Texas at San Antonio, 1987.

Teja, Jesus F. de la. "Land and Society in Eighteenth Century San Antonio de Bejar, a Community on New Spain's Northern Frontier." Ph.D. diss., University of Texas at Austin, 1988.

Tichich, Richard. "Ernst Raba: San Antonio Artist and Photographer, 1874–1951." Master's thesis, University of Texas at San Antonio, 1979.

BOOKS

Barnes, Charles Merritt. *Combats and Conquests of Immortal Heroes: Sung in Song, Told in Story.* San Antonio: Guessaz and Ferlet Co., 1910.

Belfiglio, Valentine. *The Italian Experience in Texas.* Austin: Eakin Press, 1983.

Benjamin, Gilbert Giddings. *The Germans in Texas: A Study in Imigration* [sic]. 1910. Reprint, Austin: Jenkins Publishing Company, 1974.

Bénézet, E. *Dictionnaire critique et documentaire des peintres, sculpteurs, dessinateurs et graveurs.* Rev. ed. Paris: Librairie Gründ, 1976.

Biesele, Rudolph Leopold. *The History of German Settlements in Texas, 1831–1861.* Austin: Von Boeckman and Jones, 1930.

Boyce, House. *San Antonio: City of Flaming Adventure.* 1949. Reprint, San Antonio: Naylor Publishing Company, 1968.

Brear, Holly Beachly. *Inherit the Alamo.* Austin: University of Texas Press, 1995.

Brooks, Charles H. *The Official History and Manual of the Grand United Order of Odd Fellows in America.* Freeport, N.Y.: Books for Libraries Press, 1971.

Bushick, Frank. *Glamorous Days.* San Antonio: Naylor Publishing Company, 1934.

Cardenas, Hector. *San Antonio Fire Department History.* Paducah, Ky.: Turner Publishing Company, 2000.

Chabot, Frederick C. *With the Makers of San Antonio: Genealogies of the Early Latin, Anglo-American, and German Families with Occasional Biographies; Each Group Being Prefaced with a Brief Historical Sketch and Illustrations.* San Antonio: Artes Graficas, 1937.

Corner, William. *San Antonio de Bexar: A Guide and History.* San Antonio: Bainbridge and Corner, 1890.

Crook, Cornelia E. *San Pedro Springs Park: Texas' Oldest Recreation Area.* San Antonio: Cornelia E. Crook, 1967.

Cude, Elton R. *The Wild and Free Dukedom of Bexar.* San Antonio: Munguia Printers, 1978.

Curtis, Albert. *Fabulous San Antonio.* San Antonio: Naylor Publishing Company, 1955.

Davis, John R. *San Antonio: A Historical Portrait.* Austin: Encino Press, 1978.

De León, Arnoldo. *Apuntes Tejanos: An Index of Items Related to Mexican Americans in Nineteenth Century Texas Extracted from the* San Antonio Express *(1869–1900) and the*

San Antonio Herald *(1855–1878)*. Ann Arbor: University Microfilms International, 1978.

———. *The Tejano Community, 1836–1900*. Albuquerque: University of New Mexico Press, 1982.

———. *They Called Them Greasers: Anglo Attitudes towards Mexicans in Texas, 1821–1900*. Austin: University of Texas Press, 1983.

Denier, Tony. *Parlor Tableaux, or Animated Pictures for the Use of Families, Schools and Public Exhibitions*. New York: Harold Roorback, 1868.

Everett, Donald E. *San Antonio Legacy*. San Antonio: Trinity University Press, 1979.

Fehrenbach, T. R. *The San Antonio Story*. Tulsa: Continental Heritage Press, 1978.

Fenwick, M. B., and Sara Hartman. *Directory of Societies and Ladies' Address List, San Antonio, 1897*. San Antonio: Guessaz and Ferlet, 1897.

Fisher, Lewis F. *Crown Jewel of Texas: The Story of San Antonio's River*. San Antonio: Maverick Publishing Company, 1997.

Fox, Daniel E., Dan Scurlock, and John W. Clark Jr. *Archeological Excavations at San Fernando Cathedral, San Antonio, Texas: A Preliminary Report*. Austin: Office of the State Archeologist, Texas Historical Commission, 1977.

Galleghy, Joseph. *From Alamo Plaza to Jack Harris's Saloon: O. Henry and the Southwest He Knew*. The Hague: Mouton, 1970.

Gamio, Manuel. *Mexican Immigration to the United States*. Chicago: The University of Chicago Press, 1930.

García, Pedro. *Con el cura Hidalgo en la guerra de independencia*. 1929. Reprint, Mexico City: CONAFE, 1982.

Garcia, Richard A. *Rise of the Mexican-American Middle Class: San Antonio, 1929–1941*. College Station: Texas A&M Press, 1991.

General Directory of the City of San Antonio for 1877–1878. Containing a History of the City: A Complete Index of All Societies, Associations, Corporations, etc. Also, the Full Address of All Residents, Their Occupations, Pursuits, etc. Also, a Complete Business Directory; An Exhibition of the Various Classified Kinds of Business Pursued in the City. Comp. Andrew Morrison and Mooney [sic]. Galveston: The Book and Job Office of the *Galveston News*, 1877–78.

General Directory of the City of San Antonio for 1879–80. Containing a History of the City: A Complete Index of all Societies, Associations, Corporations, etc. Also, the Full Address of All Residents, Their Occupations, Pursuits, etc. Also, a Complete Business Directory; An Exhibition of the Various Classified Kinds of Business Pursued in the City. Comp. Andrew Morrison and Fourmy [sic]. Marshall, Tex.: Jennings Bros. Binders and Blank Book Makers, 1879–80.

General Directory of the City of San Antonio for 1881–82. Containing a Historical Business Review, the Present State, County and City Governments, a Complete List of County Officials, Post Offices, Telegraph, Express and Money Order Offices in Texas; Also an Index of All Societies, Associations, Corporations, Churches, Educational Institutes, etc., the Full Name and Address of All Residents, Their Occupations or Pursuits, and a

Complete Classified Business Directory. Comp. Andrew Morrison and Fourmy [*sic*]. Austin: E. W. Swindells, Steam Printer, 1881–82.

General Directory of the City of San Antonio for 1883–84. Containing an Historical Business Review, the Present State, County and City Governments, a Complete List of All County Officials, Post Offices, Telegraph, Express and Money Order Offices in Texas, Population of the United States and Principal Cities, Population of Principal Nations and Foreign Cities; Also an Index of All Societies, Associations, Corporations, Churches, Educational Institutes, the Full Name and Address of All Residents, Their Occupations or Pursuits, and a Complete Classified Business Directory. Comp. Andrew Morrison and Fourmy [*sic*]. Galveston: Clarke and Courts, Stationer, Printers, Lithographers, 1883–84.

General Directory of the City of San Antonio for 1885–86. Containing the Present State, County and City Governments, a Complete List of All County Officials, Post Offices, Telegraph, Express and Money Order Offices in Texas; Also an Index of Societies, Associations, Corporations, Churches, Educational Institutes, the Full Name and Address of All Residents, Their Occupations or Pursuits, and a Complete Classified Business Directory. Comp. Andrew Morrison and Fourmy [*sic*]. Galveston: Clarke and Courts, Stationer, Printers, Lithographers, 1885–86.

General Directory of the City of San Antonio for 1887–88. Containing the Present State, County and City Governments, a Complete List of All County Officials, Post Offices, Telegraph, Express and Money Order Offices in Texas; Also an Index of Societies, Associations, Churches, Corporations, Educational Institutes, the Full Name and Address of All Residents, Their Occupations or Pursuits, and a Complete Classified Business Directory. Also, a Valuable Street Index or Guide. Comp. Andrew Morrison and Fourmy [*sic*]. Galveston: Morrison and Fourmy, Publishers, 1885–86.

Glassberg, David. *American Historical Pageantry: The Uses of Tradition in the Early Twentieth Century.* Chapel Hill: The University of North Carolina Press, 1990.

Gould, Stephen. *The Alamo City Guide: San Antonio, Texas. Being a Historical Sketch of the Ancient City of the Alamo and Business Review. With Notes on Present Advantages, Together with a Complete Guide to all the Prominent Points of Interest about the City, and a Compilation of Facts of Value to Visitors and Residents.* New York: McGowan and Slipper, 1882.

Green, Rena Maverick. *I Remember: Memoirs of Mary A. Maverick.* San Antonio: Alamo Printing Co., 1921.

Guerra, Mary Ann Noonan. *The Story of the San Antonio River.* San Antonio: The Alamo Press, 1987.

Haug, C. James. *Leisure and Urbanism in Nineteenth-Century Nice.* Lawrence: The Regents Press of Kansas, 1982.

Hazzard-Gordon, Katrina. *Jookin': The Rise of Social Dance Formations in African-American Culture.* Philadelphia, Temple University Press, 1990.

Hendrickson, Joe. *The Tournament of Roses: A Pictorial History.* Los Angeles: Brooke House Publishers, 1971.

Hernandez, Jose Amaro. *Mutual Aid for Survival: The Case of the Mexican American.* Malabar, Fla.: Robert E. Krieger Publishing Company, 1983.

Heusinger, Edward D. *A Chronology of San Antonio Events: Being a Concise History of the City to the End of the First Half of the Twentieth Century.* San Antonio: Standard Printing Co., 1951.
Hill, J. A. *Hill's Book of Tableaux.* 1884. Reprint, Indianapolis: Fraternity Publishing Co., 1891.
Hinojosa, Gilberto, and Gerald Poyo, eds. *Tejano Origins in Eighteenth-Century San Antonio.* Austin: University of Texas Press, 1991.
History and Guide of San Antonio, Texas. San Antonio, 1894.
The Industries of San Antonio. 1885. Reprint, Normon Brock, 1977.
Institute of Texas Cultures. *The Italian Texans.* San Antonio: Institute of Texas Cultures, 1973.
James, Vinton Lee. *Frontier and Pioneer Recollections of Early Days in San Antonio and West Texas.* San Antonio: Artes Graficas, 1938.
Jennings, Frank W. *San Antonio: The Story of an Enchanted City.* San Antonio: Express-News Corp., 1998.
Johnson, David R., John A. Booth, and Richard J. Harris. *The Politics of San Antonio: Community, Progress and Power.* Lincoln: University of Nebraska Press, 1983.
Jordan, Terry G. *German Seed in Texas Soil: Immigrant Farmers in Nineteenth-Century Texas.* Austin: University of Texas Press, 1966.
Kinser, Samuel. *Carnival American Style: Mardi Gras at New Orleans and Mobile.* Chicago: University of Chicago Press, 1990.
Landolt, Robert Garland. *The Mexican-American Workers of San Antonio.* New York: Arno Press, 1976.
Linenthal, Edward Tabor. *Sacred Ground: Americans and Their Battlefields.* Urbana: University of Illinois Press, 1991.
Lomax, Louise. *San Antonio's River.* San Antonio: Naylor Publishing Company, 1948.
Lord, Walter. *A Time to Stand.* Lincoln: The University of Nebraska Press, 1961.
Malone, Jacqi. *Steppin' on the Blues: The Visible Rhythms of African American Dance.* Urbana: University of Illinois Press, 1996.
Mason, Herbert Molloy, and Frank Brown. *A Century on Main Plaza: A History of the Frost National Bank.* San Antonio: Frost National Bank, 1968.
McComb, David G. *Galveston: A History.* Austin: University of Texas Press, 1986.
McElmore, David. *A Place in Time: A Pictorial View of San Antonio's Past.* San Antonio: Express-News Corp., 1980.
McGimsey, Mary Etta. *A Parade with a Purpose.* 1966. Rev. ed., with Mrs. Robert G. Watts., San Antonio: Battle of the Flowers Association of San Antonio, Texas, 1984.
McGuire, Jack. *A Century of Fiesta in San Antonio.* Austin: Eakin Press, 1990.
McGuire, James Patrick. *Iwonski in Texas: Painter and Citizen.* San Antonio: San Antonio Museum Association and Institute of Texan Cultures, 1976.
Meier, Matt S., ed. *Bibliography of Mexican American History.* Westport, Conn.: Greenwood Press, 1984.
Miller, Char, and Heywood T. Sanders, eds. *Urban Texas: Politics and Development.* College Station: Texas A&M University Press, 1990.

Montejano, David. *Anglos and Mexicans in the Making of Texas, 1836–1986.* Austin: University of Texas Press, 1987.

Morrison, Andrew. *The City of San Antonio, Texas.* St. Louis: George W. Engelhardt, [1890?].

Mosse, George L. *The Nationalization of the Masses: Political Symbolism and Mass Movements in Germany from the Napoleonic Wars through the Third Reich.* New York: Howard Fertig, 1975.

Münzer, Hieronymus. *Viaje por España y Portugal, 1494–1495.* Trans. José López Toro. Prologue by Manuel Gómez Moreno. Madrid: Colección Almenara, [1951?].

Newcomb, Pearson. *The Alamo City.* San Antonio: Standard Printing Co., 1926.

Nixon, Pat Ireland. *A Century of Medicine in San Antonio.* San Antonio, 1936.

Odom, Marianne, and Gaylon Finklea Young. *The Businesses That Built San Antonio.* San Antonio: Living Legacies, 1985.

Olmsted, Frederick Law. *A Journey through Texas, or A Saddle-Trip on the Southwestern Frontier: With a Statistical Appendix.* Austin: University of Texas Press, 1978.

Pinckney, Pauline A. *Painting in Texas: The Nineteenth Century.* Austin: The University of Texas Press for the Amon Carter Museum, Fort Worth, 1967.

Prather, Patricia Smith, and Jane Clement. *From Slave to Statesman, Servant to Sam Houston.* Denton: University of North Texas Press, 1993.

Ramsdell, Charles. *Reconstruction in Texas.* New York: Longmans, Green, 1910.

———. *San Antonio: A Historical and Pictorial Guide.* 1959. Reprint, Austin: University of Texas Press, 1968.

Rock, James L., and W. L. Smith. *Southern and Western Texas Guide for 1878.* Saint Louis: A. H. Granger, 1878.

Roemer, Ferdinand. *Texas: With Particular Reference to German Immigration.* Waco: Texian Press, 1967.

Ryan, Mary P. *Women in Public: Between Banners and Ballots, 1825–1880.* Baltimore: Johns Hopkins University Press, 1990.

Salins, Peter D. *Assimilation, American Style.* New York: Basic Books, 1997.

Santleben, August. *A Texas Pioneer: Early Staging and Overland Freighting Days on the Frontiers of Texas and Mexico.* New York: Neale Publishing Co., 1910.

Schindler, Henri. *Mardi Gras, New Orleans.* Paris and New York: Flammarion, 1997.

Schroeder, Susan Prendergast, and Tom W. Gläser. *Alamo Images: Changing Perceptions of a Texas Experience.* Dallas: De Golyer Library and Southern Methodist University Press, 1985.

Schucard, Ernst. *100th Anniversary of the Pioneer Flour Mills.* San Antonio: Naylor Publishing Company, 1951.

Shiffren, Gale Hamilton. *Echoes from Women of the Alamo.* San Antonio: AW Press, 1999.

Soria, Regina. *American Artists of Italian Heritage, 1776–1945: A Biographical Dictionary.* Rutherford, N.J: Fairleigh Dickinson University Press, 1993.

Spencer, Thomas M. *The St. Louis Veiled Prophet Celebration: Power on Parade, 1877–1995.* Columbia: University of Missouri Press, 2000.

Steinfeldt, Cecilia. *San Antonio Was: Seen through a Magic Lantern: Views from the Slide Collection of Albert Steves, Sr.* San Antonio: San Antonio Museum Association, 1978.
Stewart, Kenneth, and Arnoldo de León. *Not Room Enough: Mexicans, Anglos and Socio-economic Change in Texas, 1850–1900.* Albuquerque: University of New Mexico Press, 1993.
Struve, Walter. *Germans and Texans: Commerce, Migrations and Culture in the Days of the Lone Star Republic.* Austin: University of Texas Press, 1996.
Sturmberg, Robert, ed. *History of San Antonio and of the Early Days in Texas.* San Antonio: Saint Joseph's Society, 1920.
Thompson, Frank. *The Alamo: A Cultural History.* Dallas: Taylor Trade Publishing, 2001.
———. *Alamo Movies.* Plano, Tex.: Wordware Publishing Company, 1991.
Tyler, Ron, ed. *The New Texas Handbook.* 6 vols. Austin: Texas State Historical Association, 1996.
Wheeler, Kenneth W. *To Wear a City's Crown.* Cambridge: Harvard University Press, 1968.
Wiggins, William H., Jr. *O Freedom! Afro-American Emancipation Celebrations.* Knoxville: University of Tennessee Press, 1987.
Woolford, Sam. *The San Antonio Story.* Austin: Steck, 1950.
———, ed. *San Antonio: A History for Tomorrow.* San Antonio: Naylor Publishing Company, 1963.
Wright, Mrs. S. J. *San Antonio de Bejar: Historical, Traditional, Legendary.* Austin: Morgan Printing Co., 1916.
Zenderland, Leila. *Recycling the Past: Popular Uses of American History.* Philadelphia: University of Pennsylvania Press, 1978.

ARTICLES

Arkin, Lisa C., and Marian Smith. "National Dance in the Romantic Ballet." In *Rethinking the Sylph: New Perspectives on the Romantic Ballet,* ed. Lynn Garafola, 11–68. Hanover, N.H.: Wesleyan University Press, 1997.
Ballou, Ellen Bartlett. "Scudder's Journey to Texas in 1859." *Southwestern Historical Quarterly* 63 (July, 1959): 1–14.
Barr, Alwyn. "Occupation and Geographic Mobility in San Antonio, 1870–1900." *Social Science Quarterly* 51 (September, 1970): 396–403.
Beezley, William H. "The Porfirian Smart Set Anticipates Thorstein Veblen in Guadalajara." In *Rituals of Rule, Rituals of Resistance: Public Celebrations and Popular Culture in Mexico,* 173–90. Wilmington, Del.: Scholarly Research Books, 1994.
Calderón, Roberto I. "Unión, Paz y Trabajo." In *Mexican Americans in Texas History,* ed. Emilio Zamora, Cynthia Orozco, and Rodolfo Rocha, 67–70. Austin: Texas State Historical Association, 2000.
Everett, Richard. "Things in and about San Antonio." *Frank Leslie's Illustrated Newspaper,* January 15, 1859, n.p.

Harby, Lee C. "Texan Types and Contrasts." *Harper's New Monthly Magazine,* July, 1891, 229–46.

Johnson, David R. "Frugal and Sparing: Interest Groups, Politics and City Building in San Antonio, 1870–85." In *Urban Texas: Politics and Development,* ed. Char Miller and Heywood T. Sanders, 33–57. College Station: Texas A&M University Press, 1990.

King, Edward. "Glimpses of Texas—I: A Visit to San Antonio." *Scribner's Monthly: An Illustrated Magazine,* January, 1874, 320–30.

Lanier, Sidney. "San Antonio de Bexar." In *San Antonio de Bexar: A Guide and History,* by William Corner, 68–94. San Antonio: Bainbridge and Corner, 1890.

Lich, Glen E. "Goethe on the Guadalupe." In *German Culture in Texas: A Free Earth: Essays from the 1978 Southwest Symposium,* ed. Glen E. Lich and Dona B. Reeves, 29–71. Boston: Twayne Publishers, 1980.

Logan, Charles Thomas. "Quaint San Antonio." *Frank Leslie's Popular Monthly,* July, 1898, 82–85.

McGowan, Stanley S. M. "Battle or Massacre? . . . Nueces, 8/10/1862." *Southwestern Historical Quarterly* 104 (July, 2000): 64–86.

Meyer, B. H. "Fraternal Beneficiary Societies in the United States." *American Journal of Sociology* 6 (March, 1901): 647–61.

Mosebach, Fred. "Fourth of July Antedates All Celebrations in San Antonio." *San Antonio Express,* June 28, 1936, 10C.

Pecorini, Alberto. "The Italian in America, 1891–1914." In *The Italians, Social Background of an American Group,* ed. Francesco Cordasco and Eugene Bucchioni, 167–86. Clifton, N.J.: Augustus M. Kelley, 1974.

Poyo, Gerald E. "The Canary Islands Immigrants of San Antonio: From Ethnic Exclusivity to Community in Eighteenth-Century Bexar." In *Tejano Origins in Eighteenth-Century San Antonio,* ed. Gilberto Hinojosa and Gerald Poyo, 41–60. Austin: University of Texas Press, 1991.

Reese, James V. "The Early History of Labor Organization in Texas, 1838–1876." *Southwestern Historical Quarterly* 72 (July, 1968): 1–20.

Rios, Herminio, and Luoe Castillo. "Toward a True Chicano Bibliography: Mexican-American Newspapers, 1848–1942." *El Grito: A Journal of Contemporary Mexican-American Thought* 2 (summer, 1970): 17–24.

Shapiro, Harold. "The Labor Movement in San Antonio, Texas, 1865–1915." *Southwestern Social Science Quarterly* 36 (September, 1955): 160–75.

Spoffard, Harriet Prescott. "San Antonio de Bejar." *Harper's New Monthly Magazine,* November, 1877, 831–50.

Taylor, Frank H. "Through Texas," *Harper's New Monthly Magazine,* October, 1879, 712–13.

Teja, Jesus F. de la, and John Wheat. "Béxar: Profile of a Tejano Community, 1820–1832." In *Tejano Origins in Eighteenth-Century San Antonio,* ed. Gerald E. Poyo and Gilberto M. Hinojosa, 1–26. Austin: University of Texas Press, 1991.

Walker, Mack. "The Old Homeland and the New." In *German Culture in Texas: A*

Free Earth: Essays from the 1978 Southwest Symposium, ed. Glen E. Lich and Dona B. Reeves, 72–81. Boston: Twayne Publishers, 1980.

Wiggins, William H., Jr. "Juneteenth: A Red Spot Day on the Texas Calendar." In *Juneteenth, Texas: Essays in African-American Folklore*, ed. Francis Edwards Abernathy, 237–52. Denton: University of North Texas Press, 1996.

———. "'They Closed the Town Up, Man!' Reflections on the Civic and Political Dimensions of Juneteenth." In *Celebration: Studies in Festivity and Ritual*, ed. Victor Turner, 284–96. Washington, D.C.: The Smithsonian Institution Press, 1982.

INDEX

Abbot, Emma, 27
Acequia St., 4, 13, 102
Acosta, Concepción, 93
Adams, Jay E., 179, 194, 195
Alamo, 9, 12, 14, 25, 27, 32, 33, 34, 57, 146, 158, 159, 170, 171, 172, 181, 210, 213
Alamo Cement Company, 37, 114
Alamo Fire Insurance Building, 204
Alamo Heights, 33
Alamo Literary Society, 111
Alamo Mills, 57
Alamo Plaza, 3, 4, 7, 9, 12, 16, 18, 21, 22, 25, 27, 28, 31, 32, 33, 34, 38, 40, 41, 42, 43, 46, 64, 67, 114, 119, 121, 124, 127, 136, 137, 139, 141, 156, 157, 158, 159, 170, 174, 178, 186, 187, 190, 191, 196, 197, 198, 202, 209
Alamo St., 22, 49, 56, 64, 67, 163, 195
Alamo Wheelmen, 139
Alazan Creek, 53
Alexander, John S., 154, 155
Anderson, M. G., 38
Anderson, Theodore G., 40
Andrews, Colonel Henry B., 37, 121, 129, 157
Archer, Ida, 179
Arnold, Frank, 194
Arocha, Maria, 102
Aubrey, William H., 194
Austin St., 28
Avenue D, 209
Ayers, Atlee B., 178, 197

Baker, Charles, 163
Ballard, W. J., 156
balls: Calico Ball, 63, 174; Cotton Ball, 63, 179, 180, 181, 184, 185, 187; *fandango*, 75, 79, 98; Paper Carnival Ball, 185
band contest, 181
bands: Alamo Band, 48, 139; Army Band, 106; Austin Band, 181; Batista's Mexican Band, 210; Brackner Lone Star Band, 105; Carl Beck's Military Band, 7, 46, 48, 98, 133, 134, 175, 176, 181, 186, 187, 189, 207; City Band, 42; Eagle Pass Band, 130; Eighth U.S. Cavalry Band, 42, 43, 60, 86, 90, 103, 126, 127, 128, 130; Fashion Theater Band, 130; Ex-Firemen's Band, 66, 139, 169, 173; Fifth U.S. Cavalry Band, 181, Firemen's Band, 104, 139, First Texas United Cavalry Band, 48; Hallettsville Silver Cornet Band, 181, 187, 189; Hawkins Cornet Band, 71, "Karnes City Hayseed Band," 190; La Grange Band, 181; Maverick's Band, 43, McAllister City Band, 103, 126, 127; Mexican National Zapadores Band, 100, 104, 134, 137; Russi's Band, 42; Sixth U.S. Infantry Band, 187, Solis' Mexican Band, 176, Sunset Band, 57, Tenth U.S. Cavalry Band, 189, Turnverein Band, 42; Twenty-second U.S. Infantry Band, 120; Twenty-third U.S. Infantry Band, 153, 166, 172; Twenty-fifth U.S. Infantry Band, 71; U.S. Infantry Band, 104; U.S. Military Band, 139; Washington Band, 139; Yoakum Town Band, 181; York Creek Band, 181
banks: Lockwood & Kampmann Bank, 29; Maverick Bank, 22; San Antonio Loan and Trust, 204; Texas National Bank, 37

Barbarossa, Emperor Frederick, 115
Barrera, Juan E., 11, 40, 77, 80, 82, 84, 87, 89, 90
Barrera, Miguel, 94
baseball teams: 58, 62; Browns, 59; Early Birds, 59; Gray Mule Club, 59; International Reds, 59; Mascots, 59; Menger, 59; Rising Stars, 59, San Antonio Field Grays, 59, Universal Joint Club, 57
Bastille Day, xii
"Bat Cave," 12, 102
Battaglia, Angelo, 102
Battaglia, Giocchur (George), 102, 108
Battle of Flowers, xii, 49, 81, 92, 138, 108, 153, 154–93, 202, 204, 207, 209, 210, 211, 212, 213, 215
Battle of San Jacinto, 165, 166, 172, 179
Baugh, Mrs. W. P., 187
Baum, Harry, 130
Beacon Hill, 33
Bee, General Carlos, 170, 202
beer gardens: Fest's Garden, 58, 63, 89, 90, 91, 93, 113; Kirsch's Hall, 82, 138; Limburger's Garden, 67, 97, 113; Muth's Concert Garden, 27, 133; Ruppersberg's Garden, 113; Scholz' Palm Garden, 27; Wolfram's Central Gardens, 27, 81, 97, 106, 117, 118, 119, 121, 124, 126, 127, 129, 138, 142, 143, 145, 148, 150, 209
Belknap, Colonel Augustus, 124, 129
Bell, Samuel, 39
Belle View, 33
Bennett, Captain Jesse, 46
Bennett, Sam, 23
Berg, Henry, 23, 113
Berg, Louis S., 23, 113, 157
Bergstrom, Oscar, 85, 104, 166, 207
Bexar County Courthouse, 6, 31, 38
Bias (Baez), Guadalupe, 96
Blum St., 28
Bolton, John, 11
Bonham, James, 146, 170
Bonnett, R. D., 3

Booth, Edwin, 27
"Bowen's Island," 27, 117
Bowie, James, 14, 34, 76, 146, 170
Bowie, Ursula Veramendi, 34, 76
Boyd, Pastor Henry Allen, 55
Boyles, Professor A. H., 55, 62
Breckenridge, James, 89
breweries: Alamo Brewery, 144; City Brewery, 144; Lone Star Brewery, 23, 44, 130, 144, 194
Broadway, 67
Bruchner, Herman, 127
Bruni, Antonio, 78, 90, 102, 103, 106, 107
business organizations: Chamber of Commerce, 174; Liquor Dealer's Association, 174; San Antonio Businessmen's Club, 174, 175, 180, 183, 184, 186, 189, 191, 193, 194, 196, 197, 198, 214; Traveler's Protective Association, 174, 176, 177, 212; Unitec Commercial Travelers, 187

cakewalkers, 50, 70–71
Callaghan, Sr., Bryan, 76
Callaghan, Jr., Bryan, 23, 47, 78, 85, 91, 94, 103, 106, 113, 126–27, 137, 157, 166, 207
Candelaria, Madame, 127, 209
Cardenas, Juan T., 11, 78, 82, 85–89, 90, 94, 97, 103, 104, 130, 185, 207
Carnes, Rev. J. R., 57–59
Carr, James M., 44
Casino St., 18
Cassiano José Fermín, 77, 85, 157
Chabot, George, 23
Chase, Capt., 158
Chavez, Fernando, 127
Chavez, Ygnacio, 127
Chestnut St., 209
"Chihuahua," 14, 25
choirs, 113, 206; Beethoven Männerchor, 16, 48, 111, 112, 117, 131, 134, 139, 146, 150; Frohsinn Singing Society, 48, 134, 139; San Antonio Liederkrantz, 111, 112; San Antonio Deutscher Männerchor,

139, 146; San Antonio Männerchor, 131; Tyrolean Sextet, 127
churches: African Methodist Church, 42; First Baptist Church, 27; Green Chapel African Episcopal Church, 54; Macedonian Baptist Church, 55, 57; Missionary Baptist Church, 50; Mount Zion Baptist Church, 54–55; Saint James African Methodist Episcopal Church, 54, 55, 57, 66; Saint John's Church, 113; Saint Joseph's Church, 113; Saint Mark's Episcopal Church, 27; Saint Paul's Methodist Episcopal Church, 54, 57, 60, 61; Saint Peter Claver, 54; San Fernando Church (later Cathedral), 9, 12, 33, 75, 79, 105; St. Joseph's Parish Church, 105; St. Michael's Parish Church, 105; Travis Park Episcopal Church, 158
Cinco de Mayo, 99, 155, 165
City Hall, 6, 30, 33, 102, 107
Claudon, P. E., 48
Claxton, Kate, 27
cockfights, 75, 196
Columbus Day, xii, 101–109, 131, 144, 207, 212
Commerce St., 6, 7, 12, 13, 15, 18, 21, 22, 28, 33, 34, 36, 38, 42, 49, 64, 67, 105, 111, 119, 121, 136, 159, 195, 196, 198, 199, 200, 201, 203, 204, 209–10
Connor's Grove, 50
Conroy, Thomas, 194, 196, 197
Constitution Day, 99
Convention Hall, 186
Copeland, John H., 91, 93
Corner, William, 30
Coy, Jacobo, 24, 90
Crawford, Capt., 44
Crawford, Charles, 44, 78, 85, 93
Cresson, Charles, 23
Crockett Building, 22
Crockett, David, 34, 67, 146, 170, 178
Cuney, N. Wright, 62

Daggett, Professor Lurence D., 191, 198
dances. *See* balls
Daughters of the Republic of Texas, 172, 173, 179, 180, 181, 184, 185, 194, 195, 198, 202
De Zavala, Adina, 172, 181
De Zavala, Lorenzo, 22, 172
"De Zavala's Daughters," 172
Deats, Jr., Gen. George E., 36
Degener, Hans, 3, 37, 133
Díaz, Porfirio, 99
Dickey, William, 57
Dickinson, Mrs. Suzanna, 177
Diez y Seis, xii, 18, 29, 44, 62, 73–100, 102, 104, 106, 122, 139, 155, 165, 182, 191, 203, 207, 209, 210, 212
Dobrowolski, William, 7
Douai, Adolph, 112
Dreiss, Adolph, 112
Dressel, Harry, 133, 137, 138
Drought, Harry P., 161
Duerler, Gustav, 5, 18, 37, 114, 130, 158
Duerler, John J., 18
Dullnig Building, 18
Duval, Rev. Nance, 22, 54, 55
Dwyer Ave., 105
Dwyer, Jr., Edward, 78
Dwyer, Edward, Sr., 7, 76, 94, 100
Dwyer, Maj. Joseph E., 43, 46, 47

Eberhardt, Louis, 127
Ellis, Robert G., 68
Elmendorff, Henry, 79, 97
Evans, Robert, 170
Everett, Milton, 184
Everett, Richard, 9
Eyth, Louis, 170

Faust, Tony, 120
Federal Building and Post Office, 32
Feherenbach, T. R., 215
Feinberg, Sigmund, 24
Fiesta San Jacinto, 204, 215
Finnegan, Miss, 185

fire companies, 15, 18, 50, 153, 166–67, 169, 177, 202, 213; Mission Hose Company, 132; San Antonio Volunteer Fire Company, 32; Turnverein Hook and Ladder Company, 4, 37, 41, 42, 207; Volunteer Fire Company I, 4, 24, 37, 39, 42, 43, 80, 114, 127, 206; Volunteer Fire Company II, 3, 37, 39, 42, 114, 122, 127; Volunteer Fire Company III, 37, 38, 40, 44, 56, 57, 59, 60, 62, 209; Volunteer Fire Company IV, 37, 40, 56, 62
Fisher, John "King," 24, 90
Fiske, Mrs. Minnie Maddern, 27
Fitzgerald, Mr., 161
Floresm, Antonio D., 96
Flores, José Maria, 92
Flores St., 203
Fort Worth Flower Festival, 203
"forty-eighters," 110, 111, 112
Foster, Joe, 24
Fourth of July, xii, 16, 18, 19, 35–50, 79, 81, 106, 109, 115, 130, 156, 207, 209, 212
fraternal orders: Ancient Order of Hibernians, 43, 46, 105; Benevolent and Protective Order of Elks, 5, 173, 174; Gate City Lodge, 64; Grand United Order of Odd Fellows, 5, 16, 64, 66, 213; Household of Ruth, 64, 66, 68; Knights and Ladies of Honor, 48, 132, 139, 213; Knights of Pythias, 103, 153, 169, 173, 185, 213; Knights Templar, 195, 198, 202; Masons, 16, 97; Nobles of the Mystic Shrine, 195; Order of the Golden Links, 56; Order of Chosen Friends, 132, 139, 176, 179; Seven Stars of Consolidation, 64; Sons of Hermann, 5, 16, 48, 132, 139, 146, 213; Sons of Mexico, 48; Woodmen of the World, 202, 213
Frazer, Mrs. John, 172, 175, 177
Frederick's Longhorn Furniture, 120
Free Thinkers, 111, 112
French Building, 12, 80
French, James H., 41, 85, 120

French, Mrs. James H., 169
Fries, John, 170
Froboese, Sr., Edward, 78, 103
Froboese, Jr., Edward, 207
Frost, Tom C., 15
Fry, Mrs. E. A., 158

Galan, Francisco, 90
Garcia, José E., 89
Garden St., 27, 113
Garza, Colonel, 81
Garza, Leonard, 97
German-American Volksfest Association, 120, 137, 138
Geronimo, 147–48
Giles, Alfred, 31, 194
Giovannetti, Professor G., 107
Girard, François, 41
Giraud, Louis, 81
Glaser, Louis, 161
Goeth, Conrad, 7
Gonzalez-Dena, Manuel, 97, 100
Gosling, Hal, 44, 127
Gould, Stephen, 23, 25
Grand View, 33
Granger, Gen. Gordon, 51, 60
Grant, Rev. Abram, 57, 66
Grayson St., 27
Grenet, Honoré, 27, 120
Griff-Jones, Enoch, 185
Grisaffi, Professor, 108
Groos Brothers, 15
Groos, Friedrich, 76
Guanches, 74
Guenther's Mill, 5, 43
Guerguin, Leopold, 78, 81, 82
Guilbeau, Adelem, 78
Guilbeau, Edward, 81
Gutierrez, Augustín, 117

Hadra, Dr. Berthold, 15, 54, 121, 157
Hammett, Rev. E., 54,
Hammond, Benjamin, 186, 191

Harnisch and Baer Confectionary, 167
Harrison, Pres. Benjamin, 154–55, 156, 159
Harrison, Tom, 91
Hart, Sim, 130
Heilborn, Gus, 119
Hensel, Frederick, 150
Henson, Rev. Mack, 60, 61
Herff, Sr., Dr. Ferdinand, 15, 78, 84, 111, 157
Hernandez, Adele, 97
Hernandez, Eugene, 97, 202
Hernandez, Jesus, 157
Hertzberg, Anna Goodman, 177, 180, 183, 187
Hertzberg, Eleazar, 180
Hicks, E. Marshall, 100, 187, 197, 199
Hidalgo y Costilla, Fray Miguel, 73, 79, 81
Hoefling, Sr., William, 27, 81, 112, 117, 143, 150
Holder, Professor, 192
hotels: Central Hotel, 24; Hord's Hotel, 24; Menger Hotel, 4, 5, 12, 24, 32, 38, 39, 40, 161; Plaza Hotel, 12; St. Leonard's Hotel, 24
Houston, Captain, 5
Houston, Gen. Sam, 154, 210
Houston St., 6, 10, 12, 13, 14, 21, 22, 29, 46, 67, 81, 119, 138
Huddle, William, 146
Hughes, D. E., 71

Ireland, Gov. John, 89
Irvin, Zachariah, 38, 60, 66
Irvine, L. Clarke, 180
Iturbide, Agustín, 73
Iwonski, Carl von, 114

Jacobson, J., 138
James, Vinton, 39, 40
Jefferson, Joseph, 27
Johnson Charles, 56
Johnson, Doctor D.E., 66
Joske Brothers, 114
Joske, Julius, 28,

Juneteenth, xii, 16, 18, 51–72, 89, 179, 196, 207, 209, 210, 212, 214
Junta Patriótica, 62, 91, 96, 97, 214

Kalteyer, Friedrich, 15
Kalteyer, George, 87, 94, 95, 122, 129, 157
Kampmann, Hermann D., 11, 15, 22, 23, 112, 113, 157
Kampmann, Mrs. Hermann D., 158
Karber, Hermann, 126, 176
"Karnival Krewes," 189, 190
Katzenberger, Professor, 124, 127, 128
Keene, Thomas, 27
Kerbel, Frederick, 85, 90, 108, 129
"Kermess," 173–74
Kight, C. N., 186, 194, 197
King, Edward, 11
King, Sara Smith, 44
King William St., 15, 139
Klock, Alvina, 44
Knights of the Golden Circle, 53
Kokernot, Lola, 197

labor organizations: Arbeiter Verein, 38, 43, 45, 113, 120, 121, 131; Beneficiary and Laborer's Association, 4; Blacksmith's Union, 139, 202; Brotherhood of Coachmen, 68; Carpenters' Union, 139, 146; Colored Coachmen's Association, 61; Colored Laborer's Association, 4, 40; Cooks' and Waiters' Union, 202; French Workingmen's Society, 106; Gran Círculo de Obreros, 96, 97; Knights of Labor, 61, 62, 91–94, 95, 130, 189, 209, 210; Laborer's Association, 38, 112, 114; Mexican Workingmen's Club, 48; National Association of Sanitary Engineers, 195; Painters' Union, 139, 153; Restaurant and Bartenders' International League of America, 71; State Undertakers' Union, 195; Tinners' Union, 139, 146; Typographical Union, 139; Workingmen's Union, 43

Lacoste, Lucien, 43
Lanier, Sidney, 170
"Laredito," 15, 25
Laredo St., 196
Leal, Mariana, 76
Leal, Narciso, 78
"Lily Whites," 54
Lincoln, Abraham, 51, 57
Lindner, Max, 15, 117–29, 131, 133
Live Oak St., 64
"Living Flag," 187, 191, 198, 202
Logwood, William, 38, 57
Lopez, Manuel, 93
Lopez Montaldo, Andres, 97
Lozano, Ascensio, 192
Lucchese, Salvatore, 102
Luetze, Emil, 146
"Lugares Festivos," 195, 198, 199, 200, 202
Lyons, J. H., 96

Madarasz, Ladislas, 129, 130
Mahnke, Ludwig, 128–29, 131
Main Plaza, 6, 9, 12, 21, 23, 24, 28, 29, 30, 32, 33, 34, 38, 46, 64, 67, 75, 80, 98, 105, 114, 119, 124, 141, 142, 159
Mardi Gras, 119, 133, 137, 139, 153, 154, 159, 189, 192, 195, 196, 197, 211, 213, 214
Market St., 4, 10, 12, 13, 18, 21, 27
Martin, E. N., 62
Martin, Jr., James W., 60, 62, 93
Martinez, Máximo, 76
Marx, Wilhelm, 76
Mateu, Gertrudis, 117
Mauermann, Benjamin, 37, 113, 117
Maverick Building, 84, 174
Maverick, Samuel L., 13
Maverick's Grove, 57, 84
McAllister, Joseph, 127
McAllister, S. W., 40
McCullough, Sam, 170
McKibbin, General, 197, 199
McLeary, James, 103, 104
McMaster, William, 166, 170

McPherson, Clara, 68
Menger, William, 3
Mexican Opera Company, 95
Mexico City (Flower Festival), 99, 155, 159, 164, 165
Mikado, The, 168
Milam Square, 31, 67, 138, 150, 209
Military Plaza, 4, 6, 9, 12, 18, 22, 23, 25, 29, 30, 33, 36, 38, 39, 56, 67, 78, 80, 87, 90, 94, 98, 102, 107, 114, 119, 124, 141, 142, 192, 197, 205
militia companies: Alamo Rifles, 36, 38, 39, 42; Austin Capital City Light Guards, 68, 70; Austin City Rifles, 57; Belknap Rifles, 47, 58, 97, 103, 106, 130, 146, 153, 164, 166, 169, 172, 173, 176, 179, 181, 185, 186, 187, 197, 207; Excelsior Guards, 57, 58, 59, 62, 64, 66, 68, 70; Granger Guards, 60; San Antonio Rifles, 58; San Antonio Zouaves, 47, 49, 50, 97, 181, 185, 186, 187, 202; Weimar Prairie Light Guards, 130
Mitchell, Nat, 170
Moglia, Luigi, 102
Molteni, Clemente, 102
Mondragón, Epiticio, 80, 85
Montes, Epifineo, 92
Morelos, General, 81
Morrison, Andrew, 23
Mosebach, Fred, 39
Munro, D. D. 128
Murray, Ida, 70
mutual aid societies, 6; Christopher Columbus Society, 48, 96, 106, 107, 145, 146, 150, 153; French Mutual Aid Society, 48; La Unión, 48, 92, 94, 96; Sociedad Benevolencia Mexicana, 48, 49, 82–83, 89, 90–94, 96, 97; Sociedad Benito Juarez, 94, 96, 212; Sociedad Hidalgo de Señoras y Señoritas, 48, 49, 96; Sociedad Ignacio Zaragosa, 94; Sociedad Marez, 94; Sociedad Miguel Hidalgo, 94; Sociedad Morales, 96;

Sociedad Mutualista Mexicana, 43, 44, 85–89, 90, 91, 94, 95, 96, 97, 102, 104, 207, 209, 212; Società Italiano di Mutuo Soccorso, 90, 94, 96, 102, 104, 106, 108; United Mexican Societies, 100

"Nan de Mascotte," 198
National Press Association, 8
Navarro, Angel, 77, 80
Navarro, Eugenio, 95
Navarro St., 199, 204
Nelson, Richard, 62
Neraz, Bishop, 105
Newcomb, James Pearson, 40, 53, 56, 57, 59, 60, 61, 93
newspapers: *Alamo Express,* 53; *Daily Ledger and Texan,* 38; *El Hogar,* 85; *El Mexicano de Texas,* 86; *El Mexico-Tejano,* 97; *Freie Presse Fuer San Antonio,* 15, 27, 112, 113, 122; *Galveston Freemen's Journal,* 62; *La Frontizera,* 97; *New Orleans Picayune,* 139; *San Antonio Express,* 15, 27, 41, 50, 57, 60, 67, 81, 82, 95, 91, 92, 93, 98, 108, 118, 134, 135, 141, 155, 156, 173, 182, 186, 187, 190, 191, 199, 204; *San Antonio Herald,* 10, 27, 36, 41, 56, 62, 86; *San Antonio Light,* 27, 29, 53, 57, 66, 85, 89, 92, 103, 104, 108, 126, 127, 131, 135, 139, 141, 142, 160, 164, 175, 176, 199; *San Antonio Zeitung,* 10, 112; *Texas Staats-Zeitung,* 133; *Texas Vorwarts,* 130; *Weekly Toungelet,* 66, 106
Newton, Samuel, 4
Nice (Flower Carnival), 157, 159, 164, 165, 192, 193
Nieblungenleid, 138
Nolte, Professor, 138
North, Officer, 71

O'Neill, James, 33
Odd Fellow's Hall, 84
Ogden, Charles W., 130
Ogden, Duncan Campbell, 177

Ogden, Mrs. Elizabeth, 177–89, 194
Olivarri, Jose, 77
Olmstead, Frederick Law, 10
Opera Puff Cigarettes, 130
Oppenheimer, Jesse, 15, 132
Ornelas, Dr. Plutarco, 22, 78, 87, 89, 90, 91, 94, 97, 98, 132, 157

Pan American Carnival Company, 196
Park Terrace, 33
Parker, Ella Belle, 67, 68
Parkhurst, Corp. George E., 180
parks: Connor's Grove, 50; Riverside Park, 7, 30, 46, 49, 50, 66, 67, 72, 132, 214; San Pedro Springs Park, 4, 7, 10–11, 18, 29, 30, 36, 37, 38, 40, 42, 43, 46, 49, 50, 56, 57, 59, 62, 66, 67, 68, 70, 82, 83–84, 85, 87, 89, 90, 94, 95, 97, 98, 100, 102, 106, 107, 108, 113, 114, 115, 117, 129, 130, 131, 133, 209, 214
Paschal, George, 78–79, 96
Paschal Square, 6
Paaschal, Thomas, 180
Paseo St., 10
Pearl Steam Laundry, 72
Peck, Lem B., 169
Peñaloza, Antonita, 84
Peñaloza, José M., 84
Perales, Geronimo, 90
Pereida, Manuel, 82
Perez, Alejo, 3, 41, 81, 82
Perez Cordero, Gertrudis, 77
Pfefferling, 97
Pfeuffer, Cristolph, 163
Phul, Helene von, 154, 155
Polish Society, 105
political clubs: Club Mexicano-Texano, 4, 40, 80, 81; Los Bexareños Democráticos, 80, 81, 82, 84; Loyal Union League, 4, 5, 40, 56; San Pedro Club, 62, 91, 92
Porter, Shed, 60
Powderly, Terence, 91
Prospect Hill, 33

Quasso, Darius M., 102, 103, 107

railroads: International and Great Northern, 20, 196, 197; Mobile, Jackson & Kansas City Railway, 23; San Antonio & Aransas Pass, 20; Sunset Railroad (Southern Pacific Railroad), 20, 37, 122, 202
Ramón, Concepción, 20
Red Cross, 76
religious societies: Cathedral Society, 105; Catholic Knights, 105; Central Catholic Union, 45; Knights of Columbus, 145; Ladies' Aid Society (Travis Methodist Episcopal Church), 158; Protestant Home for Destitute Children, 158; Saint John's Orphanage, 105, 187; Saint Joseph's Society, 46, 105, 139; Saint Mark's Parish Aid Society, 158
Rivas, Antonio P., 11, 37, 40, 48, 77–78, 80, 81, 82, 87, 90, 97, 103, 130, 185, 206, 207
Rivas St., 10, 81
River Ave., 76
Rodriguez, Gertrudis, 76
Roosevelt, Theodore, 47, 189
Rose, Dr. G. Q. A., 177, 178, 180
Rowland, Francis, 192
Runge, Carl, 124
Russ, General, 93
Russi, David, 170
Russi, Michael, 170

Saint Mary's St., 27, 66, 113
Saint Patrick's Day, 132
San Antonio Art League, 176, 179
San Antonio International Exhibition, 132, 146, 195
San Antonio Library and Women's Exchange, 158, 179, 185, 187
San Antonio River, 4, 7, 13, 21, 111
San Antonio Street Railway Company, 21, 53
"San Jacinto Arch," 185

San Jacinto Day, 178, 213
San Pedro Creek, 6, 14, 18, 30, 33, 90, 205, 209
San Saba St., 21
Sanchez, Francisco N., 6, 11, 85, 86
Sanchez, Lino, 85, 97
sängerfests, 97, 111, 131
Santa Anna, Gen. Antonio López de, 80, 177, 210
Santleben, August, 80
Sasas, Guillermo, 11
Sayers, Gov. Joseph D., 82, 186, 189, 198, 199, 200
Schiller, Friedrich, 111, 114, 115, 128
schillerfieren, 114, 115, 124, 137
Schmeltzer, Gustav, 112, 114
schools: Colored High School, 55; Rincon (Colored) School, 5, 54, 55, 57; German-English School, 10, 112, 113; High School, 27; Peacock Military Academy, 187; Saint Peter Claver School, 105; Saint Mary's College, 105; West Texas Military Academy, 173, 179, 187
Schramm, Edgar, 104, 132–43, 199
Schramm, Milton, 141
Schwartz, Benedict, 24
Scudder, Harold, 36
Seele, Herman, 130
Seffel, Miss, 44
Shelburn, J. M., 64
Shook, Phil, 163
Sibley's Brigade, 86
Siemering, August, 11, 122
Sim Hart's Cigar Store, 24, 120
Simms, Billy, 24
Singer Sewing Machine Company, 130
Slayden, James L., 174
Slayden, Mrs. James L., 154, 158, 174
Smith, Georgie Cupples, 77
Smith, Thad W., 76, 78, 80, 156, 172
social clubs: Casino Association, 5, 7, 10, 16, 40, 96, 112, 113, 114, 119, 131, 136, 174, 207, 209; Dew Drop Club, 71; Idlewild

Club, 71; Italiana Alpini, 106; Lawn Tennis and Croquet Club, 64; Mexican Social Club, 43, 80, 84, 86, 90, 95, 100, 102, 106, 207; San Antonio Club, 25, 157, 158, 198, 209
Soledad St., 13, 22, 24, 34, 38, 67, 70
Solero, Col. Carlo A., 104
Sousa, John Philip, 210
South Center St., 67
South Heights, 33
Spoffard, Harriet, 16
Spring Carnival, 34, 186, 194–204, 207, 212, 214, 215
State Convention of Colored Men, 61
Stevens, John J., 155
Stevens, Mrs. John J., 155, 156, 158, 166, 167
Steves, Edward, 103
Steves and Sons Lumber Company, 130
stores: Alamo Music Store, 127; Bresel and Briam, 12; Chapa and Dreiss, 188, 214; Erastus Reed Furniture Store, 38; Frost and Bro., 12; Honoré Grenet's Emporium, 27; Hugo and Schmeltzer, 27, 32, 34, 170; Joske Brothers Store, 5, 27, 28, 33, 48, 181; Rhodius & Tempsky, 127; Wolff and Marx, 33; Wolfson's Emporium, 27, 33, 167, 190
Stribling, Judge Thomas, 40
Sulski, E. D., 68
Sunset Depot, 156

Talerico, Frank, 102
Teel, Maj. T. Trevanian, 44
Temple Beth El, 23, 27, 113
theaters: Beethoven Hall, 33, 179, 196, 197, 198, 199; Casino Hall, 112; Fashion Theater, 24, 92; Jack Harris' Vaudeville Theater, 24, 32, 90, 120, 164; Opera House, 25, 33, 114, 157, 198; Turner Hall, 90, 12, 117, 124
Thielepape, William C. A., 11, 41, 53, 12
Thompson, Ben, 24, 90
Tobey, G. G., 118

Tobin, Chief William, 172, 178, 179
Tobin, Jr., William, 49, 172, 173
Toepperwein, Adolf, 7
Tommassi, Antonio, 102
Tournament of Roses, 192–93, 214
Travis, Julia, 71
Travis Square, 13, 27, 32, 46, 67, 105, 113, 139, 190
Travis, William B., 34, 146, 170
Treviño, Manuel, 97, 100
Treviño St., 6
Trinidad, Cipriano, 92
Tronson, Dick, 92
Tuesday Musical Club, 180
"Twin Sisters, The," 124
Twohig, John, 38

United States military posts: Fort Sam Houston, 28, 30; Government Hill, 28; Vance Building, 10, 11
United States military units: "Rough Riders," 99; United States Eighth Cavalry, 49; United States Tenth Cavalry, 49
U.S.S. Maine, 185
Upson, Columbus, 127
utility companies: Berg Power and Electric Company, 21, 23; San Antonio Gas Company, 23; San Antonio Water Works, 23

Valley Hunt Club, 192, 193
Vance, John, 10, 12
Vance, William, 10, 12
Veiled Prophet Celebration, 120, 153, 154, 192, 197, 211, 213, 215
"Veramendi Palace," 34
Vereine, 5, 10, 16, 113, 114, 117, 119, 123, 134, 145, 150, 153, 206; Adelsverein, 110; Casino Theater Verein, 112; Elsaaser Verein, 48; Gartenverein, 111, 139, 146; Jägerlust, 48, 139; Kriegerverein, 48, 111, 116, 139, 146, 153; Scheutzenverein,

Vereine (*continued*)
  48, 111; Turnverein, 38, 39, 48, 111, 112, 114, 119, 131, 139, 169
veteran's groups: Albert Sydney Johnson Corps Veterans, 87; Black Union Veterans, 64, 66, 82; Confederate Veterans, 5, 44, 48, 106, 195, 198, 202; Grand Army of the Republic, 5, 44, 48; 106, 139, 146, 195, 198, 202; Mexican War Veterans, 44; Red Cross Veterans, 187, 189
Villareal, Fortunato, 78, 176, 206–207
volksfests, xii, 29, 67, 81, 84, 93, 106, 110–54, 165, 169, 170, 175, 176, 190, 192, 198, 200, 203, 206, 207, 209, 211, 212, 213, 214

Waco Flower Festival, 182
Wagner, Adolf, 119
Walker, Lafayette, 50, 56, 57
Warren, Santiago, 90
Washington Square, 90, 98
Washington's Birthday, 36, 37, 45
Welch, Stanley, 4
West, Emily, 77
Wieland, Cristolph, 140
Wilcox, Capt. John, 36
Wilhelm I, Kaiser, 136
Wilson, Nathan T., 177
Wilson, Mrs. Nathan T., 177, 187
Wolfson, Mrs. Abraham, 167
Womack, Rev. Joseph P., 59
Wright, Rev. Elder, 57
Wulff, A. T., 78

Young, Gen. William H., 5, 41
Yturri, Elena, 76

Zaragoza, General, 81